Design of Structural Timber

W.M.C. McKenzie B.Sc., Ph.D., C.Phys., M.Inst.P., C.Eng.

Lecturer, Napier University, Edinburgh

First published 2000 by
MACMILLAN PRESS LTD
Houndmills, Basingstoke, Hampshire RG21 6XS
and London
Companies and representatives
throughout the world.

ISBN 0–333–79236–X

A catalogue record for this book is available
from the British Library.

This book is printed on paper suitable for recycling and
made from fully managed and sustained forest sources.

10   9   8   7   6   5   4   3   2   1
09 08 07 06 05 04 03 02 01 00

Printed in Great Britain by
Antony Rowe Ltd, Chippenham,
Wiltshire.

Contents

Preface

Rationale

Existing design textbooks for undergraduate engineering students neglect, to a large extent, the importance of timber as a structural building material. As a consequence, relatively few textbooks provide information on the design of timber structures. *Design of Structural Timber* has therefore been written to:

♦ provide a comprehensive source of information on practical timber design,
♦ introduce the nature and inherent characteristics of timber given in relation to the requirements of BS 5268,
♦ introduce the use of Eurocode EC5 in structural timber design.

The book's content ranges from an introduction to timber as a material to the design of realistic structures including and beyond that usually considered essential for undergraduate study.

Readership

Design of Structural Timber is written primarily for undergraduate civil and structural engineers. Whilst Chapter 2 provides a résumé of elastic analysis techniques frequently used to determine design load effects, students will normally be expected to have covered these techniques in their courses on structural theory and analysis.

The book will also provide an invaluable reference source for practising engineers in many building, civil and architectural design offices.

Worked Examples and Review Problems

The design of structures/elements is explained and illustrated using numerous detailed, relevant and practical worked examples. These design examples are presented in a format typical of that used in design office practice in order to encourage students to adopt a methodical and rational approach when preparing structural calculations.

Review problems are included at the end of each chapter to allow the reader to test his/her understanding of the material. References are given to the relevant sections in the preceding chapter, and numerical answers given where appropriate.

Design Codes

It is essential when undertaking structural design to make frequent reference to the appropriate design codes. Students are encouraged to do this whilst using this text. It is assumed that readers will have access to either *Extracts from British Standards for Students of Structural Design* (which is a standard text in virtually all undergraduate structural design courses) or the complete versions of the necessary codes, with the exception of the Eurocode EC5. In Chapter 8 where EC 5 is discussed, appropriate extracts from the code are given to illustrate where variables, etc., have been obtained.

W.M.C. McKenzie

To Caroline, Karen and Gordon

Acknowledgements

I wish to thank Christopher Glennie of Macmillan Press and Andrew Nash for their help and advice during the preparation of this text. I am indebted to Mr. Neill McConnell of Donaldson & McConnell Ltd., Timber Engineering, Grangemouth Road, Bo'ness, for his advice and use of the cover photographs, and MARTINSONS TRA KB of Sweden. Thank you, Karen, for undertaking the tedious checking of the calculations. Finally, I wish to thank Caroline for her endless support, encouragement and proof-reading.

1. Structural Timber

> **Objective:** to introduce the inherent botanical and structural characteristics of timber in addition to the classification and philosophies used in the design process.

1.1 Introduction

The use of timber as a structural material probably dates back to primitive times when man used fallen trees to bridge streams and gain access to hunting grounds or new pastures. It is only during the latter half of the twentieth century that detailed knowledge regarding the physical properties and behaviour of timber has been developed on a scientific basis and subsequently used in design. The inherent variability of a material such as timber, which is unique in its structure and mode of growth, results in characteristics and properties which are distinct and more complex than those of other common structural materials such as concrete, steel and brickwork. Some of the characteristics which influence design and are specific to timber are:

- the moisture content,
- the difference in strength when loads are applied parallel and perpendicular to the grain direction,
- the duration of the application of the load,
- the method adopted for strength grading of the timber.

As a live growing material, every identified tree has a name based on botanical distinction, for example '*Pinus sylvestris*' is commonly known as 'Scots pine.' The botanical names have a Latin origin, the first part indicating the genus, e.g. '*Pinus*', and the second part indicating the species, e.g. '*sylvestris.*'

A general botanical classification of trees identifies two groups: endogenous and exogenous.

- **Endogenous:** This type includes trees such as palms and bamboos which are inward growing and are generally found in the tropics; they are not considered in this text.

- **Exogenous:** This type is outward growing and includes all of the commercial timbers used for construction in the UK. There is a sub-division of exogenous trees into two main groups which are familiar to most designers; they are softwoods and hardwoods. These timbers are considered in this text and in the British Standard

BS 5268 : Part 2 : 1996 'Structural use of timber.' Softwoods such as pine, Douglas fir and spruce supply the bulk of the world's commercial timber. Hardwoods including timbers such as iroko, teak, keruing and greenheart comprise the vast majority of species throughout the world.

A classification such as this is of little value to a structural designer and consequently design codes adopt a classification based on stress grading. Stress grading is discussed in Section 1.3. The growth of a tree depends on the ability of the cells to perform a number of functions, primarily conduction, storage and mechanical support. The stem (or trunk) conducts essential mineral salts and moisture from the roots to the leaves, stores food materials and provides rigidity to enable the tree to compete with surrounding vegetation for air and sunlight. Chemical processes, which are essential for growth, occur in the branches, twigs and leaves in the crown of the tree. A typical cross-section of a tree trunk is shown in Figure 1.1.

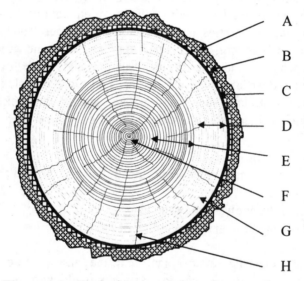

Figure 1.1   Typical cross-section of tree trunk

♦ **A: Outer bark** comprising dry dead tissue and providing general protection against external elements.
♦ **B: Inner bark** comprising moist, soft material which conducts food synthesised by the leaves to all growing parts of the tree.
♦ **C: Cambium layer** comprising a microscopic layer on the inside of the inner bark. Cell division within this layer is responsible for growth in the thickness of the tree.
♦ **D: Sapwood** comprising the younger growth containing living cells which store foods and conduct moisture from the roots to the leaves. This zone of wood is normally lighter in colour than the inner heartwood and varies in thickness from approximately 30 mm in Western red cedar and Douglas fir to thicknesses in excess of 75 mm in maples, white ash and some pines.

- ◆ **E: Heartwood** comprising the inner layers in which the sapwood has become inert, with the cells dying and the remaining food stores undergoing chemical change to produce substances such as tannin, a colourless amorphous mass. The main function of the inactive heartwood tissue is to provide mechanical rigidity to the tree.
- ◆ **F: Pith** comprising the core of the tree about which the first wood growth takes place.
- ◆ **G: Growth rings** which occur in timber grown in climates having distinct seasonal changes. These rings are the result of cycles of growth and rest, where changes occur in the tissues formed between the beginning and the end of the growing season. In general, tissues formed at the beginning of a season conduct moisture, whilst toward the end of a season the demand for moisture diminishes and the conduction vessels become smaller with proportionately thicker walls. A consequence of this is that springwood tends to be light, porous and relatively weak and summerwood stronger and more dense.
- ◆ **H: Rays** comprising narrow bands of tissue running radially across the growth rings. Their purpose is to store and conduct food to the various layers between the pith and the bark.

1.2 Moisture Content

Unlike most structural materials, the behaviour of timber is significantly influenced by the existence and variation of its moisture content. The moisture content, as determined by oven drying of a test piece, is defined in *Annex H* of BS 5268 as:

$$w = 100(m_1 - m_2)/m_2$$

where:
m_1 is the mass of the test piece before drying (in g)
m_2 is the mass of the test piece after drying (in g)

Moisture contained in 'green' timber is held both within the cells (free water) and within the cell walls (bound water). The condition where all free water has been removed but the cell walls are still saturated is known as the 'fibre saturation point' (FSP). At levels of moisture above the FSP, most physical and mechanical properties remain constant. Variations in moisture content below the FSP cause considerable changes to properties such as weight, strength, elasticity, shrinkage and durability. The controlled drying of timber is known as seasoning. There are two methods generally used:

- ◆ **Air seasoning** in which the timber is stacked and layered with air-space in open sided sheds to promote natural drying. This method is relatively inexpensive with very little loss in the quality of timber if carried out correctly. It has the disadvantage that the timber and the space which it occupies are unavailable for long periods. In addition, only a limited control is possible by varying the spaces between the layers and/or by using mobile slatted sides to the sheds.

♦ **Kiln drying** in which timber is dried out in a heated, ventilated and humidified oven. This requires specialist equipment and is more expensive in terms of energy input. The technique does offer a more controlled environment in which to achieve the required reduction in moisture content and is much quicker.

The anisotropic nature of timber and differential drying out caused by uneven exposure to drying agents such as wind, sun or applied heat can result in a number of defects such as *twisting*, *cupping*, *bowing* and *cracking* as shown in Figure 1.2.

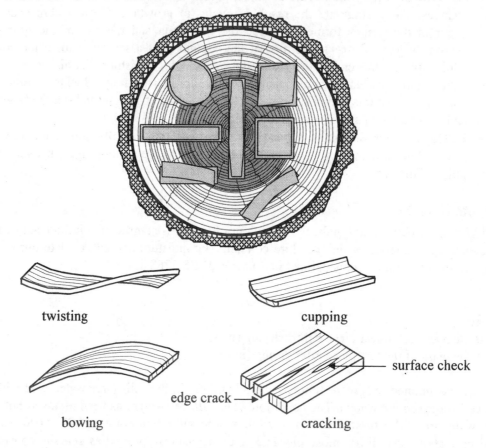

Figure 1.2   Distortions due to differential directional shrinkage

1.3 Defects in Timber

In addition to the defects indicated in Figure 1.2 there are a number of naturally occurring defects in timber. The most common and familiar of such defects is a **knot** (see Figure 1.3). Normal branch growth originates near the pith of a tree and consequently its base develops new layers of wood each season which develop with the trunk. The cells of the new wood grow into the lower parts of the branches, maintaining a flow of moisture to the leaves. The portion of a branch which is enclosed within the main trunk constitutes a *live* or *intergrown* knot and has a firm connection with surrounding wood.

When lower branches in forest trees die and drop off as a result of being deprived of sunlight, the dead stubs become overgrown with new wood but have no connection to it. This results in dead or enclosed knots which are often loose and, when cut, fall out.

The presence of knots is often accompanied by a decrease in the physical properties of timber such as the tensile and compressive strength. The reduction in strength is primarily due to the distortion of the grain passing around the knots and the large angle between the grain of the knot and the piece of timber in which it is present. During the seasoning of timber, checks often develop around the location of knots.

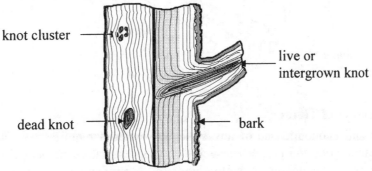

Figure 1.3 Defects due to knots

In a mill when timber is converted from a trunk into suitable commercial sizes (see Figure 1.4) a *wane* can occur when part of the bark or rounded periphery of the trunk is present in a cut length as shown in Figure 1.5. The effect of a wane is to reduce the cross-sectional area with a resultant reduction in strength.

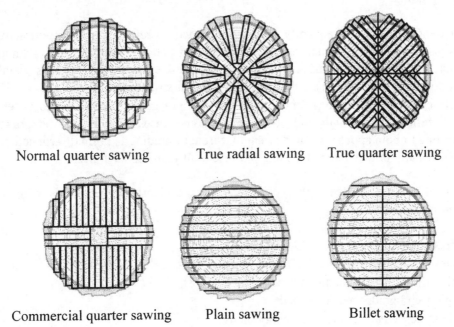

Figure 1.4 Typical sawing patterns

A ***shake*** is produced when fibres separate along the grain: this normally occurs between the growth rings, as shown in Figure 1.5. The effect of a shake in the cross-section is to reduce the shear strength of beams; it does not significantly affect the strength of axially loaded members.

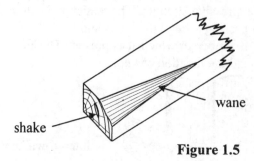

Figure 1.5

1.4 Classification of Timber

The efficient and economic use of any structural material requires a knowledge of its physical characteristics and properties such that a representative mathematical model can be adopted to predict behaviour in qualitative terms. Manufactured materials such as steel and concrete, in which quality can be tightly controlled and monitored during production, readily satisfy this. As a natural product, timber is subject to a wide range of variation in quality which cannot be controlled.

Uniformity and reliability in the quality of timber as a structural material is achieved by a process of selection based on established grading systems, i.e. appearance grading and strength grading:

♦ appearance grading is frequently used by architects to reflect the warm, attractive features of the material such as the surface grain pattern, the presence of knots, colour, etc. In such circumstances the timber is left exposed and remains visible after completion and may be either structural or non-structural,

♦ all structural (load-bearing) timber must be strength graded according to criteria which reflect its strength and stiffness. In some cases timber may be graded according to both appearance and strength. Strength grading is normally carried out either visually or mechanically, using purpose built grading machines.

Every piece of strength graded timber should be marked clearly and indelibly with the following information:

♦ grade/strength class (e.g. GS,SS,C16,C24),
♦ species or specific combination (e.g. ER – *redwood*, B/D – *Douglas fir (British)*),
♦ number of the British Standard used (e.g. BS 4978),
♦ company and grader/machine used,
♦ company logo/mark of the certification body,
♦ timber condition (e.g. KD – *kiln dried*, WET).

A typical grading mark/stamp is illustrated in Figure 1.6.

Certification body logo or mark	Grader/machine and/or company reference	Species or species group
abc	**1234**	**B/DF**
		GS
BS 4978	**KD**	**C16**
British Standard reference	Timber condition	Strength class and/or Grade

Figure 1.6

1.4.1 Visual Strength Grading

As implied by the name, this method of grading is based on the physical observation of strength-reducing defects such as knots, rate of growth, cracks, wane, bowing, etc. Since the technique is based on the experience and judgement of the grader it is inherently subjective. In addition, important properties such as density, which has a significant influence on stiffness, and strength are not considered. Numerous grading rules and specifications have been developed throughout Europe, Canada and the USA during the last fifty years. In the UK, visual grading is governed by the requirements of BS 4978 : 1996 'Specification for softwood grades for structural use' and the Eurocode EN 518 : 1995 'Structural timber – Grading – Requirements for visual grading standards.'

Visual defects considered when assessing timber strength include: location and extent of knots, slope of grain, rate of growth, fissures, wane, distortions such as bowing, springing, twisting, cupping, resin and bark pockets, and insect damage. Two strength grades are specified: General Structural (GS) and Special Structural (SS), the latter being the higher quality material. Timber which contains abnormal defects such as compression wood (see Section 1.4), insect damage such as worm holes, or fungal decay (not sapstain), or which is likely to impair the serviceability of the pieces, is excluded from the grades.

1.4.2 Machine Strength Grading

The requirements for machine strength grading are specified in BS EN 519 : 1995 *'Structural Timber' – Grading – Requirements for machine strength graded timber and grading machines.* Timber is classified into:

- nine classes of poplar and coniferous species ranging from the weakest grade C14 to the highest grade C40,
- six classes for deciduous species ranging from the weakest grade D30 to the highest grade D70.

In each case the number following either the 'C' or the 'D' represents the characteristic bending strength of the timber. In BS 5268 : Part 2 : 1996 an additional strength class, TR26, is also given; this is intended for use in the design of trussed rafters.

The inherently subjective nature of visual strength grading results in a lower yield of higher strength classes than would otherwise be achieved. Machine strength grading is generally carried out by conducting bending tests on planks of timber which are fed continuously through a grading machine. The results of such tests produce a value for the modulus of elasticity. The correlation between the modulus of elasticity and strength properties such as bending, tensile and compressive strength can be used to define a particular grade/class of timber.

Visual grading enables a rapid check on a piece of timber to confirm, or otherwise, an assigned grade; this is not possible with machine grading. The control and reliability of machine grading is carried out either by destructive testing of output samples (output controlled systems), or regular and strict control/adjustments of the grading machine settings. In Europe the latter technique is adopted since this is more economic than the former when using a wide variety of species and relatively low volumes of production.

1.5 Material Properties

The strength of timber is due to certain types of cells (called tracheids in softwoods and fibres in hardwoods) which make up the many minute hollow cells of which timber is composed. These cells are roughly polygonal in cross-section and the dimension along the grain is many times larger than across it. The principal constituents of the cells are cellulose and lignin. Individual cell walls comprise four layers, one of which is more significant with respect to strength than the others. This layer contains chains of cellulose which run nearly parallel to the main axis of the cell. The structure of the cell enhances the strength of the timber in the grain direction.

Density, which is expressed as mass per unit volume, is one of the principal properties affecting strength. The heaviest species, i.e. those with most wood substance, have thick cell walls and small cell cavities. They also have the highest densities and consequently are the strongest species. Numerous properties in addition to strength, e.g. shrinkage, stiffness and hardness, increase with increasing density.

When timber is seasoned the cell contents dry out leaving only cell walls. Shrinkage occurs during the drying process as absorbed moisture begins to leave the cell walls. The cell walls become thinner as they draw closer together. However the length of the cell layers is only marginally affected. A consequence of this is that as shrinkage occurs the width and thickness change but the length remains the same. The degree to which shrinkage occurs is dependent upon its initial moisture content value and the value at which it stabilises in service. A number of defects such as bowing, cupping, twisting and surface checks are a direct result of shrinkage.

Since timber is hygroscopic, and can absorb moisture whilst in service, it can also swell until it reaches an equilibrium moisture content.

Anisotropy is a characteristic of timber because of the long fibrous nature of the cells and their common orientation, the variation from early to late wood, and the differences between sapwood and hardwood. The elastic modulus of a fibre in a direction *along* its axis is considerably greater than that *across* it, resulting in the strength and elasticity of timber parallel to the grain being much higher than in the radial and tangential directions.

The slope of the grain can have an important effect on the strength of a timber member. Typically a reduction of 4% in strength can result from a slope of 1 in 25, increasing to an 11% loss for slopes of 1 in 15.

The strength of timber is also affected by the ratio of growth as indicated by the width of the annual growth rings. For most timbers the number of growth rings to produce the optimum strength is approximately in the range of 6–15 per 25 mm measured radially. Timber which has grown either much more quickly or much more slowly than that required for the optimum growth rate is likely to be weaker.

In timber from a tree which has grown with a pronounced lean, wood from the compression side (compression wood) is characterised by much greater shrinkage than normal. In softwood planks containing compression wood, bowing is likely to develop in the course of seasoning and the bending strength will be low. In hardwoods, the tension wood has abnormally high longitudinal shrinkage and although stronger in tension is much weaker in longitudinal compression than normal wood.

Like many materials, e.g. concrete, the stress–strain relationship demonstrated by timber under load is linear for low stress values. For all species the strains for a given load increase with moisture content. A consequence of this is that the strain in a beam under constant load will increase in a damp environment and decrease as it dries out again.

Timber demonstrates viscoelastic behaviour (creep) as high stress levels induce increasing strains with increasing time. The magnitude of long-term strains increases with higher moisture content. In structures where deflection is important, the duration of the loading must be considered. This is reflected in BS 5268 : Part 2 : 1996 by the use of modifying factors applied to admissible stresses depending on the type of loading, e.g. long-term, medium-term, short- and very short-term.

The cellular structure of timber results in a material which is a poor conductor of heat. The air trapped within its cells greatly improves its insulating properties. Heavier timbers having smaller cell cavities are better conductors of heat than lighter timbers. Timber does expand when heated but this effect is more than compensated for by the shrinkage caused by loss of moisture.

The fire resistance of timber generally compares favourably with other structural materials and is often better than most. Steel is subject to loss of strength, distortion, expansion and collapse, whilst concrete may spall and crack.

Whilst small timber sections may ignite easily and support combustion until reduced to ash, this is not the case with large structural sections. At temperatures above 250°C material at the exposed surface decomposes, producing inflammable gases and charcoal. These gases, when ignited, heat the timber to a greater depth and the fire continues. The charcoal produced during the fire is a poor conductor and will eventually provide an insulating layer between the flame and the unburned timber. If there is sufficient heat, charcoal will continue to char and smoulder at a very slow rate, particularly in large timber sections with a low surface to mass ratio. Fire authorities usually consider that a normal timber door will prevent the spread of fire to an adjoining room for about 30 minutes. The spread of fire is then often due to flames and hot gases permeating between the door and its frame or through cracks between door panels and styles produced by shrinkage (see BS 5268 : Part 4 – Fire resistance of timber structures).

The durability of timbers to resist the effects of weathering, chemical or fungal attack varies considerably from one species to another. In general the heartwood is more durable to fungal decay than the sapwood. This is due to the presence of organic compounds within the cell walls and cavities which are toxic to fungi and insects. Provided timber is kept dry, or is continuously immersed in fresh water, decay will generally not be a problem. Where timber is used in seawater, particularly in harbours, there is always a risk of severe damage due to attack by molluscs. The pressure impregnation of timber with suitable preservatives will normally be sufficient to prevent damage due to fungal, insect or mollusc attack.

1.6 Preservative Treatments

A number of chemical treatments are available to prevent the degeneration of timber due to fungi, insect or mollusc attack. The extent to which a structural member is susceptible to attack is dependent on several factors including the species and the environmental conditions. The treatments can be classified into three types:

- ◆ tar oil preservatives,
- ◆ organic solvents,
- ◆ water borne preservatives.

Tar oil preservatives such as creosote are restricted in their use to a limited type of external members (railway sleepers, telegraph poles, fences etc.) because of their eco-toxicological characteristics.

Organic solvent preservatives are widely used and have the advantage of being readily absorbed by the timber, even when applied using simple techniques such as brushing, spraying or dipping,

Water borne solvents, e.g. chromated copper arsenate, are the most widely used preservatives and are normally introduced into the timber under pressure.

1.7 Design Philosophies

A fundamental requirement of any design is that the resulting structure should possess an acceptable 'margin of safety'. Absolute safety cannot be guaranteed regardless of the design philosophy adopted. This was expressed by Freudenthal (12) in the following terms: *'Failure cannot be prevented with certainty but only with a high degree of probability which may approach certainty very closely but can never attain it.'* A margin of safety is by definition a statistical concept.

A margin of safety is required for a number of reasons:

- ◆ uncertainty of the material properties. There are considerable differences in the variability of constituent materials and/or manufacturing process of materials, e.g. steel, concrete, masonry and timber,

♦ uncertainty of the applied loading in any given circumstance, e.g. imposed loads due to wind or intermittent and changing occupation of a building are much more variable than dead loads due to self-weight,
♦ uncertainty of the calculated shears, moments, axial loads and stresses. Mathematical modelling of structures is based on presumed material properties, physical restraints and simplified structural behaviour resulting in approximate answers.

Generally there are three design philosophies which have been adopted to reflect a desired margin of safety:

♦ permissible stress design,
♦ load factor design,
♦ limit state design.

1.7.1 Permissible Stress Design

When using permissible stress design, the margin of safety is introduced by considering structural behaviour under working/service load conditions and comparing the stresses so induced with permissible values. The permissible values are obtained by dividing the failure stresses by an appropriate factor of safety. The applied stresses are determined using elastic analysis techniques, i.e.

$$stress\ induced\ by\ working\ loads \le \frac{failure\ stress}{factor\ of\ safety}$$

This is the philosophy adopted in the current timber design code BS 5268 : Part 2 : 1996 as used in this text.

1.7.2 Load Factor Design

When using load factor design, the margin of safety is introduced by considering structural behaviour at collapse load conditions. The ultimate capacities of sections based on yield strength (e.g. axial, bending moment and shear force capacities), are compared with the design effects induced by the ultimate loads. The ultimate loads are determined by multiplying the working/service loads by a factor of safety. Plastic methods of analysis are used to determine section capacities and design load effects. Despite being acceptable, this method has never been widely used.

$$\begin{matrix} Ultimate\ design\ load\ effects\ due\ to \\ (working\ loads \times factor\ of\ safety) \end{matrix} \le \begin{matrix} Ultimate\ capacity\ based\ on\ the \\ failure\ stress\ of\ the\ material \end{matrix}$$

1.7.3 Limit State Design

When using limit state design, the margin of safety is introduced by considering structural behaviour at collapse load conditions. The ultimate capacities of sections (e.g. axial, bending moment and shear force capacities), are compared with the design effects induced by the ultimate loads. The ultimate capacities are determined by dividing the failure stresses by a *partial safety factor* and the ultimate loads are determined by multiplying the working/service loads by a different *partial safety factor*. The working/service loads are normally referred to as *characteristic loads*. In addition to the member capacities other limit states are also considered, e.g. under service conditions the deflection, vibration or cracking may need to be checked and limited to prescribed values.

Plastic or Elastic methods of analysis can be used to determine the load effects.

It is important when using plastic design to ensure that the material has sufficient ductility to develop plastic hinges and that adequate restraint is provided to prevent failure due to secondary effects such as local buckling.

Ultimate design load effects due to (characteristic loads × partial factor of safety)	$\leq$	*Ultimate capacity based on the failure stress of the material divided by a partial safety factor*

This philosophy is more realistic in its representation of structural behaviour than either permissible stress or load factor design. The load types and their magnitude and material characteristics are subject to differing partial safety factors which reflect more accurately their individual statistical variations.   This technique is adopted in most modern design codes, including Eurocode 5 for timber.

1.8 Structural Loading

All structures are subjected to loading from various sources. The main categories of loading are: dead, imposed and wind loads. In some circumstances there may be other loading types which should be considered such as settlement, fatigue, temperature effects, dynamic loading, or impact effects (e.g. when designing bridge decks, crane-gantry girders or maritime structures). In the majority of cases design considering combinations of dead, imposed and wind loads is the most appropriate.

The definition of dead and imposed loading is given in BS 6399 : Part 1 : 1996, whilst wind loading is defined in BS 6399 : Part 2 : 1997. Part 2 is a technical revision of, and supersedes CP3 : Chapter V : Part 2 : 1972.

1.8.1 Dead Loads: BS 648 : 1964

Dead loads are loads which are due to the effects of gravity, i.e. the self-weight of all permanent construction such as beams, columns, floors, walls, roofs and finishes.

If the position of permanent partition walls is known, their weight can be assessed and included in the dead load. In speculative developments, internal partitions are regarded as imposed loading.

1.8.2 Imposed Loads: BS 6399 : Part 1 : 1996 (Clauses 5.0 and 6.0)

Imposed loads are loads which are due to variable effects such as the movement of people, furniture, equipment and traffic. The values adopted are based on observation and measurement and are inherently less accurate than the assessment of dead loads.

Clause 5.0 and Table 1 defines the magnitude of uniformly distributed and concentrated point loads which are recommended for the design of floors, ceilings and their supporting elements. Loadings are considered in the following categories:

A   Domestic and residential activities
B   Offices and work areas not covered elsewhere
C   Areas where people may congregate
D   Shopping areas
E   Areas susceptible to the accumulation of goods (e.g. warehouses)
F   Vehicle and traffic areas (Light)
G   Vehicle and traffic areas (Heavy)

Most floor systems are capable of lateral distribution of loading and the recommended concentrated load need not be considered. In situations where lateral distribution is not possible the effects of the concentrated loads should be considered with the load applied at locations which will induce the most adverse effect, e.g. maximum bending moment, shear and deflection. In addition, local effects such as crushing and punching should be considered where appropriate.

In multi-storey structures it is very unlikely that all floors will be required to carry the full imposed load at the same time. Statistically it is acceptable to reduce the total floor loads carried by a supporting member by varying amounts depending on the number of floors or floor area carried. This is reflected in Clause 6.2 and Tables 2 and 3 of BS 6399 : Part 1 in which a percentage reduction in the total distributed imposed floor loads is recommended when designing columns, piers, walls, beams and foundations.

1.8.3 Imposed Roof Loads: BS 6399 : Part 3 : 1988

Imposed loading caused by snow is included in the values given in this part of the code which relates to imposed roof loads. Flat roofs, sloping roofs and curved roofs are also considered.

1.8.4 Wind Loads: BS 6399 : Part 2 : 1997

Environmental loading such as wind loading is clearly variable and its source is outwith human control. In most structures the dynamic effects of wind loading are small, and static methods of analysis are adopted. The nature of such loading dictates that a statistical approach is the most appropriate in order to quantify the magnitudes and directions of the related design loads. The main features which influence the wind loading imposed on a structure are:

♦ geographical location   -   London, Edinburgh, Inverness, Chester, ...
♦ physical location   -   city centre, small town, open country, ...
♦ topography   -   exposed hill top, escarpment, valley floor, ...

- ◆ altitude   - height above mean sea level,
- ◆ building shape   - square, rectangular, cruciform, irregular, ...
- ◆ roof pitch   - shallow, steep, mono-pitch, duo-pitch, multi-bay...
- ◆ building dimensions
- ◆ wind speed and direction
- ◆ wind gust peak factor.

Tabulated procedures enable these features to be evaluated and hence produce a system of equivalent static forces which can be used in the analysis and design of the structure.

1.9   Review Problems

    1.1   Identify and describe the main components of a tree trunk.
        (see Section 1.1)

    1.2   Identify the principal defects which occur in timber.
        (see Section 1.3)

    1.3   Discuss the classification and grading of structural timber.
        (see Section 1.4)

    1.4   Identify the differences between permissible stress, load factor and
        limit state design.
        (see Section 1.7)

---

2. Elastic Analysis Techniques

Objective: to provide a résumé of the modification factors, load distribution and elastic methods of stress analysis most commonly used when designing structural timber elements to BS 5268 : Part 2 : 1996.

2.1 Introduction

Since BS 5268 is a permissible stress design code, mathematical modelling of the behaviour of timber elements and structures is based on assumed elastic behaviour. In Clause 1.6.1.1 it is stated that *'The design requirements of this part of BS 5268 (i.e. Part 2) should be satisfied either by calculation, using the laws of structural mechanics, or by load testing in accordance with section 8'*.

The laws of structural mechanics referred to are those well established in recognised 'elastic theory', i.e.

- The material is *homogeneous,* which implies that its constituent parts have the same physical properties throughout its entire volume. This assumption is clearly violated in the case of timber. The constituent fibres are large in relation to the mass of which they form a part when compared with a material such as steel in which there are millions of very small crystals per square centimetre, randomly distributed and of similar quality creating an amorphous mass. In addition, the presence of defects such as knots, shakes etc. as described in Sections 1.2 and 1.3 represent the inclusion of elements with differing physical properties.

- The material is *isotropic,* which implies that the elastic properties are the same in all directions. The main constituent of timber is cellulose, which occurs as long chain molecules. The chemical/electrical forces binding the molecules together in these chains are much stronger than those which hold the chains to each other. A consequence of this is that considerable differences in elastic properties occur according to the grain orientation. Timber exhibits a marked degree of anisotropic behaviour. The design of timber is generally based on an assumption of orthotropic behaviour with three principal axes of symmetry: the longitudinal axis (parallel to the grain) the radial axis and the tangential axis, as shown in Figure 2.1. The properties relating to the tangential and radial directions are often treated together and regarded as properties perpendicular to the grain.

- The material obeys *Hooke's Law*, i.e. when subjected to an external force system the deformations induced will be directly proportional to the magnitude of the applied force. A typical stress/strain curve for a small wood specimen (with as few variations or defects as possible and loaded for a short-term duration) exhibits linearity prior to failure when loaded in tension or compression as indicated in Figures 2.2(a) and 2.2(b).

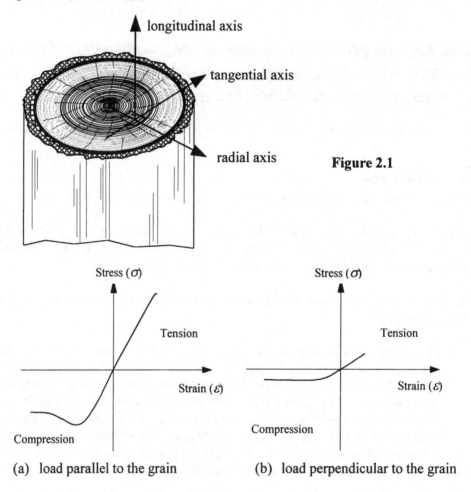

Figure 2.1

Figure 2.2

In Figure 2.2(a) the value of tensile strength is greater then the compressive strength. In both compression and tension linear behaviour occurs. In the case of compression ductility is present before failure occurs, whilst in tension a brittle, sudden failure occurs. These characteristics are reflected in the interaction behaviour of timber elements designed to resist combined bending and axial stresses as discussed in Chapter 5.0.

♦   The material is *elastic*, which implies that it will recover completely from any deformation after the removal of load. Elastic behaviour is generally observed in timber subject to compression up to the limit of proportionality. The elastic properties of timber in tension are more sensitive to the level of moisture content.

Permanent strain occurs at very low stress levels in timber which contains a high percentage of moisture.

♦ The *modulus of elasticity* is the same in tension and compression. This assumption is reasonable for both compression and tension. The value is much lower when the load is applied perpendicular to the grain than when it is applied parallel to the grain, as shown in Figure 2.2. Two values of modulus of elasticity are given in the code for each timber grade; $E_{minimum}$ and E_{mean}. The value to be used in any given circumstance is given in the code in the pertinent clauses.

♦ *Plane sections remain plane* during deformation. During bending this assumption is violated and is reflected in a non-linear bending stress diagram throughout cross-sections subject to a moment.

The behaviour and properties of timber do not satisfy the basic assumptions used in simple elastic theory. These deficiencies are accommodated in the design processes by the introduction of numerous modification factors and a factor of safety which are applied to produce an admissible stress which is then compared with the applied stress induced by the applied load system calculated using elastic theory. Extensive research and development during the latter half of the twentieth century has resulted in more representative mathematical models of timber behaviour and is reflected in Eurocode 5 which adopts a limit state approach to design. This code will eventually be utilised for timber design in the UK and is summarised in Chapter 8 of this text.

2.2 Modification Factors

The inherently variable nature of timber and its effects on structural material properties such as stress/strain characteristics, elasticity and creep has resulted in more than eighty different modification factors which are used in converting grade stresses (see Section 1.3) to permissible stresses for design purposes. In general, when designing to satisfy strength requirements (e.g. axial, bending or shear strength) the following relationship must be satisfied:

applied stress $\leq$ *permissible stress*

The applied stresses are calculated using elastic theory and the permissible stresses are determined from the code using the appropriate values relating to the strength classification multiplied by the modification factors which are relevant to the stress condition being considered. Symbols are defined relating to stresses and other variables in Clause 1.4 of BS 5268 : Part 2 : 1996 as follows:

a	distance;
A	area;
b	breadth of beam, thickness of web, or lesser transverse dimension of a tension or compression member;
d	diameter;
E	modulus of elasticity;
F	force or load;

h depth of member, greater transverse dimension of a tension or compression member;

i radius of gyration;

K modification factor (always with a subscript);

L length; span;

m mass;

M bending moment;

n number;

r radius of curvature;

t thickness; thickness of laminations;

u fastener slip;

α angle between the direction of the load and the direction of the grain;

η eccentricity factor;

θ angle between the longitudinal axis of a member and a connector axis;

λ slenderness ratio;

σ stress;

τ shear stress;

ω moisture content.

In many instances subscripts are also used to identify various types of force, stress or geometry; these are as follows:

a) type of force, stress etc.:
- c   compression;
- m   bending;
- t   tension;

b) significance:
- a   applied;
- adm   permissible;
- e   effective;
- mean   arithmetic mean;

c) geometry:
- apex   apex;
- r   radial;
- tang   tangential;
- || parallel (to the grain);
- $\perp$ perpendicular (to the grain);
- α angle.

The following examples illustrate the use of these symbols and subscripts:

$\sigma_{m,a,\perp}$ $\equiv$ applied bending stress perpendicular to the grain

$\sigma_{m,adm,\perp}$ $\equiv$ permissible bending stress perpendicular to the grain

$\sigma_{c,a,||}$ $\equiv$ applied compressive stress parallel to the grain

$\sigma_{c,adm,||}$ ≡ permissible compressive stress parallel to the grain

τ_a ≡ applied shear stress

Whilst not given in this Clause the subscript 'g' is often used to identify grade stresses. As mentioned previously, the permissible stress is evaluated by multiplying the grade stress for a particular strength class by the appropriate modification factors, e.g.

$$\sigma_{m,adm,||} = \sigma_{m,g,||} \times K_2 \times K_3 \times K_6 \times K_7 \times K_8$$

where:

K_2 relates to the *moisture content* of the timber;

K_3 relates to the *duration of the load* on the timber;

K_6 relates to the *shape of the cross-section* of the element being considered;

K_7 relates to the *depth* of the section being considered;

K_8 relates to the existence of structural elements enabling *load sharing*.

In each case a definition and the method of evaluating a coefficient is given in the code. In this text a table is given in each chapter which identifies each coefficient and reference clause number for the coefficients which are pertinent to the structural elements being considered. Three of the most frequently used coefficients are K_2, K_3 and K_8:

K_2:   The value of K_2 is governed by the average moisture content likely to be attained in service conditions. This is allowed for in the code by identifying a '*service class*' for the particular element being designed as given in Clause 1.6.4. The service classes are:

Service Class 1:   This is characterized by a moisture content in the materials corresponding to a temperature of 20°C and the relative humidity of the surrounding air only exceeding 65% for a few weeks per year. In such moisture conditions most timber will attain an average moisture content not exceeding 12%.

Service Class 2:   This is characterized by a moisture content in the materials corresponding to a temperature of 20°C and the relative humidity of the surrounding air only exceeding 85% for a few weeks per year. In such moisture conditions most timber will attain an average moisture content not exceeding 20%.

Service Class 3:   This is characterized, due to climatic conditions, by moisture contents higher than service class 2.

In Table 13 of the code values of K_2 are given varying from 0.6 in the case of compression parallel and perpendicular to the grain to 0.9 for shear parallel to the grain. These values reflect the non-uniform influence of moisture content on the mechanical properties of timber.

K_3:   The grade stresses given in the code relate to the strength of timber subject to long-term permanent loads. Extensive research and testing has established that the short-term strength of timber is considerably higher than can be expected in the long-term. The value of K_3 used is therefore dependent on the duration of loading being considered, i.e. long-term, medium-term, short-term or very short-term as defined in Table 14 of the code, e.g.

Long-term: dead + permanent imposed
Medium-term: dead + snow, dead + temporary imposed
Short-term: dead + imposed + wind,   dead + imposed + snow + wind
Very short-term: dead + imposed + wind

Each of these examples is qualified in the notes relating to Table 14 in the code.

K_8:   When designing structures in which four or more members, which are no greater than 610 mm apart, are connected by structural elements which provide lateral distribution of load (i.e. load-sharing) the grade stresses can be enhanced by multiplying by K_8 as indicated in Clause 2.9. Typical elements, which provide lateral distribution of load, are purlins, binders, boarding, battens etc.

    In addition, the mean modulus of elasticity can be used to calculate the displacements induced by both dead and imposed loads. *This does not apply to flooring systems which support mechanical plant and equipment or storage of systems which are subject to vibrations.*

    Provisions for built-up beams, trimmer joists, lintels and laminated beams are given separately in Clause 2.10.10, 2.10.11 and Section 3 of the code.

    The use of K_8 does not extend to the calculation of factor K_{12} in which the E value is used when designing load-sharing columns.

2.3 Shear Force and Bending Moment

Two parameters which are fundamentally important to the design of beams are '*shear force*' and '*bending moment.*' These quantities are the resultant of internal forces acting on the material of a beam in response to an externally applied load system.

2.3.1 Example 2.1 Beam with Point Loads

Consider a simply supported beam as shown in Figure 2.3 carrying a series of secondary beams each imposing a point load of 4 kN.

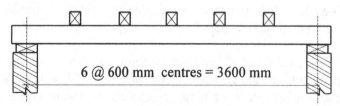

Figure 2.3

This structure can be represented as a line diagram, as shown in Figure 2.4.

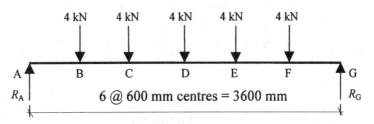

Figure 2.4

Since the externally applied force system is in equilibrium, the three equations of static equilibrium must be satisfied, i.e.

+ve ↑ $\Sigma F_y = 0$ The sum of the vertical forces must equal zero.

+ve ↻ $\Sigma M = 0$ The sum of the moments of all forces about '*any*' point on the plane of the forces must equal zero.

+ve → $\Sigma F_x = 0$ The sum of the horizontal forces must equal zero.

The assumed positive direction is as indicated. In this particular problem there are no externally applied horizontal forces and consequently the third equation is not required. (**Note:** It is still necessary to provide horizontal restraint to a structure since it can be subject to a variety of load cases, some of which may have a horizontal component.)

Consider the vertical equilibrium of the beam:

+ve ↑ $\Sigma F_y = 0$

$+ R_A - (5 \times 4.0) + R_G = 0$ $\therefore R_A + R_G = 20 \text{ kN}$ (i)

Consider the rotational equilibrium of the beam:

+ve ↻ $\Sigma M_A = 0$

Note: The sum of the moments is taken about one end of the beam (end A) for convenience. Since one of the forces (R_A) passes through this point it does not produce a moment about A and hence does not appear in the equation. It should be recognised that the sum of the moments could have been considered about *any* known point in the same plane.

$+ (4.0 \times 0.6) + (4.0 \times 1.2) + (4.0 \times 1.8) + (4.0 \times 2.4) + (4.0 \times 3.0) - (R_G \times 3.6) = 0$

$\therefore R_G = 10 \text{ kN}$ (ii)

Substituting into equation (i) gives $\therefore R_A = 10 \text{ kN}$

This calculation was carried out considering only the externally applied forces, i.e.

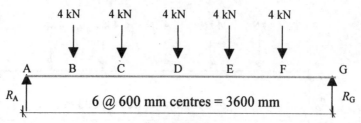

Figure 2.5

The structure itself was ignored; however the applied loads are transferred to the end supports through the material fibres of the beam. Consider the beam to be cut at section X-X producing two sections each of which is in equilibrium as shown in Figure 2.6.

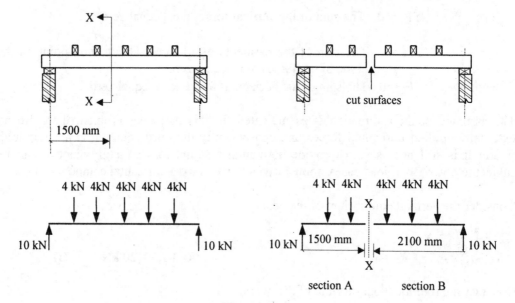

Figure 2.6

Clearly if the two sections are in equilibrium there must be internal forces acting on the cut surfaces to maintain this; these forces are known as the '*shear force*' and the '*bending moment*' as illustrated in Figure 2.7.

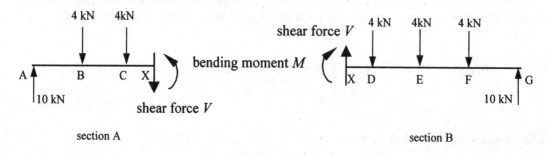

Figure 2.7

The force V and moment M are equal and opposite on each surface. The magnitude and direction of V and M can be determined by considering two equations of static equilibrium for either of the cut sections; both will give the same answer.

Consider the left-hand section with the 'assumed' directions of the internal forces V and M as shown in Figure 2.8.

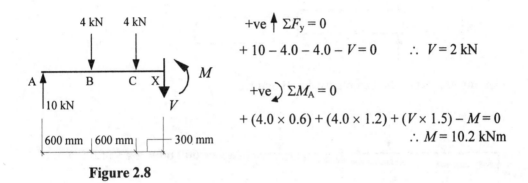

$$+ve \uparrow \Sigma F_y = 0$$
$$+ 10 - 4.0 - 4.0 - V = 0 \qquad \therefore \ V = 2 \text{ kN}$$

$$+ve \ \text{)} \ \Sigma M_A = 0$$
$$+ (4.0 \times 0.6) + (4.0 \times 1.2) + (V \times 1.5) - M = 0$$
$$\therefore \ M = 10.2 \text{ kNm}$$

Figure 2.8

2.4 Shear Force Diagram

In a statically determinate beam, the numerical value of the shear force can be obtained by evaluating the algebraic sum of the vertical forces to one side of the section being considered. The convention normally adopted to indicate positive and negative shear forces is shown in Figure 2.9.

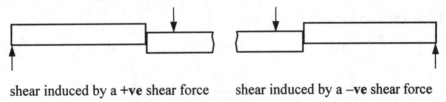

shear induced by a **+ve** shear force   shear induced by a **−ve** shear force

Figure 2.9

The calculation carried out to determine the shear force can be repeated at various locations along a beam and the values obtained plotted as a graph; this graph is known as the '*shear force diagram.*' The shear force diagram indicates the variation of the shear force along a structural member.

Consider any section of the beam between A and B:

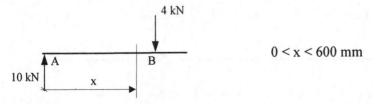

$$0 < x < 600 \text{ mm}$$

Note: the value immediately under the point load at the cut section is not being considered.

The shear force at any position x   =   Σ vertical force to one side
                                                =   +10.0 kN

This value is a constant for all values of x between zero and 600 mm: the graph will therefore be a horizontal line equal to 10.0 kN. This force produces a +ve shear effect, i.e.

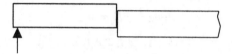

Consider any section of the beam between B and C:

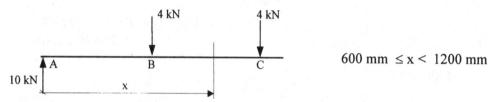

600 mm $\leq$ x $<$ 1200 mm

The shear force at any position x   =   Σ vertical force to one side
                                                =   +10.0 − 4.0 = 6.0 kN

This value is a constant for all values of x between 600 mm and 1200 mm: the graph will therefore be a horizontal line equal to 6.0 kN. This force produces a +ve shear effect.

Similarly for any section between C and D:

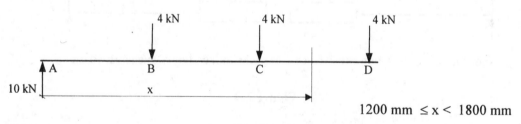

1200 mm $\leq$ x $<$ 1800 mm

The shear force at any position x   =   Σ vertical force to one side
                                                =   +10.0 − 4.0 − 4.0 = 2.0 kN

Consider any section of the beam between D and E:

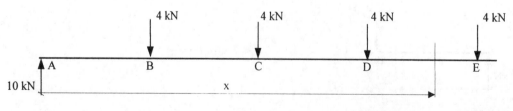

1800 mm $\leq$ x $<$ 2400 mm

The shear force at any position x = Σ vertical force to one side

  = +10.0 – 4.0 – 4.0 – 4.0 = – 2.0 kN

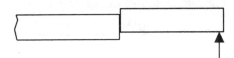

In this case the shear force is negative

Similarly between E and F 2400 mm < x < 3000 mm

The shear force at any position x = Σ vertical force to one side

  = +10.0 – 4.0 – 4.0 – 4.0 – 4.0 = – 6.0 kN

and

between F and G 3000 mm < x < 3600 mm

The shear force at any position x = Σ vertical force to one side

  = +10.0 – 4.0 – 4.0 – 4.0 – 4.0 – 4.0 = – 10.0 kN

In each of the cases above the value has not been considered at the point of application of the load.

Consider the location of the applied load at B, as shown in Figure 2.10.

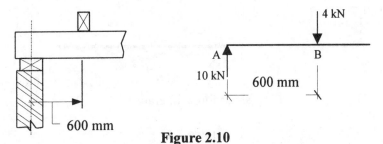

Figure 2.10

The 4.0 kN is not instantly transferred through the beam fibres at B but instead over the width of the actual secondary beam. The change in value of the shear force between x < 600 mm and x > 600 mm occurs over this width, as shown in Figure 2.11.

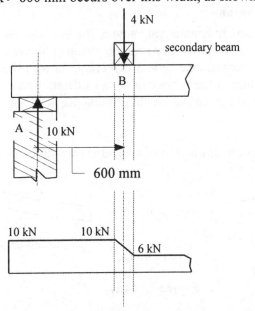

Figure 2.11

The width of the secondary beam is insignificant when compared with the overall span and the shear force is assumed to change instantly at this point, producing a vertical line on the shear force diagram as shown in Figure 2.12.

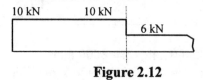

Figure 2.12

The full shear force diagram can therefore be drawn as shown in Figure 2.13.

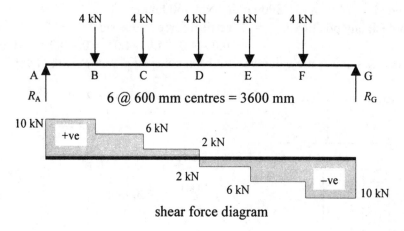

shear force diagram

Figure 2.13

The same result can be obtained by considering sections from the right-hand side of the beam.

2.5 Bending Moment Diagram

In a statically determinate beam, the numerical value of the bending moment (i.e. moments caused by forces which tend to bend the beam) can be obtained by evaluating the algebraic sum of the moments of the forces to 'one' side of a section. As with shear forces either the left-hand or the right-hand side of the beam can be considered. The convention normally adopted to indicate positive and negative bending moments is shown in Figures 2.14(a) and (b).

Bending inducing **tension on the underside** of a beam is considered **positive**.

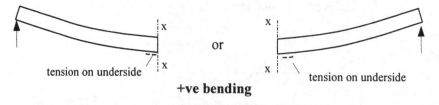

Figure 2.14 (a)

Bending inducing **tension on the top** of a beam is considered **negative**.

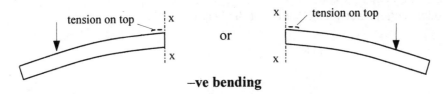

−ve bending

Figure 2.14 (b)

*Note: clockwise/anti-clockwise moments **do not** define +ve or −ve **bending** moments. The sign of the bending moment is governed by the location of the tension surface at the point being considered.*

As with shear forces the calculation for bending moments can be carried out at various locations along a beam and the values plotted on a graph; this graph is known as the '*bending moment diagram.*' The bending moment diagram indicates the variation in the bending moment along a structural member.

Consider sections between A and B of the beam as before:

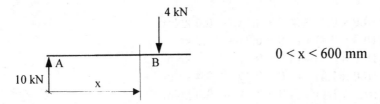

$0 < x < 600$ mm

In this case when $x = 600$ mm the 4.0 kN load passes through the section being considered and does not produce a bending moment and can therefore be ignored.

Bending moment $= \Sigma$ (algebraic sum of the moments of the forces to 'one' side of a section)

$= \Sigma$ (force × lever arm)

$M = 10.0 \times x = 10.0x$ kNm

Unlike the shear force, this expression is not a constant and depends on the value of 'x' which varies between the limits given. This is a linear expression which should be reflected in the calculated values of the bending moment.

x = 0	$M = 10.0 \times 0$	$= 0$ kNm
x = 100 mm	$M = 10.0 \times 0.1$	$= 1.0$ kNm
x = 200 mm	$M = 10.0 \times 0.2$	$= 2.0$ kNm
x = 300 mm	$M = 10.0 \times 0.3$	$= 3.0$ kNm
x = 400 mm	$M = 10.0 \times 0.4$	$= 4.0$ kNm
x = 500 mm	$M = 10.0 \times 0.5$	$= 5.0$ kNm
x = 600 mm	$M = 10.0 \times 0.6$	$= 6.0$ kNm

Clearly the bending moment increases linearly from zero at the simply supported end to a value of 6.0 kNm at point B.

Consider sections between B and C of the beam:

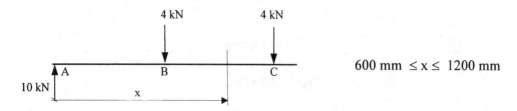

Bending moment = Σ (algebraic sum of the moments of the forces to 'one' side of a section)

$$M = +(10.0 \times x) \quad - (4.0 \times [x - 0.6])$$

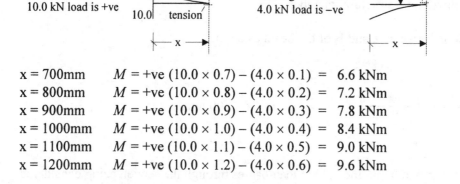

bending effect of 10.0 kN load is +ve

bending effect of 4.0 kN load is −ve

x = 700mm $M = +ve\ (10.0 \times 0.7) - (4.0 \times 0.1) = 6.6$ kNm
x = 800mm $M = +ve\ (10.0 \times 0.8) - (4.0 \times 0.2) = 7.2$ kNm
x = 900mm $M = +ve\ (10.0 \times 0.9) - (4.0 \times 0.3) = 7.8$ kNm
x = 1000mm $M = +ve\ (10.0 \times 1.0) - (4.0 \times 0.4) = 8.4$ kNm
x = 1100mm $M = +ve\ (10.0 \times 1.1) - (4.0 \times 0.5) = 9.0$ kNm
x = 1200mm $M = +ve\ (10.0 \times 1.2) - (4.0 \times 0.6) = 9.6$ kNm

As before, the bending moment increases linearly, i.e. from 6.6 kNm at x = 700 mm to a value of 9.6 kNm at point C.

Since the variation is linear it is only necessary to evaluate the magnitude and sign of the bending moment at locations where the slope of the line changes, i.e. each of the point load locations.

Consider point D:

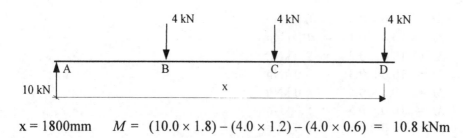

x = 1800mm $M = (10.0 \times 1.8) - (4.0 \times 1.2) - (4.0 \times 0.6) = 10.8$ kNm

Consider point E:

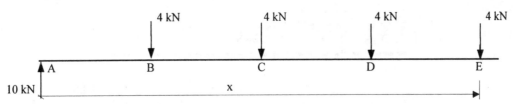

x = 2400mm $M = (10.0 \times 2.4) - (4.0 \times 1.8) - (4.0 \times 1.2) - (4.0 \times 0.6) = 9.6$ kNm
Similarly at point F:
x = 3000mm $M = (10.0 \times 3.0) - (4.0 \times 2.4) - (4.0 \times 1.8) - (4.0 \times 1.2) - (4.0 \times 0.6)$
            $= 6.0$ kNm
The full bending moment diagram can therefore be drawn as shown in Figure 2.15.

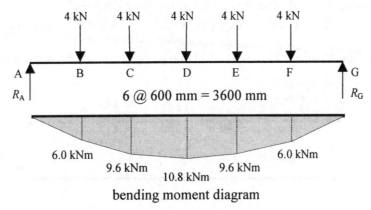

bending moment diagram

Figure 2.15

The same result can be obtained by considering sections from the right-hand side of the beam.
The value of the bending moment at any location can also be determined by evaluating the area under the shear force diagram.
Consider point B:

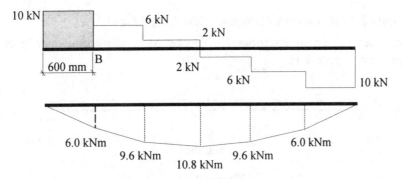

bending moment at B = shaded area on the shear force diagram
            $M_B = (10.0 \times 0.6) = 6.0$ kNm   as before

Consider a section at a distance of x = 900 mm along the beam between B and C:

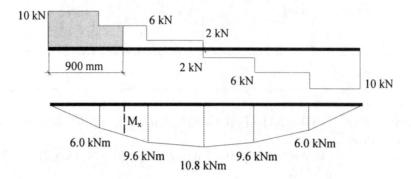

bending moment at x = shaded area on the shear force diagram

$$M_x = (10.0 \times 0.6) + (6.0 \times 0.3) = 7.8 \text{ kNm} \qquad \text{as before}$$

Consider a section at a distance of x = 2100 mm along the beam between B and C:

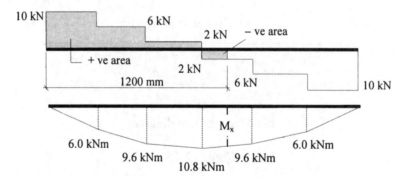

bending moment at x = shaded area on the shear force diagram

$$M_x = (10.0 \times 0.6) + (6.0 \times 0.6) + (2.0 \times 0.6) - (2.0 \times 0.3)$$
$$= 10.2 \text{ kNm}$$

Note that a maximum bending moment occurs at the same position as a zero shear force.

2.5.1   Example 2.2   Beam with Uniformly Distributed Load (UDL)

Consider the beam shown in Example 2.1 supporting a uniformly distributed load of 5 kN/m as shown in Figure 2.16.

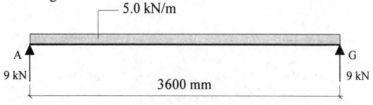

Figure 2.16

The shear force at any section a distance 'x' from the support at A is given by:

$$V_x = \text{algebraic sum of the vertical forces}$$

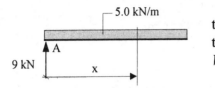

the force inducing +ve shear = 9.0 kN
the force inducing −ve shear = $(5.0 \times x)$ = 5.0x kN
V_x = +9.0 − 5.0x

This is a linear equation in which 'V_x' decreases as 'x' increases. The points of interest are at the supports where the maximum shear forces occur and at the locations where the maximum bending moment occurs, i.e. the point of zero shear.

$$V_x = 0 \quad \text{when} \quad +9.0 - 5.0x = 0 \qquad \therefore x = 1.8 \text{ m}$$

Any intermediate value can be found by substituting the appropriate value of 'x' in the equation for the shear force; e.g.

x = 600 mm $\quad V_x$ = +9.0 − (5.0 × 0.6) = +6.0 kN
x = 2100 mm $\quad V_x$ = +9.0 − (5.0 × 2.1) = −1.5 kN

The shear force can be drawn as before, as shown in Figure 2.17.

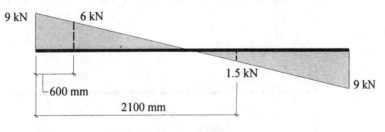

shear force diagram

Figure 2.17

The bending moment can be determined as before using either an equation or evaluating the area under the shear force diagram. Using an equation:

Bending moment at x = M_x = + (9.0 × x) − [(5.0 × x) × (x/2)] = $(9.0x - 2.5x^2)$

In this case the equation is *not* linear, and the bending moment diagram will therefore be *curved*.
Consider several values:
x = 0 $\qquad M_x$ = 0

$x = 600$ mm $M_x = +(9.0 \times 0.6) - (2.5 \times 0.6^2)$ $= 4.5$ kNm
$x = 1800$ mm $M_x = +(9.0 \times 1.8) - (2.5 \times 1.8^2)$ $= 8.1$ kNm
$x = 2100$ mm $M_x = +(9.0 \times 2.1) - (2.5 \times 2.1^2)$ $= 7.88$ kNm

Using the shear force diagram:
$x = 600$ mm

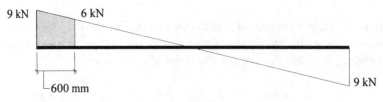

$M_x =$ shaded area $= +[0.5 \times (9.0 + 6.0) \times 0.6] = 4.5$ kNm

$x = 1800$ mm

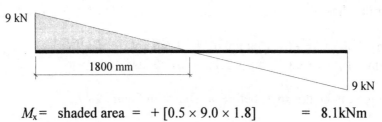

$M_x =$ shaded area $= +[0.5 \times 9.0 \times 1.8]$ $= 8.1$kNm

$x = 2100$ mm

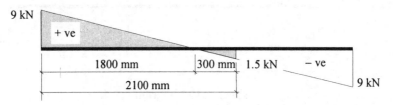

$M_x =$ shaded area $= +[8.1 - (0.5 \times 0.3 \times 1.5)] = 7.88$ kNm

The bending moment diagram is shown in Figure 2.18.

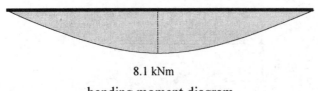

8.1 kNm

bending moment diagram

Figure 2.18

The UDL loading is a 'standard' load case which occurs in numerous beam designs and can be expressed in general terms using 'L' for the span and 'w' for the applied load/metre or W_{total} for the total uniformly distributed applied load, as shown in Figure 2.19.

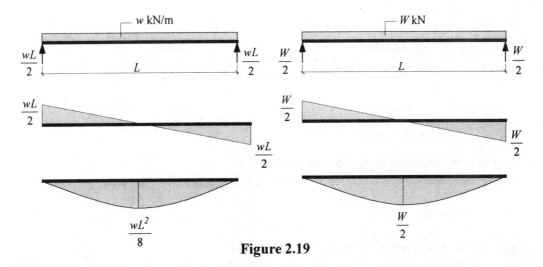

Figure 2.19

Clearly both give the same magnitude of support reactions, shear forces and bending moments.

2.5.2 Example 2.3 Beam with Combined Point Loads and UDL's

A simply supported beam ABCD carries a uniformly distributed load of 3.0 kN/m between A and B, point loads of 4 kN and 6 kN at B and C respectively, and a uniformly distributed load of 5.0 kN/m between B and D, as shown in Figure 2.20. Determine the support reactions, sketch the shear force diagram and determine the position and magnitude of the maximum bending moment.

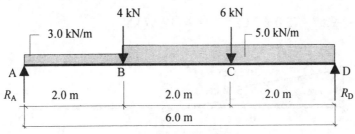

Figure 2.20

Consider the vertical equilibrium of the beam:

+ve $\uparrow$ $\Sigma F_y = 0$

$R_A - (3.0 \times 2.0) - 4.0 - 6.0 - (5.0 \times 4.0) + R_D = 0$ $\therefore R_A + R_D = 36$ kN   (i)

Consider the rotational equilibrium of the beam:

+ve $\downarrow$ $\Sigma M_A = 0$

$(3.0 \times 2.0 \times 1.0) + (4.0 \times 2.0) + (6.0 \times 4.0) + (5.0 \times 4.0 \times 4.0) - (R_D \times 6.0) = 0$ (ii)

$\therefore R_D = 19.67$ kN

Substituting into equation (i) gives $\therefore R_A = 16.33$ kN

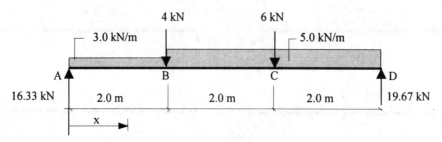

Shear force = algebraic sum of the vertical forces
Consider the shear force at a section 'x' from the left-hand end of the beam:

$x = 0$ $V_x = 0$

At position 'x' to the left of B before the 4.0 kN load
$$V_x = + 16.33 - (3.0 \times 2.0) \quad = \; + 10.33 \text{ kN}$$

At position 'x' to the right of B after the 4.0 kN load
$$V_x = + 10.33 - 4.0 \qquad\qquad = \; + 6.33 \text{ kN}$$

At position 'x' to the left of C before the 6.0 kN load
$$V_x = + 6.33 - (5.0 \times 2.0) \qquad = \; - 3.67 \text{ kN}$$

At position 'x' to the right of C after the 6.0 kN load
$$V_x = - 3.67 - 6.0 \qquad\qquad = \; - 9.67 \text{ kN}$$

$x = 6.0 \text{ m} \quad V_x = -9.67 - (5.0 \times 2.0) \qquad = \; - 19.67 \text{ kN}$

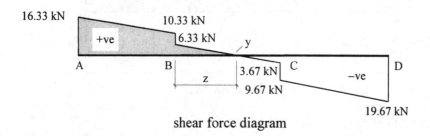

shear force diagram

The maximum bending moment occurs at the position of zero shear, i.e. point 'y' on the shear force diagram. The value of 'z' can be determined from the shear force and applied loads:

$$z = \frac{6.33}{5.0} = 1.266 \text{ m}$$

Note: the slope of the shear force diagram between B and C is equal to the UDL of 5 kN/m.

Maximum bending moment M = shaded area
$$= [0.5 \times (16.33 + 10.33) \times 2.0] + [0.5 \times 1.266 \times 6.33]$$
$$= 30.67 \text{ kNm}$$

Alternatively, consider the beam cut at this section:

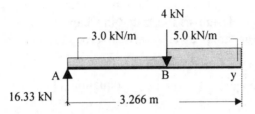

$$M_y = +(16.33 \times 3.266) - (3.0 \times 2.0 \times 2.266) - (4.0 \times 1.266) - [(5.0 \times 1.266) \times (0.633)]$$
$$= +30.67 \text{ kNm}$$

2.6 Elastic Shear Stress Distribution

The shear forces induced in a beam by an applied load system generate shear stresses in both the horizontal and vertical directions. At any point in an elastic body, the shear stresses in two mutually perpendicular directions are equal to each other in magnitude.

Consider an element of material subject to shear stresses along the edges, as shown in Figure 2.21.

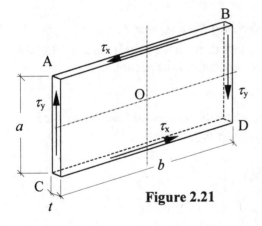

Force on surface AB = F_{AB} = $\tau \times bt$
Force on surface CD = F_{CD} = $\tau \times bt$
Force on surface AC = F_{AC} = $\tau \times at$
Force on surface BD = F_{BD} = $\tau \times at$.

+ve $\uparrow \Sigma F_y = 0$

$$F_{AC} = F_{BD}$$

+ve $\rightarrow \Sigma F_x$ =

$$F_{AB} = F_{CD}$$

Figure 2.21

+ve $\circlearrowright \Sigma M_O = 0$

$$- (F_{AB} \times \frac{a}{2}) - (F_{CD} \times \frac{a}{2}) + (F_{AC} \times \frac{b}{2}) + (F_{BD} \times \frac{b}{2}) = 0$$

Substitute for F_{CD} and F_{BD}:
$$- (F_{AB} \times a) + (F_{AC} \times b) = 0 \qquad \therefore F_{AB}a = F_{AC}b$$
$$(\tau_x bt)a = (\tau_y at)b$$
$$\tau_x = \tau_y$$

The two shear stresses are equal and complementary. In timber beam design, vertical shear stresses across the grain are always accompanied by horizontal shear stresses parallel to the grain and of equal magnitude. The shear strength of timber parallel to the grain ($\tau_{||}$) is considerably less than the value across the grain. The grade shear stress given in BS 5268 is based on the $\tau_{||}$ value. When considering ply-web beams, horizontal shear stresses occur between the web and the flanges in addition to those in the web; both stress conditions must be considered in design, as illustrated in Chapter 3.

The magnitude of the shear stress at any vertical cross-section on a beam can be determined using;

$$\tau \;=\; \frac{VA\bar{y}}{Ib} \qquad\qquad \text{equation (1)}$$

where:

V the vertical shear force at the section being considered,
A the area of the cross-section above (or below) the 'horizontal' plane being considered (**Note:** The shear stress varies throughout the depth of a cross-section for any given value of shear force),
$\bar{y}$ the distance from the elastic neutral axis to the centroid of the area A,
b the breadth of the beam at the level of the horizontal plane being considered,
I the second moment of area of the full cross-section about the elastic neutral axis.

The intensity of shear stress throughout the depth of a section is not uniform and is a maximum at the level of the neutral axis.

2.6.1   *Example 2.4   Shear Stress Distribution in a Rectangular Beam*

The rectangular beam shown in Figure 2.22 is subject to a vertical shear force of 3.0 kN. Determine the shear stress distribution throughout the depth of the section.

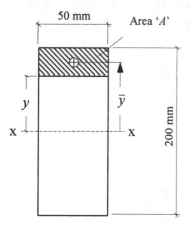

The shear stress at any horizontal level a distance 'y' from the neutral axis is given by:

$\tau \quad = \quad \dfrac{VA\bar{y}}{Ib}$

$V \quad = \quad$ shear force $= \; 3.0$ kN

$I \quad = \quad \dfrac{bd^3}{12} \; = \; \dfrac{50\times200^3}{12} \; = \; 33.33 \times 10^6 \; \text{mm}^4$

$b \quad = \quad 50$ mm   (for all values of 'y')

Figure 2.22

Consider the shear stress at a number of values of 'y',

$y \;=\; 100$ mm $A\bar{y} \;=\; 0$ (since $A = 0$)

$\tau_{100} \;=\; 0$

$y \;\; = \;\; 75 \text{ mm}$

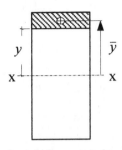

$$A \;\; = \;\; 50 \times 25 \;\; = \;\; 1250 \text{ mm}^2$$
$$\bar{y} \;\; = \;\; 75 + 12.5 = \;\; 87.5 \text{ mm}$$
$$A\bar{y} \;\; = \;\; 109.375 \times 10^3 \text{ mm}^3$$
$$\tau_{75} \;\; = \;\; \frac{3 \times 10^3 \times 109.375 \times 10^3}{33.3 \times 10^6 \times 50} \;\; = \;\; 0.197 \text{ N/mm}^2$$

$y \;\; = \;\; 50 \text{ mm}$

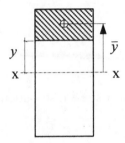

$$A \;\; = \;\; 50 \times 50 \;\; = \;\; 2500 \text{ mm}^2$$
$$\bar{y} \;\; = \;\; 50 + 25 \;\; = \;\; 75 \text{ mm}$$
$$A\bar{y} \;\; = \;\; 187.5 \times 10^3 \text{ mm}^3$$
$$\tau_{50} \;\; = \;\; \frac{3 \times 10^3 \times 187.5 \times 10^3}{33.3 \times 10^6 \times 50} \;\; = \;\; 0.338 \text{ N/mm}^2$$

$y \;\; = \;\; 25 \text{ mm}$

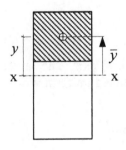

$$A \;\; = \;\; 50 \times 75 \;\; = \;\; 3750 \text{ mm}^2$$
$$\bar{y} \;\; = \;\; 25 + 37.5 = \;\; 62.5 \text{ mm}$$
$$A\bar{y} \;\; = \;\; 234.375 \times 10^3 \text{ mm}^3$$
$$\tau_{25} \;\; = \;\; \frac{3 \times 10^3 \times 234.375 \times 10^3}{33.3 \times 10^6 \times 50} \;\; = \;\; 0.422 \text{ N/mm}^2$$

$y \;\; = \;\; 0 \text{ mm}$

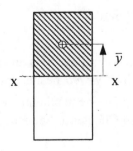

$$A \;\; = \;\; 50 \times 100 \;\; = \;\; 5000 \text{ mm}^2$$
$$\bar{y} \;\; = \;\; 50 \text{ mm}$$
$$A\bar{y} \;\; = \;\; 250 \times 10^3 \text{ mm}^3$$
$$\tau_0 \;\; = \;\; \frac{3 \times 10^3 \times 250 \times 10^3}{33.3 \times 10^6 \times 50} \;\; = \;\; 0.45 \text{ N/mm}^2$$

$y = -25$ mm

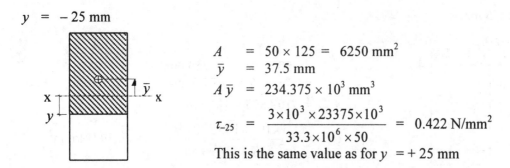

$$A = 50 \times 125 = 6250 \text{ mm}^2$$
$$\bar{y} = 37.5 \text{ mm}$$
$$A\bar{y} = 234.375 \times 10^3 \text{ mm}^3$$

$$\tau_{-25} = \frac{3 \times 10^3 \times 23375 \times 10^3}{33.3 \times 10^6 \times 50} = 0.422 \text{ N/mm}^2$$

This is the same value as for $y = +25$ mm

The cross-section (and hence the stress diagram) is symmetrical about the elastic neutral axis as shown in Figure 2.23.

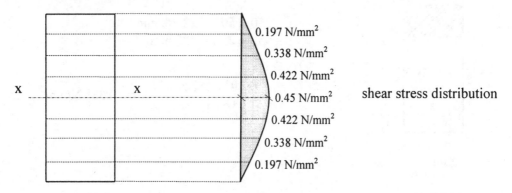

0.197 N/mm²
0.338 N/mm²
0.422 N/mm²
0.45 N/mm²
0.422 N/mm²
0.338 N/mm²
0.197 N/mm²

shear stress distribution

Figure 2.23

The maximum value occurs at the same level as the elastic neutral axis. The 'average' shear stress for a cross-section is equal to the applied force distributed uniformly over the entire cross-section, i.e.

$$\tau_{\text{average}} = \frac{Force}{Area} = \frac{V}{A} = \frac{3.0 \times 10^3}{50 \times 200} = 0.3 \text{ N/mm}^2$$

For a *rectangular* section:

$$\tau_{\text{maximum}} = 1.5 \times \tau_{\text{average}} = \frac{1.5V}{A} = 1.5 \times 0.3 = 0.45 \text{ N/mm}^2$$

In timber design, rectangular sections are the most frequently used cross-sections and the maximum shear stress can be evaluated using ($1.5 \times \tau_{\text{average}}$). In ply-web beams where I-sections and box-sections are often used it is necessary to determine the maximum value using equation (1) as in Example 2.4. This is further illustrated in Chapter 3, Sections 3.4 and 3.5.

2.7   Elastic Bending Stress Distribution

The bending moments induced in a beam by an applied load system generate bending stresses in the material fibres, which vary from a maximum in the extreme fibres to a minimum at the level of the neutral axis, as shown in Figure 2.24.

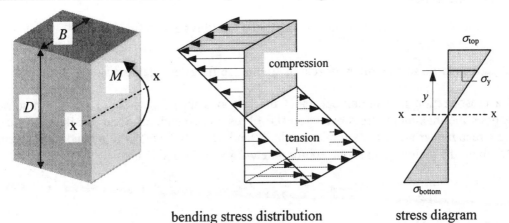

bending stress distribution   stress diagram

Figure 2.24

The magnitude of the bending stresses at any vertical cross-section can be determined using the simple theory of bending from which the following equation is derived:

$$\frac{M}{I} = \frac{E}{R} = \frac{\sigma}{y} \qquad \therefore \ \sigma = \frac{My}{I} \qquad \text{equation (2)}$$

where:
M   the applied bending moment at the section being considered,
E   the value of Young's modulus of elasticity,
R   the radius of curvature of the beam,
σ the bending stress,
y   the distance measured from the elastic neutral axis to the level on the cross-section at which the stress is being evaluated,
I   the second moment of area of the full cross-section about the elastic neutral axis.

It is evident from equation (2) that for any specified cross-section in a beam subject to a known value of bending moment (i.e. *M* and *I* constant) the bending stress is directly proportional to the distance from the neutral axis; i.e.

$$\sigma = \text{constant} \times y \quad \therefore \ \sigma \propto y$$

This is shown in Figure 2.24, in which the maximum bending stress occurs at the extreme fibres, i.e. $y_{maximum} = D/2$.

In design it is usually the extreme fibre stresses relating to the $y_{maximum}$ values at the top and bottom which are critical. These can be determined using:

$$\sigma_{top} = \frac{M}{Z_{top}} \quad \text{and} \quad \sigma_{bottom} = \frac{M}{Z_{bottom}}$$

where:

σ and M are as before,

Z_{top} the elastic section modulus relating to the top fibres and defined as $\dfrac{I_{xx}}{y_{top}}$

Z_{bottom} the elastic section modulus relating to the top fibres and defined as $\dfrac{I_{xx}}{y_{bottom}}$

If a cross-section is symmetrical about the x-x axis then $Z_{top} = Z_{bottom}$. In asymmetric sections the maximum stress occurs in the fibres corresponding to the smallest Z value. For a rectangular cross-section of breadth 'B' and depth 'D' subject to a bending moment 'M' about the major x-x axis, the appropriate values of I, y and Z are:

$$I = \frac{BD^3}{12} \qquad y_{maximum} = \frac{D}{2} \qquad Z_{minimum} = \frac{BD^2}{6}$$

In the case of bending about the minor y-y axis:

$$I = \frac{DB^3}{12} \qquad y_{maximum} = \frac{B}{2} \qquad Z_{minimum} = \frac{DB^2}{6}$$

The maximum stress induced in a cross-section subject to bi-axial bending is given by:

$$\sigma_{maximum} = \frac{M_x}{Z_{x\,minimum}} + \frac{M_y}{Z_{y\,minimum}}$$

where M_x and M_y are the applied bending moments about the x and y axes respectively.

2.7.1   Example 2.5   *Bending Stress Distribution in a Rectangular Beam*

The rectangular beam shown in Figure 2.25 is subject to a bending moment of 2.0 kNm. Determine the bending stress distribution throughout the depth of the section.

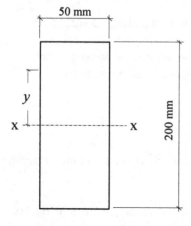

The bending stress at any horizontal level a distance 'y' from the neutral axis is given by:

$$\sigma = \frac{My}{I}$$

M = bending moment   = 2.0 kNm

$$I = \frac{bd^3}{12} = \frac{50 \times 200^3}{12} = 33.33 \times 10^6 \text{ mm}^4$$

Figure 2.25

Consider the bending stress at a number of values of 'y',

$y = 100$ mm $\qquad \sigma_{100} = \dfrac{2.0 \times 10^6 \times 100}{33.33 \times 10^6} = 6.0$ N/mm^2

$y = 75$ mm $\qquad \sigma_{75} = \dfrac{2.0 \times 10^6 \times 75}{33.33 \times 10^6} = 4.5$ N/mm^2

$y = 50$ mm $\qquad \sigma_{50} = \dfrac{2.0 \times 10^6 \times 50}{33.33 \times 10^6} = 3.0$ N/mm^2

$y = 25$ mm $\qquad \sigma_{25} = \dfrac{2.0 \times 10^6 \times 25}{33.33 \times 10^6} = 1.5$ N/mm^2

$y = 0$ $\qquad \sigma_0 = 0$

$y = -25$ mm $\qquad \sigma_{-25} = \dfrac{2.0 \times 10^6 \times 25}{33.33 \times 10^6} = 1.5$ N/mm^2

The cross-section (and hence the stress diagram) is symmetrical about the elastic neutral axis.

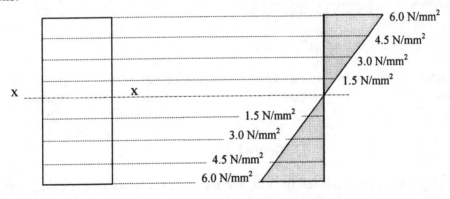

bending stress diagram

Figure 2.26

2.8 Transformed Sections

Beams such as ply-web and box-beams in timber (see Figure 3.1) are generally fabricated from different materials, e.g. ply-wood webs and softwood flanges fastened together. During bending, the stresses induced in such sections are shared among all the component parts. The extent to which sharing occurs is dependent on the method of connection at the interfaces. This connection is normally designed such that '*no slip*' occurs between the different materials during bending. The resulting structural element is a composite section which is non-homogeneous; this invalidates the simple theory of bending in which homogeneity is assumed.

A useful technique often used when analysing such composite sections is the '*transformed section*' method. When using this method an equivalent homogeneous section is considered in which all components are assumed to be of the same material. The simple theory of bending is then used to determine the stresses in the transformed sections, which are subsequently modified to determine the stresses in the '*actual*' materials.

Consider the composite section shown in Figure 2.27(a) in which a steel plate has been securely fastened to the underside face. There are two possible transformed sections which can be considered:

(i) an equivalent section in terms of timber; Figure 2.27(b) or
(ii) an equivalent section in terms of steel; Figure 2.27(c).

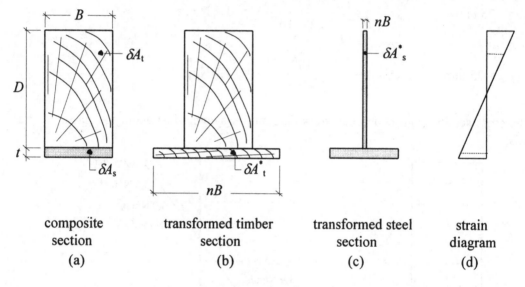

composite	transformed timber	transformed steel	strain
section	section	section	diagram
(a)	(b)	(c)	(d)

Figure 2.27

To obtain an equivalent section made from timber, the same material as the existing timber must replace the steel plate. The dimension of the replacement timber must be modified to reflect the different material properties. The equivalent '*transformed*' section properties are shown in Figure 2.27(b).

The overall depth of both sections is the same $(D + t)$. The '*strain*' in element 'δA_s' in the original section is equal to the strain in element δA_t^* of the transformed section;

$$\varepsilon_{steel} = \varepsilon_{timber}$$

but $\quad strain = \dfrac{stress}{modulus\ (E)} = \dfrac{\sigma}{E} \qquad \therefore \varepsilon = \dfrac{\sigma}{E}$

$$\dfrac{\sigma_s}{E_s} = \dfrac{\sigma_t}{E_t} \qquad \therefore \dfrac{\sigma_s}{\sigma_t} = \dfrac{E_s}{E_t}$$

The force in each element must also be equal:

$$force = stress \times area \quad P_s = P_t$$
$$\sigma_s \delta A_s = \sigma_t \delta A_t^*$$

$$\delta A^*_t = \frac{\sigma_s}{\sigma_t} \delta A_s = \frac{E_s}{E_t} \delta A_s$$

This indicates that in the transformed section:

Equivalent area of transformed timber $= n \times$ original area of steel

where:

n is the '*modular ratio*' of the materials and is equal to $\dfrac{E_s}{E_t}$

The equivalent area of timber must be subject to the same value of strain as the original material it is replacing, i.e. it is positioned at the same distance from the elastic neutral axis. The simple equation of bending, equation (2), can be used with the transformed section properties to determine the bending stresses. The '*actual*' stresses in the steel will be equal to 'n' $\times$ equivalent timber stresses. The use of this method is illustrated in Example 2.6 and in the design of ply-web beams and stressed-skin panels in Chapter 3. A similar, alternative analysis can be carried out using a transformed steel section as shown in Figure 2.27(c).

2.8.1   Example 2.6   Composite Timber/Steel Section

A timber beam is enhanced by the addition of two steel plates, as shown in Figure 2.28. Determine the maximum timber and steel stresses induced in the cross-section when the beam is subjected to a bending moment of 70 kNm.

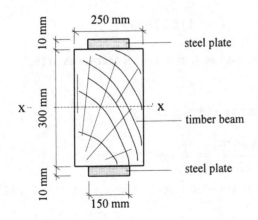

$E_{\text{timber}} = 8200 \ \text{N/mm}^2$
$E_{\text{steel}} = 205 \times 10^3 \ \text{N/mm}^2$

Figure 2.28

(a)   Transformed section based on '*timber*'

Equivalent width of timber to replace the steel plate $= n \times 150$ mm
where:

$$n = \frac{E_{\text{steel}}}{E_{\text{timber}}} = \frac{205 \times 10^3}{8200} = 25 \qquad nB = 25 \times 150 = 3750 \ \text{mm}$$

The maximum stresses occur in the timber when $y = 150$ mm, and in the steel (or equivalent replacement timber) when $y = 160$ mm.

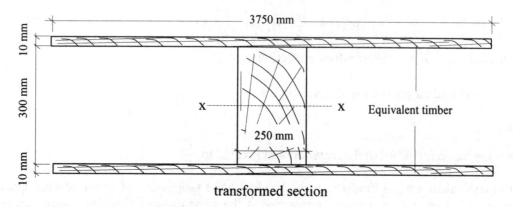

transformed section

$$I_{xx \text{ transformed}} = \left\{ \frac{3750 \times 320^3}{12} - \frac{3500 \times 300^3}{12} \right\} = 2.365 \times 10^9 \text{ mm}^4$$

Maximum bending stress in the *timber* is given by:

$$\sigma_{\text{timber}} = \frac{My_{150}}{I} = \frac{70 \times 10^6 \times 150}{2.365 \times 10^9} = 4.43 \text{ N/mm}^2$$

Maximum bending stress in the *equivalent timber* is given by:

$$\sigma = \frac{My_{160}}{I} = \frac{70 \times 10^6 \times 160}{2.365 \times 10^9} = 4.74 \text{ N/mm}^2$$

This value of stress represents a maximum value of stress in the steel plates given by:

$$\sigma_{\text{steel}} = n \times \sigma = 25 \times 4.74 = 118.5 \text{ N/mm}^2$$

Alternatively, the above stresses can be determined assuming a steel section as in (b).

(b)   Transformed section based on '*steel*'
Equivalent width of steel to replace the timber beam $= n \times 150$ mm
where:

$$n = \frac{E_{\text{timber}}}{E_{\text{steel}}} = \frac{1}{25} \qquad nB = \frac{1 \times 250}{25} = 10 \text{ mm}$$

The maximum stresses occur in the timber (or equivalent replacement steel) when $y = 150$ mm, and in the steel when $y = 160$ mm.

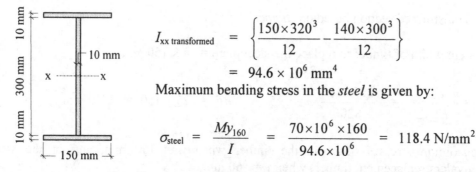

$$I_{xx \text{ transformed}} = \left\{ \frac{150 \times 320^3}{12} - \frac{140 \times 300^3}{12} \right\}$$

$$= 94.6 \times 10^6 \text{ mm}^4$$

Maximum bending stress in the *steel* is given by:

$$\sigma_{\text{steel}} = \frac{My_{160}}{I} = \frac{70 \times 10^6 \times 160}{94.6 \times 10^6} = 118.4 \text{ N/mm}^2$$

Maximum bending stress in the *equivalent steel* is given by:

$$\sigma = \frac{My_{150}}{I} = \frac{70 \times 10^6 \times 150}{94.6 \times 10^6} = 111 \text{ N/mm}^2$$

This value of stress represents a maximum value of stress in the timber given by:

$$\sigma_{\text{timber}} = n \times \sigma = \left(\frac{1}{25} \times 111\right) = 4.44 \text{ N/mm}^2$$

Normally when using this method in the design of ply-web beams the plywood webs are replaced by softwood timber of equivalent thickness to give the required transformed section; as indicated in Example 2.6 both transformed sections produce the same result.

2.9 Deflection of Beams

Structural design encompasses a wide range of considerations in addition to strength criteria as evaluated using permissible stresses. One of the most important of these is the stiffness of a structure or structural element. The stiffness is reflected in the deformations and deflections induced by the applied load system. There are large variations in what are considered by practising engineers to be acceptable deflections for different circumstances, e.g. limitations on the deflections of beams are necessary to avoid consequences such as:

- ♦ damage to finishes e.g. to brittle plaster or ceiling tiles,
- ♦ unnecessary alarm to occupants of a building,
- ♦ misalignment of door frames causing difficulty in opening,

If situations arise in which a designer considers the recommendations given in the design codes are too lenient or too severe (e.g. conflicting with the specification of suppliers or manufacturers), then individual engineering judgement must be used. There are well established analytical methods for calculating theoretical deflections, in most cases computer analysis is adopted.

In a simply supported beam, the maximum deflection induced by the applied loading always approximates the mid-span value if it is not equal to it. A number of standard, frequently used load cases for which the elastic deformation is required are given in Table 2.1 of this text. In the case indicated with '*' the actual maximum deflection will be approximately equal to the value given (i.e. within 2.5%).

In many cases beams support complex load arrangements which do not lend themselves to either an individual load case or a combination of the load cases given in Table 2.1. Provided that deflection is not the governing design criterion, a calculation which gives an approximate answer is usually adequate. The equivalent UDL method is a useful tool for estimating the deflection in a simply supported beam with a complex loading.

Load Case	Deflection	Load Case	Deflection
W_{Total} over span L	$\dfrac{5WL^3}{384EI}$	W_{Total} over span L (fixed ends)	$\dfrac{WL^3}{384EI}$
W_{Total} over b, with a, b, c; span L	$\dfrac{WL^3}{384EI}\alpha_1$	P at centre, $L/2$ and $L/2$ (fixed ends)	$\dfrac{PL^3}{192EI}$
P at centre, $L/2$ and $L/2$	$\dfrac{PL^3}{48EI}$	P at a, b, $b>a$ (fixed ends)	$\dfrac{2\,Pa^2b^3}{3\,EI\beta}$
* P at a, b, $b>a$; span L	$\approx\dfrac{PL^3}{48EI}\alpha_2$	W_{Total} over a, b (fixed end)	$-\dfrac{Wa^2b}{24EI}$
W_{Total} over a, then b (cantilever)	$\dfrac{Wa^3}{8EI}\alpha_3$	W_{Total} over b, with a (cantilever)	$\dfrac{Wb^4}{8EI}+\dfrac{Wab^3}{6EI}$
P over a, b (cantilever)	$\dfrac{Pa^3}{3EI}\alpha_4$	P at b, with a (cantilever)	$\dfrac{Wb^3}{3EI}+\dfrac{Wab^2}{3EI}$

$$\alpha_1 = (L^3 + 2L^2a + 4La^2 - 8a^3) \qquad \alpha_2 = \left[\frac{3a}{L} - 4\left(\frac{a}{L}\right)^3\right] \qquad \alpha_3 = \left(1 + \frac{4b}{3a}\right) \qquad \alpha_4 = \left(1 + \frac{3b}{2a}\right)$$

$$\beta = (3L - 2a)^2$$

Table 2.1

2.9.1 Equivalent UDL Technique.

To estimate deflection, consider a single-span, simply supported beam carrying a *non-uniform* loading which induces a maximum bending moment of *M*, as shown in Figure 2.29:

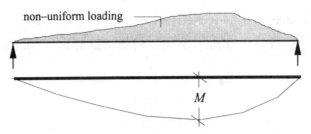

bending moment diagram

Figure 2.29

The equivalent UDL (W_e) which would induce the same *magnitude* of maximum bending moment (**Note:** the position may be different) on a simply supported span carrying a *uniform* loading can be determined from:

Maximum bending moment $M = \dfrac{W_e L^2}{8}$

$\therefore$ $W_e = \dfrac{8M}{L^2}$

where W_e is the equivalent uniform distributed load.

The maximum deflection of the beam carrying the uniform loading will occur at the mid-span and be equal to $\delta = \dfrac{5W_e L^4}{384EI}$ (see Table 2.1)

Using this expression, the maximum deflection of the beam carrying the non-uniform loading can be estimated by substituting for the W_e term, i.e.

$$\delta \approx \frac{5W_e L^4}{384E\,I} = \frac{5 \times \left(\dfrac{8M}{L^2}\right) L^4}{384\ EI} = \frac{0.104\ M L^2}{EI}$$

2.10 Résumé of Analysis Techniques

The following résumé gives a brief summary of the most common manual techniques adopted to determine the forces induced in the members of statically determinate pin-jointed frames. There are numerous structural analysis books available which give comprehensive detailed explanations of these techniques.

2.10.1 Method of Sections

The method of sections involves the application of the three equations of static equilibrium to two-dimensional plane frames. The sign convention adopted to indicate ties and struts in frames is as shown in Figure 2.30.

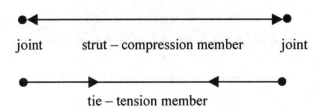

Figure 2.30

The method involves considering an imaginary section line which cuts the frame under consideration into two parts A and B, as shown in Figure 2.33.

Since only three independent equations are available, any section taken through a frame must not include more than three members for which the internal force is unknown.

Consideration of the equilibrium of the resulting force system enables the magnitude and sense of the forces in the cut members to be determined.

2.10.2 Joint Resolution

This is a particular case of the *'method of sections'* in which a series of sections are considered, each isolating an individual joint as shown in Section 2.11.1. Since all of the forces at a joint are coincident, the moment equation of equilibrium cannot be used and hence only two unknown forces can be determined at any given section.

2.11 Example 2.7   Pin-Jointed Truss

A pin-jointed truss simply supported by a pinned support at A and a roller support at E carries three loads at nodes G, H and I, as shown in Figure 2.31. Determine the magnitude and sense of the forces induced in members X, Y and Z as indicated.

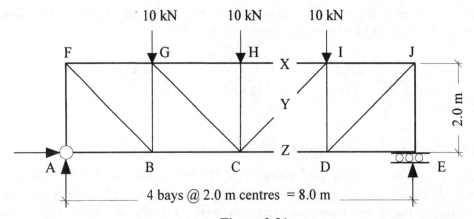

Figure 2.31

Step 1: Evaluate the support reactions. It is not necessary to know any information regarding the frame members at this stage other than dimensions as shown in Figure 2.32, since only externally applied loads and reactions are involved.

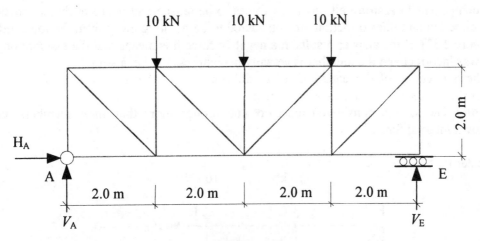

Figure 2.32

Apply the three equations of static equilibrium to the force system.

+ve ↑	$\Sigma F_y = 0$	$V_A - (10 + 10 + 10) + V_E = 0$	$V_A + V_E = 30 \text{ kN}$
+ve →	$\Sigma F_x = 0$		$\mathbf{H_A} = \mathbf{0}$
+ve ↗	$\Sigma M_A = 0$	$(10 \times 2.0) + (10 \times 4.0) + (10 \times 6.0) - (V_E \times 8.0) = 0$	
			$\mathbf{V_E} = \mathbf{15 \text{ kN}}$
		hence	$\mathbf{V_A} = \mathbf{15 \text{ kN}}$

Step 2: Select a section through which the frame can be considered to be cut, and using the same three equations of equilibrium determine the magnitude and sense of the unknown forces (i.e. the internal forces in the cut members).

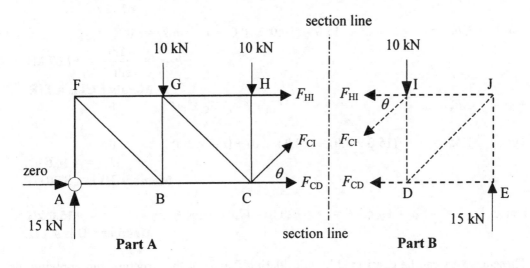

Figure 2.33

It is convenient to **assume** all unknown forces to be tensile and hence at the cut section their direction and lines of action are considered to be pointing away from the joint (refer to Figure 2.33). If the answer results in a negative force this means that the assumption of a tie was incorrect and the member is actually in compression, i.e. a strut.

The application of the equations of equilibrium to either part of the cut frame will enable the forces X, Y and Z to be evaluated.

Note: The section considered must not cut through more than three members with unknown internal forces.

Consider Part A:

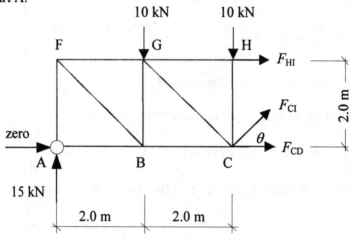

Figure 2.34

Note: $\sin\theta = \dfrac{1}{\sqrt{2}} = 0.707,$ $\cos\theta = \dfrac{1}{\sqrt{2}} = 0.707,$

+ve ↑ $\Sigma F_y = 0$ $15.0 - (10.0 + 10.0) + F_{CI}\sin\theta = 0$

$$F_{CI} = \frac{5.0}{\sin\theta} = +7.07 \text{ kN}$$

Member CI is a TIE

+ve → $\Sigma F_x = 0$ $F_{HI} + F_{CD} + F_{CI}\cos\theta = 0$

+ve ⤢ $\Sigma M_C = 0$ $(15.0 \times 4.0) - (10.0 \times 2.0) + (F_{HI} \times 2.0) = 0$

$$F_{HI} = -20.0 \text{ kN}$$

Member HI is a STRUT

hence $F_{CD} = -F_{HI} - F_{CI}\cos\theta = -(-20.0) - (7.07 \times \cos\theta)$ $= +15.0 \text{ kN}$

Member CD is a TIE

These answers can be confirmed by considering Part B of the structure and applying the equations as above.

2.11.1 Joint Resolution

Considering the same frame using joint resolution highlights the advantage of the method of sections when only a few member forces are required.

In this technique (which can be considered as a special case of the method of sections) sections are taken which isolate each individual joint in the frame in turn, e.g.

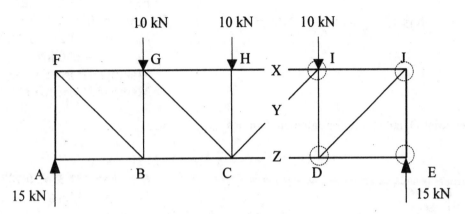

Figure 2.35

In Figure 2.35 four sections are shown, each of which isolates a joint in the structure as indicated in Figure 2.36.

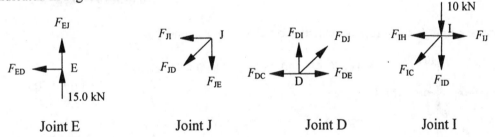

Figure 2.36

Since in each case the forces are coincident, the moment equation is of no value: hence only two independent equations are available. It is necessary when considering the equilibrium of each joint to do so in a sequence which ensures that there are no more than two unknown member forces in the joint under consideration. This can be carried out until all member forces in the structure have been determined.

Consider Joint E:

$$+\text{ve} \uparrow \ \Sigma F_y \ = 0 \qquad +15.0 + F_{EJ} \quad = 0$$

$$F_{EJ} \ = \ -\mathbf{15.0 \ kN}$$

$$+\text{ve} \rightarrow \Sigma F_x \ = 0 \qquad -F_{ED} = 0$$

Member ED is a zero member
Member EJ is a strut

Consider Joint J: substitute for calculated values, i.e. F_{JE} (direction of force is into the joint):

$$+ve \uparrow \ \Sigma F_y \ = 0 \qquad +15.0 - F_{JD} \cos\theta \ = \ 0$$
$$F_{JD} \qquad = \ + 15.0 / 0.707$$
$$F_{JD} \qquad = \ + \mathbf{21.21 \ kN}$$
$$+ve \rightarrow \Sigma F_x \ = 0 \qquad -F_{JI} - F_{JD} \sin\theta \ = \ 0$$
$$F_{JI} \quad = \ - 21.21 \times 0.707$$
$$F_{JI} \quad = \ - \mathbf{15.0 \ kN}$$

Member JD is a tie
Member JI is a strut

Consider Joint D: substitute for calculated values, i.e. F_{DJ} and F_{DE}:

$$+ve \uparrow \ \Sigma F_y \ = 0 \qquad + F_{DI} + 21.21 \sin\theta = \ 0$$
$$F_{DI} \quad = \ - 21.21 \times 0.707$$
$$F_{DI} \quad = \ - \mathbf{15.0 \ kN}$$
$$+ve \rightarrow \Sigma F_x \ = 0 \qquad - F_{DC} + 21.21 \cos\theta = \ 0$$
$$F_{DC} \quad = \ + 21.21 \times 0.707$$
$$F_{DC} \quad = \ + \mathbf{15.0 \ kN}$$

Member DI is a strut
Member DC is a tie

Consider Joint I: substitute for calculated values, i.e. F_{ID} and F_{IJ}:

$$+ve \uparrow \ \Sigma F_y = 0 \quad +15.0 - 10.0 - F_{IC} \cos\theta \ = \ 0$$
$$F_{IC} \quad = \ + 5.0 / 0.707$$
$$F_{IC} \quad = \ + \ \mathbf{7.07 \ kN}$$
$$+ve \rightarrow \Sigma F_x = 0 \quad -F_{IH} - 15.0 \ - F_{IC} \sin\theta = \ 0$$
$$\mathbf{F_{IH}} \quad = \ \mathbf{-20.0 \ kN}$$

Member IC is a tie
Member IH is a strut

This process can be continued until all the member forces in the frame have been determined.

2.11.2 Secondary Bending

The top and bottom chords of trusses are normally continuous members. The points of application of the applied loads often do not coincide with the joint positions. In such circumstances the chords are subjected to combined axial and secondary bending effects. The magnitudes of the axial loads are determined using standard pin-jointed frame analysis assuming a simple static distribution of all the loads to adjacent nodes, as shown in Figure 2.37 (b). The secondary bending moments can be determined assuming the chord to be a multi-span beam, as shown in Figure 2.37 (c).

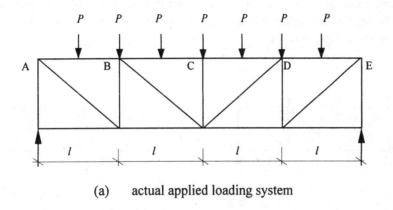

(a)   actual applied loading system

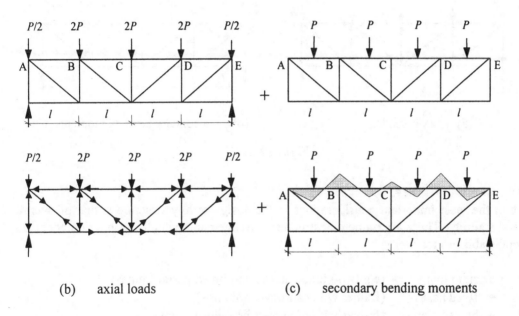

(b)   axial loads

(c)   secondary bending moments

Figure 2.37

In situations where the applied loads are due to numerous, closely spaced members or continuous decking, it is convenient to consider the chord to be supporting a uniformly distributed load, as shown in Figure 2.38.

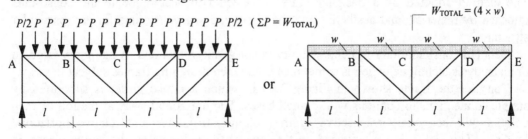

actual applied loading system

Figure 2.38

A similar analysis can be carried out assuming a multi-span beam with a distributed load to determine the secondary bending moments; the axial loads are evaluated as before, as indicated in Figure 2.39 (a) and (b).

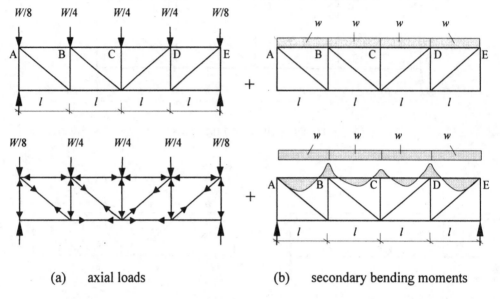

(a)   axial loads   (b)   secondary bending moments

Figure 2.39

2.12 Frames with sway

One of the most important considerations in the design of any structure is that of overall lateral stability. There are numerous structural arrangements which can provide adequate lateral stability such as:

- rigid joints   (e.g two-pinned and three-pinned portal frames),
- fixed bases   (frames with cantilever columns),
- braced frames   (frames with triangular bracing systems),
- membrane action within frames,

or combinations of the above.

The method adopted by a designer must be selected to accommodate the constraints imposed by materials and aesthetics and the client and site constraints for any particular structure.

Detailed consideration of lateral stability is not given in this text. A summary is given of an analysis technique which is sometimes used when designing frames subject to sway.

Consider the frame shown in Figure 2.40 in which a lattice girder is supported by simple connections to columns with pinned bases. The horizontal sway at the top of each column will be equal, irrespective of the column stiffnesses and relative horizontal loading. This deflection is imposed on the tops of the columns by the lattice girder, in which axial shortening of the members is negligible.

In column AB the horizontal deflection at B relative to the base at A is equal to the combined effects of a point load (H_1) and a UDL (W_1) acting on a cantilever.

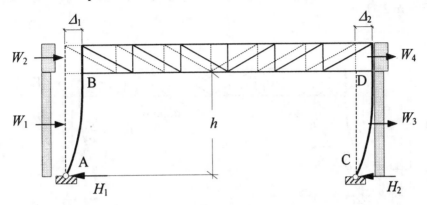

Figure 2.40

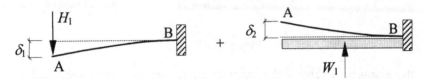

Relative deflection between A and B

$$\Delta_1 = \delta_1 - \delta_2$$

$$\Delta_1 = \frac{H_1 h^3}{3EI} - \frac{W_1 h^3}{8EI}$$

Similarly for the relative deflection between C and D:

$$\Delta_2 = \frac{H_2 h^3}{3EI} - \frac{W_3 h^3}{8EI}$$

The horizontal sway at the top of each column is equal, irrespective of the column stiffnesses and relative loadings.

$$\Delta_1 = \Delta_2$$

$$\frac{H_1 h^3}{3EI} - \frac{W_1 h^3}{8EI} = \frac{H_2 h^3}{3EI} - \frac{W_3 h^3}{8EI}$$

$$H_1 = \frac{3EI}{h^3}\left\{ \frac{H_2 h^3}{3EI} - \frac{W_3 h^3}{8EI} + \frac{W_1 h^3}{8EI} \right\}$$

$$H_1 = (H_2 - 0.375W_3 + 0.375W_1) \qquad \text{equation (1)}$$

In addition, consider the horizontal equilibrium of the entire frame:

$+ve \rightarrow \quad \Sigma F_x = 0 \qquad W_1 + W_2 - H_1 + W_3 + W_4 - H_2 = 0 \qquad \text{equation (2)}$

$$H_2 = (W_1 + W_2 + W_3 + W_4) - H_1$$

Substitute in equation (1)

$$H_1 = (W_1 + W_2 + W_3 + W_4 - H_1 - 0.375W_3 + 0.375W_1)$$

$$2H_1 = (1.375W_1 + W_2 + 0.625W_3 + W_4)$$

$$\mathbf{H_1 = (0.688W_1 + 0.5W_2 + 0.313W_3 + 0.5W_4)}$$

$$\mathbf{H_2 = (0.312W_1 + 0.5W_2 + 0.687W_3 + 0.5W_4)}$$

A similar analysis can be carried out for frames in which the bases are fixed. In this case a *point of contraflexure* (i.e. a point of zero moment) is assumed in each of the columns as shown in Figure 2.41.

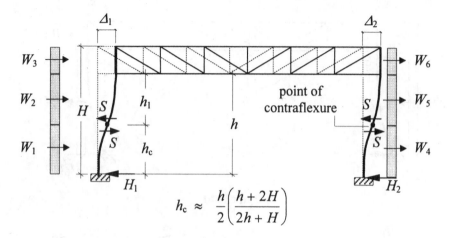

$$h_c \approx \frac{h}{2}\left(\frac{h+2H}{2h+H}\right)$$

Figure 2.41

h_c is the assumed height of the point of contraflexure, above the fixed base. This assumption is sufficiently accurate for design purposes, even when the loading on each column is not equal.

The magnitude of the horizontal shear force (S) is equal to the sum of the horizontal loadings above the points of contraflexure, distributed between the columns in proportion to their stiffnesses. In most instances both columns are the same, resulting in the following relationships:

$$S = \frac{W_2 + W_3 + W_5 + W_6}{2}$$

$$\Delta_1 = \frac{1}{EI}\left\{\frac{Sh_1^3}{3} - \frac{W_2 h_1^3}{8} + \frac{Sh_c^3}{3} + \frac{W_1 h_c^3}{8}\right\}$$

$$\Delta_2 = \frac{1}{EI}\left\{\frac{Sh_1^3}{3} - \frac{W_5 h_1^3}{8} + \frac{Sh_c^3}{3} + \frac{W_4 h_c^3}{8}\right\}$$

As before:

$$\Delta_1 = \Delta_2 \quad \text{and} \quad H_1 = S - W_1 \qquad H_2 = S + W_4$$

The use of this analysis is illustrated in Example 5.2 in Chapter 5.

2.13 Review Problems

2.1 Compare the stress/strain characteristics of timber subject to tensile or compressive stress parallel to the grain and perpendicular to the grain. (see Section 2.1)

2.2 Describe the purpose of modification factors used in timber design. (see Section 2.2)

2.3 Identify and distinguish between the Service Classes adopted in BS 5268 : Part 2 : 1996. (see Section 2.2)

2.4 Identify and distinguish between the various load duration criteria used in BS 5268 : Part 2 : 1996. (see Section 2.2)

2.5 Explain the term '*load-sharing*' as used in timber design. (see Section 2.2)

2.6 Determine the maximum shear stress induced in the cross-section shown in Figure 2.42 when it is subjected to a shear force of 12.0 kN.

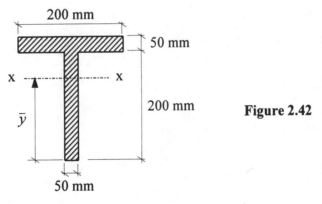

Figure 2.42

($\bar{y} = 162.5$ mm; $I_{xx} = 113.54 \times 10^6$ mm^4; $\tau_{max} = 1.39$ N/mm^2 see Section 2.4)

2.7 Determine the maximum bending moment which can be applied about the x-x axis in the section shown in Figure 2.42 such that the maximum bending stress does not exceed 18 N/mm^2. ($M_{max} = 12.5$ kNm – see Section 2.5)

2.8 A composite section comprising two steel plates firmly attached to a solid timber beam is shown in Figure 2.43. Assuming an applied moment of 120 kNm and elastic moduli for the timber and steel as 10 kN/mm^2 and 200 kN/mm^2 respectively, determine the maximum stress induced in the timber and steel, considering:

(a) a transformed timber section, and
(b) a transformed steel section.

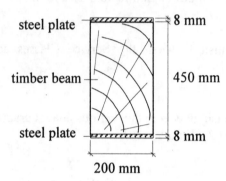

steel plate ⟶ 8 mm

timber beam ⟶ 450 mm

steel plate ⟶ 8 mm

200 mm

Figure 2.43

(For timber section: $I_{xx} = 4875 \times 10^6$ mm^4
For steel section: $I_{xx} = 243.76 \times 10^6$ mm^4
$\sigma_{timber} = 5.56$ N/mm^2; $\sigma_{steel} = 114.7$ N/mm^2; – see Section 2.6)

3. Flexural Members

Objective: *to illustrate the design of flexural members considering solid, composite I-beam, composite box-beam, glued-laminated beams and stressed skin panels.*

3.1 Introduction

Beams are the most commonly used structural elements, for example as floor joists, trimmer joists around openings, rafters etc. The cross-section of a timber beam may be one of a number of frequently used sections such as those indicated in Figure 3.1.

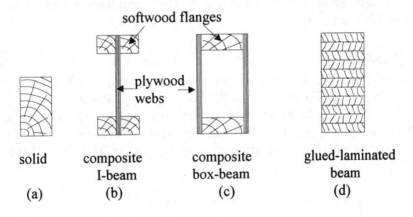

Figure 3.1

The principal considerations in the design of all beams are:

- shear,
- bending,
- deflection,
- bearing, and
- lateral stability.

In the case of ply-web beams such as the composite I and box beams shown in Figures 3.1(b) and (c), the additional phenomenon of rolling shear, which is specific to plywood, must also be considered.

The size of timber beams may be governed by the requirements of:

♦ the elastic section modulus (Z), to limit the bending stresses and ensure that neither lateral torsional buckling of the compression flange nor fracture of the tension flange induces failure,

♦ the cross-section, to ensure the vertical and/or horizontal shear stresses do not induce failure,

♦ the second moment of area, to limit the deflection induced by bending and/or shear action to acceptable limits.

Generally, the bearing area actually provided at the ends of a beam is much larger than is necessary to satisfy the permissible bearing stress requirement. Whilst lateral stability should be checked it is frequently provided to the compression flange of a beam by nailing of floor boards, roof decking etc. (see Section 3.3.5). Similarly the proportions of solid timber beams are usually such that lateral instability is unlikely.

The detailed design of solid, ply-web and glued laminated beams is explained and illustrated in the examples given in Sections 3.3, 3.4 and 3.5 respectively. In each case the relevant modification factors (K values), their application and value/location are summarised in each section.

3.2   Effective Span

Most timber beams are designed as simply supported and the effective span which should be used is defined in *Clause 2.10.3* of BS 5268 : Part 2 : 1996 as: '........ *the distance between the centres of bearings. Where members extend over bearings which are longer than is necessary, the span may be measured between the centres of bearings of a length which should be adequate in accordance with this Part of BS 5268.*' This is illustrated in Figure 3.2.

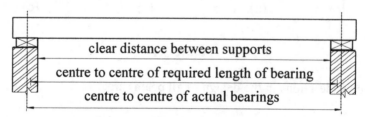

Figure 3.2

Since the required bearing length on most beams is relatively small when compared with the actual span it is common practice to assume an effective span equal to:

♦ the clear distance between the supports + 50 mm for solid beams, and
♦ the clear distance between supports + 100 mm for ply-web beams.

In the case of long span beams (e.g. in excess of 10.0 m), or heavily loaded beams with consequently larger end reactions, the validity of this assumption should be checked.

3.3 Solid Rectangular Beams

The modification factors, which are pertinent when designing solid timber beams, are summarized in Table 3.1.

3.3.1 Shear (Clause 2.10.4)

The grade and hence permissible stresses given in the BS relate to the maximum shear stress parallel to the grain for a particular species or strength class. As indicated in Section 2.2, in solid beams of rectangular cross-section the maximum horizontal shear stress occurs at the level of the neutral axis and is equal to 1.5 × the average value:

$$\tau_{a,||} = \frac{1.5V}{A}$$

where:

$\tau_{a,||}$ maximum applied horizontal shear stress,
V maximum applied vertical shear force,
A cross-sectional area.

The magnitude of $\tau_{a,||}$ must not exceed $\tau_{adm,||}$ given by:

$$\tau_{adm,||} = \tau_{g,||} \times K_2 \times K_3 \times K_5 \times K_8$$

where:

$\tau_{g,||}$ grade stress parallel to the grain
K_2, K_3, K_5 and K_8 are modification factors used when appropriate (see Section 3.3.6.1 for notched beams).

$$\tau_{a,||} \leq \tau_{adm,||}$$

Factors	Application	Clause Number	Value/Location
K_2	service class 3 sections (wet exposure): all stresses	2.6.2	Table 13
K_3	load duration : all stresses (does not apply to E or G)	2.8	Table 14
K_4	bearing stress	2.10.2	Table 15
K_5	shear at notched ends : shear stress	2.10.4	Equations given
K_6	cross-section shape : bending stress	2.10.5	1.18 for ○ 1.41 for ◆
K_7	depth of section : bending stress	2.10.6	Equations given
K_8	load-sharing : all stresses	2.9	1.1
K_9	load-sharing : modulus of elasticity of trimmer joists and lintels	2.10.11	Table 17

Table 3.1 Modification Factors - solid beams

3.3.2   Bending

As indicated in Section 2.3 the applied bending stress is determined using simple elastic bending theory:

$$\sigma_{m,a,||} = \frac{M_a}{Z}$$

where:

$\sigma_{m,a,||}$ maximum applied bending stress parallel to the grain,
M_a maximum applied bending moment,
Z elastic section modulus about the axis of bending, (usually the x-x axis).

The permissible bending stress is given by:

$$\sigma_{m,adm,||} = \sigma_{m,g,||} \times K_2 \times K_3 \times K_6 \times K_7 \times K_8$$

where:

$\sigma_{m,g,||}$ grade bending stress parallel to the grain,
K_2, K_3, K_6, K_7 and K_8 are modification factors used when appropriate (see Table 3.1) and Section 2.2). **Note:** $K_6 = 1.0$ for rectangular cross-sections.

$$\sigma_{m,a,||} \leq \sigma_{m,adm,||}$$

3.3.3   Deflection (Clause 2.10.7)

In the absence of any special requirements for deflection in buildings, it is customary to adopt an arbitrary limiting value based on experience and good practice. The recommended value adopted in BS 5268 : Part 2 is *0.003 × span* when fully loaded. In the case of domestic floor joists there is an additional recommendation of limiting deflection to less than or equal to 14 mm. These limitations are intended to minimize the risk of cracking/damage to brittle finishes (e.g. plastered ceilings), unsightly sagging or undesirable vibration under dynamic loading. The magnitude of the actual deflection induced by the applied loading can be estimated using the coefficients given in Table 2.1 or the equivalent uniform load technique described in Section 2.9.1.

   The calculated deflection for solid beams is usually based on the bending action of the beam ignoring the effects of shear deflection (this is considered when designing ply-web beams in Section 3.4).

$$\delta_{actual} \leq 0.003 \times span \quad \text{and}$$
$$\leq 14 \text{ mm for domestic floor joists}$$

3.3.4   Bearing (Clause 2.10.2)

The behaviour of timber under the action of concentrated loads, e.g. at positions of support, is complex and influenced by both the length and location of the bearing, as shown in Figures 3.3 (a) and (b). The grade stress perpendicular to the grain is used to determine the permissible bearing stress.

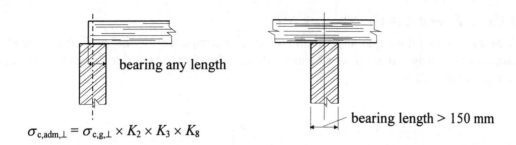

$$\sigma_{c,adm,\perp} = \sigma_{c,g,\perp} \times K_2 \times K_3 \times K_8$$

bearing any length

bearing length > 150 mm

Figure 3.3 (a)

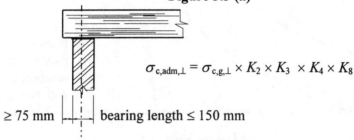

$$\sigma_{c,adm,\perp} = \sigma_{c,g,\perp} \times K_2 \times K_3 \times K_4 \times K_8$$

≥ 75 mm   bearing length ≤ 150 mm

Figure 3.3 (b)

Note: In case (b), an additional modification factor 'K_4' for bearing stress has been included.

The actual bearing stress is determined from:

$$\sigma_{c,a,\perp} = \frac{P}{A_b}$$

where:

P applied concentrated load,

A_b actual bearing area provided.

$$\sigma_{c,a,\perp} \leq \sigma_{c,adm,\perp}$$

The actual bearing area is the net area of the contact surface and allowance must be made for any reduction in the width of bearing due to wane, as shown in Figure 3.4. In timber engineering, the presence of wane is frequently excluded and consequently this can often be ignored.

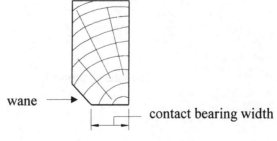

wane →

contact bearing width

Figure 3.4

3.3.5   Lateral Stability (Clause 2.10.8)

A beam in which the depth and length are large in comparison to the width (i.e. a slender cross-section) may fail at a lower bending stress value due to lateral torsional buckling, as shown in Figure 3.5.

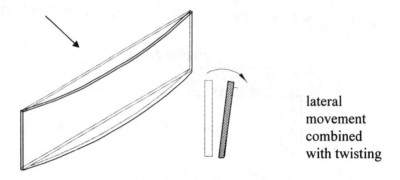

lateral
movement
combined
with twisting

Figure 3.5

The critical value of bending moment which induces this type of failure is dependent on several parameters such as: the relative cross-section dimensions (i.e. aspect ratio), shape, modulus of elasticity (E), shear modulus (G), span, degree of lateral restraint to the compression flange, and the type of loading.

This problem is accommodated in BS 5628 : Part 2 : 1996 by using a simplified approach based on practical experience, in which limiting ratios of **maximum depth to maximum breadth** are given relating to differing restraint conditions. In *'Table 16'* of BS 5268, values of limiting ratios are given varying from '2', when no restraint is provided to a beam, to a maximum of '7', for beams in which the top and bottom edges are fully laterally restrained. These conditions are illustrated in Figure 3.6 (a) to (f).

Provision is made in the BS for designers to undertake a rigorous analysis, if desired, to determine the critical moment which will induce lateral torsional buckling of a beam. The vast majority of beams which are designed are of such proportions and have such restraint conditions that this analysis is unnecessary. The calculations relating to the critical moment are outwith the scope of this text: further reference can be found in the *'Timber Designers' Manual'* (13), or *'STEP 2: Structural Timber Education Programme'* (15).

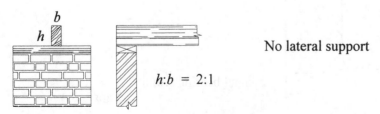

No lateral support

$h:b = 2:1$

Figure 3.6 (a)

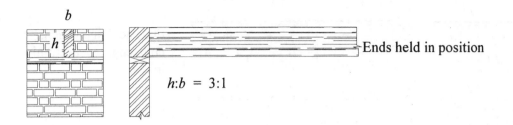

$h{:}b = 3{:}1$

Ends held in position

Figure 3.6 (b)

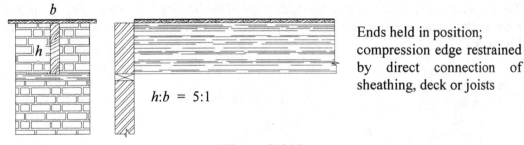

$\leq 30h$ $\leq 30h$ $\leq 30h$

$h{:}b = 4{:}1$

Ends held in position; spacing of restraints (e.g. tie rods or purlins) $\leq 30h$

Figure 3.6 (c)

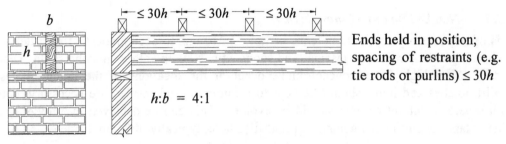

$h{:}b = 5{:}1$

Ends held in position; compression edge restrained by direct connection of sheathing, deck or joists

Figure 3.6 (d)

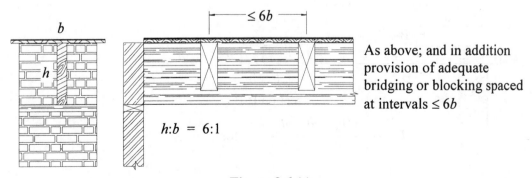

$\leq 6b$

$h{:}b = 6{:}1$

As above; and in addition provision of adequate bridging or blocking spaced at intervals $\leq 6b$

Figure 3.6 (e)

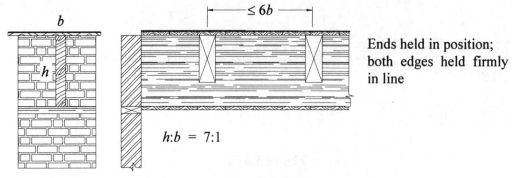

$h{:}b = 7{:}1$

Figure 3.6 (f)

Ends held in position; both edges held firmly in line

3.3.6   *Notched Beams (Clause 2.10.9)*

It is often necessary to create notches or holes in beams to accommodate fixing details such as gutters, reduced fascias and connections with other members. In such circumstances high stress concentrations occur at the locations of the notches/holes. Whilst notches and holes should be kept to a minimum, when they are necessary, cuts with square re-entrant corners should be avoided. This can be achieved by providing a fillet or taper or cutting the notch to a pre-drilled hole, typically of 8 mm diameter.

3.3.6.1   *Effect on shear strength (Clause 2.10.4)*

The projection of a notch beyond the inside edge of the bearing line at the point of support reduces the shear capacity of a beam. There are two situations to consider, as shown in Figure 3.7.

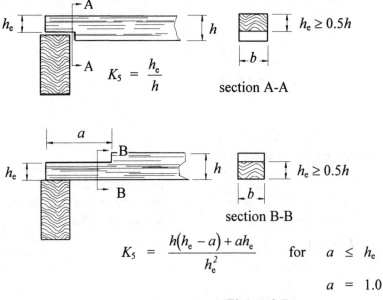

$$K_5 = \frac{h_e}{h}$$

section A-A

$h_e \geq 0.5h$

$$K_5 = \frac{h(h_e - a) + ah_e}{h_e^2} \quad \text{for} \quad a \leq h_e$$

$$a = 1.0$$

Figure 3.7

The reduction in shear capacity is reflected in the use of the net area and a reduction factor K_5, as indicated in Figure 3.7.

$$\text{shear capacity} \; = \; \tau_{\text{adm, ||}} \times h_e \times b$$

where:

$\tau_{\text{adm, ||}}$ permissible shear stress   (see Section 3.3.1),
h_e effective depth of the beam,
b breadth of the beam.

3.3.6.2   *Effect on bending strength* *(Clause 2.10.9)*

The calculated bending strength of notched beams is based on the net cross-section, as shown in Figure 3.8.

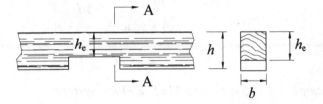

section A-A

Net cross-sectional area $= b \times h_e$

Net section modulus $\quad = \dfrac{b \times h_e^2}{6}$

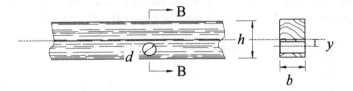

section B-B

Net cross-sectional area $= b \times (h - d)$

Net section modulus $\quad = \dfrac{b}{6h}\left[h^3 - d^2 - 12dy^2\right]$

Figure 3.8

When considering simply supported floor and roof joists which are not more than 250 mm deep and which satisfy the restrictions indicated in Figure 3.9, the effects of notches and holes can be neglected.

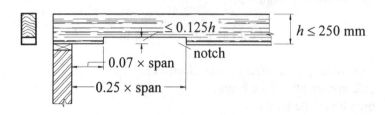

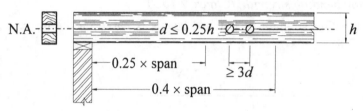

Figure 3.9

3.3.7   Example 3.1   Suspended Timber Floor System

Consider the design of a suspended timber floor system in a domestic building in which the joists are simply supported on 200 mm wide timber wall plates on load-bearing brickwork, as shown in Figure 3.10 (a).

♦ Determine a suitable section size for the tongue and groove floor boards.
♦ Determine a suitable section size for the main joists.
♦ Assuming one end of the joists to be notched and supported by a wall plate as shown in Figure 3.10 (b), check the shear capacity of the joists.

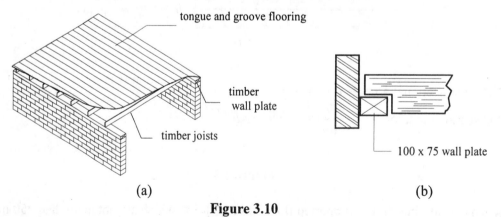

(a)   (b)

Figure 3.10

Design data:

Centre of timber joists	450 mm
Clear distance between the inner faces of the brickwork wall	5.0 m
Strength class of timber for joists and tongue and groove boarding	C16
Imposed loading	4.0 kN/m^2

3.3.7.1 Solution to Example 3.1

Contract : Solid beams **Job Ref. No. :** Example 3.1 **Part of Structure :** Suspended floor system **Calc. Sheet No. :** 1 of 6		**Calcs. by : W.McK.** **Checked by :** **Date :**

References	Calculations	Output

BS 5268
Clause 2.6
Table 7
	Structural use of timber
	Bending parallel to grain $\sigma_{m,g,\parallel}$ = 5.3 N/mm^2
	Compression perpendicular to grain
	                          $\sigma_{c,g,\perp}$ = 1.7 N/mm^2
	Shear parallel to grain $\tau_{m,g,\parallel}$ = 0.67 N/mm^2
	Modulus of elasticity E_{mean} = 8800 N/mm^2
	Modulus of elasticity E_{min} = 5800 N/mm^2
	Average density ρ_k = 370 kg/m^3
	Note: a value of characteristic density is also given for use
	            when designing joints.
	
	Tongue and groove floor boarding:
	Consider 1.0 m width of flooring and 19 mm thick boarding:
	
	————— 1000 mm width —————
	
	Self-weight = $\dfrac{(0.019 \times 370) \times 9.81}{10^3}$ = 0.07 kN/m^2
	Imposed loading = <u>4.0 kN/m^2</u>
	Total load = (4.0 + 0.07) = 4.07 kN/m^2	

Clause 2.10	**Bending:** *Permissible stress* $\sigma_{m,adm,\parallel}$ = $\sigma_{m,g,\parallel} \times K_2 \times K_3 \times K_6 \times K_7 \times K_8$	

Clause 2.6.2
Clause 2.8
Table 14 (note 1)
Clause 2.10.5
Clause 2.10.6
Clause 2.9
	K_2 – wet exposure does not apply in this case
	K_3 – load duration for uniformly distributed imposed
	                           floor loads
	K_6 – shape factor does not apply in this case
	K_7 – depth of section < 300 mm
	K_8 – load sharing stresses tongue and groove boarding has
	                           adequate provision for lateral load
	                           distribution
	
	$\sigma_{m,adm,\parallel}$ = 5.3 × 1.0 × 1.17 × 1.1 = 6.82 N/mm^2
	
	span of boards = joist spacing = 450 mm
		K_3 = 1.0
		
		K_7 = 1.17
		
		K_8 = 1.1

Contract : Solid beams Job Ref. No. : Example 3.1	Calcs. by : W.McK.
Part of Structure : Suspended floor system	Checked by :
Calc. Sheet No. : 2 of 6	Date :

References	Calculations	Output
	Allowing for the continuity of the boards over the supports reduces the bending moment	

Max. bending moment $\approx \dfrac{wL^2}{10} = \dfrac{4.07 \times 0.45^2}{10} = 0.082$ kNm

Minimum section modulus required:

$$Z_{min} \geq \frac{\text{Maximum bending moment}}{\text{permissible stress}} = \frac{0.082 \times 10^6}{6.82}$$

$$\approx 12.02 \times 10^3 \text{ mm}^3/\text{metre width}$$

$$Z = \frac{bh^2}{6} \quad \therefore \ h = \sqrt{\frac{6z}{b}} \quad \therefore \ h = \sqrt{\frac{6 \times 12.02 \times 10^3}{1000}}$$

$h = 8.05$ mm;   assume an additional 3 mm for wear

BS 1297

$h \approx 8.05 + 3 = 11.05$ mm   try 16 mm thick

Clause 2.10.7
Clause 2.9

Deflection:
Since load-sharing exists use E_{mean} to calculate deflection.
Since the boards are continuous, assume the end span deflection (i.e. a propped cantilever) is approximately equal to 50% of a simply supported span:

$$\delta_{max} \approx (0.5 \times \delta_{\text{simply supported span}}) = \frac{1}{2}\left(\frac{5W_{total}L^3}{384\,EI}\right)$$

$$\delta_{max} = 0.5 \times \frac{5 \times 4.07 \times 0.45 \times 10^3 \times 450^3}{384 \times 8800 \times \left(\dfrac{1000 \times 16^3}{12}\right)} \approx 0.36 \text{ mm}$$

$$\delta_{\text{permissible}} \leq 0.003 \times 450 = 1.35 \text{ mm}$$

$$\delta_{max} \ll \delta_{\text{permissible}}$$

Output: Adopt a minimum thickness of 16 mm for the tongue and groove boarding

Joists at 450 centres:

Dead load due to self-weight of joist: assume	=	0.1 kN/m
Dead load due to t & g boarding = 0.07×0.45	=	0.03 kN/m
Imposed loading = 4.0×0.45	=	1.8 kN/m
Total load = $(0.1 + 0.03 + 1.8)$	=	1.93 kN/m

Clause 2.10

Bending:
Permissible stress

$$\sigma_{m,adm,||} = \sigma_{m,g,||} \times K_2 \times K_3 \times K_6 \times K_7 \times K_8$$

Clause 2.6.2 K_2 – wet exposure   does not apply in this case

Clause 2.8 K_3 – load duration   for uniformly distributed imposed

Table 14 (note 1)   floor loads

Output: $K_3 = 1.0$

Contract : Solid beams Job Ref. No. : Example 3.1 Part of Structure : Suspended floor system Calc. Sheet No. : 3 of 6	Calcs. by : W.McK. Checked by : Date :

References	Calculations	Output
Clause 2.10.5 Clause 2.10.6 Clause 2.9	K_6 – shape factor; does not apply in this case K_7 – depth of section; assume $h \leq 300$ mm This assumption should be checked at a later stage and modified if necessary. K_8 – load sharing stresses; this applies since tongue and groove boarding provides adequate lateral distribution of loading and the spacing of the joists ≤ 610 mm $\sigma_{m,adm,\|\|} = 5.3 \times 1.0 \times 1.0 \times 1.1 = 5.83$ N/mm^2 Span of joists: assume centre-to-centre of bearings $L = 5.0 + 0.2 = 5.2$ m maximum bending moment $= \dfrac{wL^2}{8} = \dfrac{1.93 \times 5.2^2}{8} = 6.5$ kNm $Z_{min} \geq \dfrac{6.5 \times 10^6}{5.83} = 1.12 \times 10^6$ mm^3	$K_7 = 1.0$ $K_8 = 1.1$
Clause 2.10.7 Clause 2.9	**Deflection:** $\delta_{permissible} \leq 0.003 \times span = 0.003 \times 5200 = 15.6$ mm ≤ 14.0 mm Since load-sharing exists and assuming floor is *not* intended for mechanical plant and equipment, storage or subject to vibration (e.g. a gymnasium), use E_{mean} to calculate the deflection. $\delta_{maximum} \approx \dfrac{5W_{total}L^3}{384E_{mean}I}, \qquad E_{mean} = 8800$ N/mm^2 $= \dfrac{5 \times (5.2 \times 1.93 \times 10^3) \times 5200^3}{384 \times 8800 \times I_{xx}} = \dfrac{2.088 \times 10^9}{I_{xx}}$ since $\delta_{maximum} \leq 14.0,$ $\dfrac{2.088 \times 10^9}{I_{xx}} \leq 14.0$ $I_{xx} \geq \dfrac{2.088 \times 10^9}{14.0} = 149 \times 10^6$ mm^4 try a 100 mm x 300 mm joist or change to higher Strength Class $A = 30.0 \times 10^3$ mm^2 Section modulus $Z_{xx} = 1.5 \times 10^6$ mm^3 Second moment of area $= I_{xx} = 225 \times 10^6$ mm^4	

Contract : Solid beams Job Ref. No. : Example 3.1 Part of Structure : Suspended floor system Calc. Sheet No. : 4 of 6	Calcs. by : W.McK. Checked by : Date :

References	Calculations	Output
Clause 2.10.8 Table 16 Clause 2.10	$\dfrac{h}{b} = \dfrac{300}{100} = 3.0 \quad < \quad 5.0$ **Bearing:** 100 mm End reaction $= (1.93 \times 5.2)/2$ $\qquad\qquad\quad = 5.02$ kN 200 mm Bearing area $= 200 \times 100$ 5.02 kN $\qquad\qquad\qquad = 20 \times 10^3$ mm^2 $\sigma_{c,a,\perp} = \dfrac{5.02 \times 10^3}{20 \times 10^3} = 0.251$ N/mm^2 $\sigma_{c,adm,\perp} = \sigma_{c,g,\perp} \times K_2 \times K_3 \times K_4 \times K_8$	Lateral support is adequate
Clause 2.6.2 Clause 2.8 Table 14 (note 1) Clause 2.10.2 Clause 2.9	As before K_2 does not apply $K_3 = 1.0$ bearing length $> \quad 150$ mm $\qquad \therefore \; K_4$ does not apply since load-sharing applies $\qquad\qquad K_8 = \quad 1.1$ $\sigma_{c,adm,\perp} \quad = \quad 1.7 \times 1.0 \times 1.1 \; = \; 1.87$ N/mm^2 $\qquad\qquad\qquad\qquad \sigma_{c,a,\perp} \; << \; \sigma_{c,adm,\perp}$	Joist is adequate with respect to bearing
Section 3.3.1 of this text	**Shear:** Maximum shear stress on rectangular section $\quad \tau \; = \; \dfrac{1.5\,V}{A}$ where $V \quad = \quad$ design value of shear force $= \quad 5.02$ kN $\tau_{a,||} \quad = \quad \dfrac{1.5 \times 5.02 \times 10^3}{30 \times 10^3} \quad = \quad 0.25$ N/mm^2 $\tau_{adm,||} \; = \; \tau_{g,||} \times K_2 \times K_3 \times K_5 \times K_8$ As before K_2 does not apply and $K_3 = \quad 1.0$ Since the end of the beam is not notched, K_5 does not apply	

Contract : Solid beams Job Ref. No. : Example 3.1 Part of Structure : Suspended floor system Calc. Sheet No. : 5 of 6	Calcs. by : W.McK. Checked by : Date :

References	Calculations	Output
Clause 2.9	load-sharing applies $\therefore$ $K_8 = 1.1$ $\tau_{adm,\|\|} = 0.67 \times 1.1 = 0.74$ N/mm^2 $\qquad \tau_{a,\|\|} < \tau_{adm,\|\|}$ **Note:** A 45° dispersion of load from the centre line of the bearing could have been assumed and the applied shear force evaluated at this location, i.e.: $V_{modified} = 5.02 - (0.3 \times 1.93) = 4.4$ kN	Joist is adequate with respect to shear Adopt 100 x 300 Grade C16 Timber Joïsts at 450 mm centres
Clause 2.10.4 Clause 2.9	Assume a notched beam at the end load-sharing applies $\therefore$ $K_8 = 1.1$ $\tau_{adm,\|\|} = 0.67 \times 1.1 = 0.74$ N/mm^2 $\qquad \tau_{a,\|\|} < \tau_{adm,\|\|}$ **Note:** A 45° dispersion of load from the centre line of the bearing could have been assumed and the applied shear force evaluated at this location, i.e.: $V_{modified} = 5.02 - (0.3 \times 1.93) = 4.4$ kN	Joist is adequate with respect to shear Adopt 100 x 300 Grade C16 Timber Joïsts at 450 mm centres

References	Calculations	Output

Contract : Solid beams   **Job Ref. No. :** Example 3.1   **Calcs. by :** W.McK.
Part of Structure : Suspended floor system   **Checked by :**
Calc. Sheet No. : 6 of 6   **Date :**

References	Calculations	Output
Clause 2.10.4	Assume a notched beam at the end 100 x 75 wall plate 75 100 $K_5 = \dfrac{h_e}{h} = \dfrac{225}{300} \quad 0.75$ $\tau_{adm,\parallel} = 0.67 \times 1.1 \times K_5 = 0.74 \times 0.75 = 0.56\,\text{N/mm}^2$ $\tau_{a,\parallel} = \dfrac{1.5 \times 5.02 \times 10^3}{100 \times (300 - 75)} = 0.33\,\text{N/mm}^2$ $\tau_{a,\parallel} \; < \; \tau_{adm,\parallel}$	Joist is adequate with respect to shear
Clause 2.10.9	**Note:** In certain circumstances the effects of notches need not be calculated, see Section 3.3.6 and Figure 3.9 of this text.	

3.3.8   *Example 3.2 Trimmer Beam*

Consider the design of a trimmer beam inserted to create an opening, as shown in Figure 3.11. Assuming materials and loading to be the same as in (a), determine a suitable size of trimmer beam. (**Note:** the joists supporting the trimmer beam are normally made 25 mm thicker than the other standard joists.)

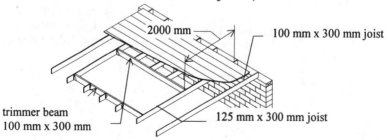

2000 mm   100 mm x 300 mm joist

trimmer beam
100 mm x 300 mm   125 mm x 300 mm joist

Figure 3.11

3.3.8.1 Solution to Example 3.2

References	Calculations	Output
	Contract : Solid beams **Job Ref. No. :** Example 3.2 **Calcs. by :** W.McK.	

Contract : Solid beams   **Job Ref. No. :** Example 3.2
Part of Structure : Trimmer Beam
Calc. Sheet No. : 1 of 3

Calcs. by : W.McK.
Checked by :
Date :

References	Calculations	Output
	Trimmer beam design	

Trimmer beam design
The trimmed joists provide lateral restraint to the compression flange of the beam

The same grade stresses apply as for the main joists
Assume the trimmer is a 100 mm x 300 mm solid section

$$\text{Self-weight of trimmer} = \frac{(0.1 \times 0.3 \times 370 \times 9.81)}{10^3}$$

$$= 0.11 \text{ kN/m}$$

P is the load imposed by each trimmer joist.
Area of floor supported by *trimmed* joist $= 2.0 \times 0.45$
$= 0.9 \text{ m}^2$

Dead load due to joist $= 0.11 \times 2.0$ $= 0.22$ kN
Dead load due to t&g boarding $= 0.07 \times 0.45 \times 2.0 = 0.06$ kN

Imposed load $= 4.0 \times 0.45 \times 2.0$ = <u>3.6 kN</u>
   Total load $= 3.88$ kN

End reaction from trimmed joist on trimmer beam $= \dfrac{3.88}{2}$
$= 1.94$ kN

Contract : Solid beams **Job Ref. No. :** Example 3.2		**Calcs. by :** W.McK.
Part of Structure : Trimmer Beam		**Checked by :**
Calc. Sheet No. : 2 of 3		**Date :**

References	Calculations	Output
Clause 2.10	**Bending:**	
	Maximum bending moment= $\left(2.91 \times \dfrac{1.675}{2}\right) - (1.94 \times 0.45)$	
	$\qquad\qquad\qquad\qquad = 1.56$ kNm	
Clause 2.9	K_8 – load sharing does not apply in this case since there is only a single member resisting the load	
	$\sigma_{m,adm,\|\|} = 5.3 \times 1.0 \times 1.0 = 5.3$ N/mm^2	
	$\sigma_{m,a,\|\|} = \dfrac{1.56 \times 10^6}{1.5 \times 10^6} = 1.04$ N/mm$^2 < \sigma_{m,adm,\|\|}$	Trimmer is adequate with respect to bending
Clause 2.10.7	**Deflection:**	
	$\delta_{permissible} \le 0.003 \times$ span $= 0.003 \times 1675 = 5$ mm	
	$\qquad\qquad \le 14.0$ mm	
Clause 2.9	Since load-sharing does not exist, use $E_{minimum}$ to calculate the deflection.	
See Section 2.9.1	$\delta_{maximum} \approx \dfrac{0.104 \times B.M_{maximum} \times L^2}{E_{minimum} \times I}$,	
	$E_{minimum} = 5800$ N/mm^2	
	$\delta_{maximum} = \dfrac{0.104 \times 1.56 \times 10^6 \times 1675^2}{5800 \times 225 \times 10^6} = 0.35$ mm	
	$\delta_{maximum} \le 5$ mm	Trimmer is adequate with respect to deflection
Clause 2.10	**Bearing:**	
	End reaction $= 2.91$ kN	
	$\sigma_{c,adm,\perp} = \sigma_{c,g,\perp} \times K_2 \times K_3$	
	(Neglect the coefficient K_4 relating to the length of bearing)	
	$\sigma_{c,adm,\perp} = 1.7 \times 1.0 = 1.7$ N/mm^2	
	Minimum bearing area required $= \dfrac{2.91 \times 10^3}{1.7} = 1712$ mm^2	

References	Calculations	Output
	Contract : Solid beams **Job Ref. No. :** Example 3.2 **Calcs. by : W.McK.** **Part of Structure :** Trimmer Beam **Checked by :** **Calc. Sheet No. :** 3 of 3 **Date :**	

References	Calculations	Output
	pressed steel hanger $b > \dfrac{1712}{100} = 17.12$ mm $100 \leftarrow b \rightarrow$	Trimmer is supported on a pressed steel hanger and is adequate with respect to bearing
	Shear: Maximum shear stress on rectangular section $\tau = \dfrac{1.5\,V}{A}$ where $V =$ design value of shear force $= 2.91$ kN $\tau_{a,\parallel} = \dfrac{1.5 \times 2.91 \times 10^3}{100 \times 300} = 0.15$ N/mm^2 $\tau_{adm,\parallel} = \tau_{g,\parallel} \times K_3 = 0.67 \times 1.0 = 0.67$ N/mm^2 $\tau_{a,\parallel} < \tau_{adm,\parallel}$	Trimmer is adequate with respect to shear Lateral support is adequate
Clause 2.10.8	$\dfrac{h}{b} = \dfrac{300}{100} = 3.0 \quad < \quad 4.0 \quad$ **Adopt 100 x 300 joist**	

3.4 Ply-web Beams

In situations where heavy loads and/or long spans require beams of strength and stiffness which are not available as solid sections, ply-web construction of I- or Box-section are frequently used (see Figure 3.1). The increased size of ply-web beams (e.g. 500 mm deep) and consequent strength/weight characteristics permit larger spacings (typically 1.2 m to 4.0 m) than solid beams, but can still be sufficiently close to enable the use of standard cladding and ceiling systems. In addition, they are frequently able to accommodate services, and insulation materials. The expansion of timber framed housing in the U.K. has resulted in the use of smaller ply-web beams, typically 200 mm to 400 mm deep for floor joists and roof framing. A considerable saving in weight can be achieved over solid timber joists, and problems often associated with warping, cupping, bowing, twisting and splitting of sawn timber joists can be significantly reduced.

In most cases, since ply-web beams are hidden, the surface finishes including features such as nail heads, holes and glue marks need not be disguised. If desired, surface treatment can be carried out to enhance the appearance, however this will incur additional cost. The construction of ply-web beams comprises four principal components:

♦ web,
♦ stiffeners,
♦ flanges,
♦ joints between flanges and the web.

The manufacture should comply with the requirements of *BS 6446 : 1984 ' Manufacture of glued structural components of timber and wood based panel products.'*
The modification factors appropriate to plywood beams are given in Table 3.2.

Factors	Application	Clause Number	Value/Location
K_2	Service class 3 sections (wet exposure) : all stresses. Does not apply to plywood	2.6.2	Table 13
K_3	Load duration : all stresses. Does not apply to plywood	2.8	Table 14
K_4	Bearing stress	2.10.2	Table 15
K_5	Shear at notched ends : shear stress	2.10.4	Equations given
K_8	Load-sharing : all stresses	2.9	1.1
K_{36}	Load-duration and service classes for plywood	4.5	Table 33
K_{37}	Stress concentration factor - rolling shear	4.6	0.5

Table 3.2   Modification Factors for ply-web beams

3.4.1   Web

The primary purpose of the **web** is to resist stresses induced by shear forces. In the majority of cases the material used for the web is plywood; other wood-based panel materials such as particle board and fibreboard are also suitable. The most commonly used material is Finnish birch-faced plywood (also known as Combi), in which the outer veneers are always birch whilst the inner plies alternate between birch and softwood. This type of plywood is more readily available than for example Finnish all-birch plywood which may be more appropriate when the web is highly stressed. There are a number of alternative timbers such as Canadian Douglas fir, Swedish softwood and American construction and industrial plywoods which can also be used. The appropriate grade stresses for the materials are given in Tables 34 to 47 of BS 5268 : Part 2 : 1996.

The construction of the webs is normally carried out such that butt end joints do not occur at the mid-span location and full 2440 mm panels are used where possible. In Finnish birch-faced plywood the face grain is normally perpendicular to the span whilst in cases where Douglas fir is used the face grain is normally parallel to the span.

There are two types of shear stress which must be resisted by the web of a ply-web beam, they are:

♦ panel shear,   and
♦ rolling shear.

3.4.1.1   Panel Shear

The maximum horizontal shear stress induced in a beam subjected to bending and vertical shear forces occurs at the level of the neutral axis, as shown in Figure 3.12, and can be determined as shown in Section 2.2 using the following equation:

$$\tau_{a,||} = \frac{VA\bar{y}}{bI_{\text{N.A.}}}$$

where:

$\tau_{a,||}$ maximum applied horizontal shear stress,
V maximum applied vertical shear force,
$A\bar{y}$ first moment of area of the material above the neutral axis,
$I_{N.A.}$ second moment of area of the cross-section,
b thickness of the web at the position of the section being considered.

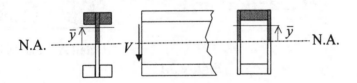

Figure 3.12

Note: If a section is designed on the basis of a transformed section in terms of the flange material as discussed in Section 2.7, then $\tau_{a,||}$ must be modified using the modular ratio to obtain equivalent plywood stresses, i.e.

$$\tau_{a,||\ \text{plywood}} = \tau_{a,||\ \text{transformed}} \times \alpha$$

where:

α the modular ratio equal to $\dfrac{E_w}{E_f}$

This is illustrated in Examples 3.3 and 3.4.

The magnitude of $\tau_{a,||\ \text{plywood}}$ must not exceed $\tau_{\text{adm},||\ \text{plywood}}$, given by:

$$\tau_{\text{adm},||} = \tau_{g,||} \times K_8 \times K_{36}$$

where:

$\tau_{g,||}$ grade stress of plywood given in *Tables 34 to 37* of the code
K_8 modification factor to allow for load sharing,
K_{36} modification factor to allow for differing load-duration and/or different service classes.

3.4.1.2   Rolling Shear

The physical construction of plywood, in which alternate veneers have grain directions which are mutually perpendicular, enables a mode of failure called '*rolling shear*' to occur (see Figure 3.13); there is a tendency for the material fibres to roll across each other creating a horizontal shear failure plane. This phenomenon can occur at locations where plywood is joined to other members/materials, either at the interface with the plywood or between adjacent veneers of the plywood. In ply-web beams the rolling shear must be checked at the connection of the web to the flanges and sufficient thickness (T) of flange must be available to transfer the horizontal shear force at this location.

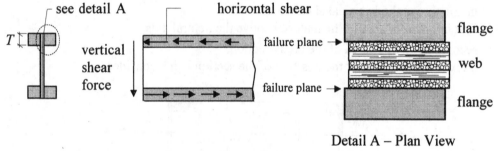

Figure 3.13

The magnitude of the rolling shear stress can be determined using the same equation as for panel shear with the critical section considered being section *x-x* at the interface between the web and the flange, as shown in Figure 3.14.

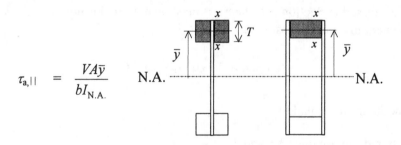

$$\tau_{a,||} = \frac{VA\bar{y}}{bI_{N.A.}}$$

Figure 3.14

where V, $A\bar{y}$ and $I_{N.A.}$ are as before. The value of b is equal to (flange thickness × no. of interfaces between the flange and the web). In the beam shown above $b = 2T$.

As for panel shear, when using a transformed section the calculated value of τ should be modified using the modular ratio to obtain equivalent plywood stresses.

$$\tau_{a,rolling} = \tau_{a,rolling,transformed} \times \alpha$$
$$\tau_{adm,rolling} = \tau_g \times K_8 \times K_{36} \times K_{37}$$

As before the actual stress must be less than or equal to the permissible value:

$$\tau_{a,rolling} \leq \tau_{adm,rolling}$$

where: α, K_8 and K_{36} are as previously defined, and K_{37} is a stress concentration factor given in Clause 4.6 and is equal to 0.5.

3.4.1.3 Web Stiffeners (Clause 2.10.10)

Where webs are slender and at locations such as supports and points of application of concentrated load, there is the possibility of failure caused by buckling of the web. BS 5268 : Part 2 : 1996 does not give any guidance on the design of either non-loadbearing (intermediate) or loadbearing web stiffeners other than to indicate that they are required where appropriate. Most proprietary suppliers of ply-web beams advise web stiffener details based on the results of full scale tests of their product. Design methods are illustrated in various publications, notably by the Council of Forest Industries of British Columbia (COFI) publication *Fir Plywood Web Beam Design* (9) *and Timber Designers' Manual* (13). Reference should be made to these publications for further information regarding stiffeners.

3.4.2 Flanges

The primary purpose of the **flanges** is to resist tensile and compressive stresses induced by bending effects and/or axial loads. Their construction is normally carried out using continuous or finger-jointed structural timber such as European whitewood, Douglas fir-larch or redwoods; the first of these being the most commonly used. Alternatively plywood or glued-laminated components can be used.

3.4.2.1 Bending

There are a number of techniques which can be used to determine the bending moment capacity of a ply-web beam. The method adopted in this text assumes that the full cross-section, i.e. the web and the flanges, contribute to the bending resistance. Analysis to determine bending stresses is carried out assuming a transformed section as indicated in Section 2.8, where:

$$\sigma_{m,a} = \frac{bending\ moment}{transformed\ elastic\ section\ modulus} = \frac{M}{Z}$$

When using this method it is necessary to ensure that:

- the calculated stresses in the extreme fibres of the flanges do not exceed the permissible bending stress parallel to the grain as indicated in Section 3.3.2 for solid beams;

$$\sigma_{m,a} \leq \sigma_{m,adm,||}$$

where:

$$\sigma_{m,adm,||} = \sigma_{m,g,||} \times K_2 \times K_3 \times K_8$$

- the tension and compressive stresses induced by the bending moment in the plywood web do not exceed the appropriate values for the face grain orientation as indicated in Tables 34 to 47 and Clause 4.6 of the Code.

i.e.

$$\sigma_{t,a} = \frac{M}{Z} \times \alpha \leq \sigma_{t,adm} \quad \text{and}$$

$$\sigma_{c,a} = \frac{M}{Z} \times \alpha \leq \sigma_{c,adm}$$

where:

$\sigma_{t,adm} = \sigma_{t,g} \times K_8 \times K_{36},$
$\sigma_{c,adm} = \sigma_{c,g} \times K_8 \times K_{36},$
Z is the value of section modulus for the transformed section,
α is the modular ratio of the web and flange materials.

The above equations relating to the plywood apply to face grain in either the parallel or the perpendicular directions.

In many cases load-sharing will not occur and the K_8 value of 1.1 will not apply. This is a conservative interpretation of Clause 2.9 relating to load-sharing systems. Some designers interpret this Clause more widely and include the K_8 value when lateral load distribution does exist and the number of individual pieces of timber within a cross-section is greater than four.

Note: the *bending* stresses given in Tables 34 to 47 apply to stresses induced when bending is about either axis *in the plane* of the board, as indicated in Figure 3.15.

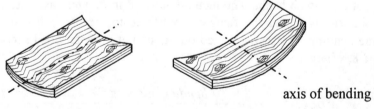

axis of bending   axis of bending

Figure 3.15   In-plane axes of bending

In the case of ply-web beams the axis of bending is perpendicular to the plane of the board as shown in Figure 3.16, and consequently the *tensile* and *compressive* stresses are used.

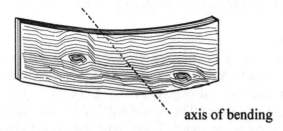

axis of bending

Figure 3.16   Out-of-plane axis of bending

In most cases the governing criteria will relate to the flange material.

3.4.2.2   Deflection (Clauses 2.10.7 and 4.6)

Traditionally when calculating the deflection of beams, only the component due to the bending action is considered. This is due to the fact that in other materials, for example steel, the shear modulus is considerably higher as a percentage of the true elastic modulus than is the case in timber. A consequence of this is that when considering the deflection of timber beams the effect of shearing deformation may be significant. In *Clause 4.6* the code indicates that shear deflection should be taken into account when designing ply-web beams such that:

$$\delta_{actual} \approx (\delta_{bending} + \delta_{shear}) \leq 0.003 \times \text{span}$$

3.4.2.2.1   Bending deflection $(\delta_{bending})$

The calculation of the bending component of the overall deflection is based on elastic deformation using the standard deflection formulae given in Table 2.1, or the equivalent UDL technique discussed in Section 2.9.1. The bending rigidity (*EI*) of the section must be determined using the modular ratio to account for the different elastic moduli of the flange and web materials. This can be achieved using the following expression:

$$EI = (EI)_{flange} + (EI)_{web\ transformed}$$
$$EI = E_{flange}(I_{flange} + \alpha I_{web})$$

3.4.2.2.2   Shear deflection (δ_{shear})

A number of factors such as the cross-sectional dimensions, the shear modulus of the web (G_{web}), and the position and intensity of the loads influence the shear deflection of a beam. A number of complex analytical expressions have been developed to determine the magnitude of the shear deflection – see Roark(16), COFI(9), – however a simplified equation may be used to give an acceptable, approximate value:

$$\delta_{shear} \approx \frac{M}{G_{web} A_w}$$

where:

M bending moment at mid-span,

A_w area of the web,

G_{web} modulus of rigidity of the web given in Tables 34 to 47 of the code.

3.4.3   *Lateral stability (Clauses 2.10.8 and 2.10.10)*

The lateral stability of a built-up beam can be assessed by calculation assuming the compression flange to be a column subject to sideways buckling between points of lateral restraint. An alternative is also given in the Code in which differing lateral restraint conditions are required depending on the ratio of the second moment of area in the x-x direction to that in the y-y direction. These requirements are given in paragraphs *a)* to *f)* of *Clause 2.10.10* of the Code and are summarised here in Table 3.3. This is similar to those given in *Table 16* for solid and laminated beams which are dependent on the depth/breadth ratio.

Clause in BS 5268	Ratio	Requirement
2.10.10 (a)	$\dfrac{I_{xx}}{I_{yy}} \leq 5$	no lateral support required
2.10.10 (b)	$5 < \dfrac{I_{xx}}{I_{yy}} \leq 10$	ends of beam to be held in position at the bottom flange at supports
2.10.10 (c)	$10 < \dfrac{I_{xx}}{I_{yy}} \leq 20$	beam to be held in line at the ends
2.10.10 (d)	$20 < \dfrac{I_{xx}}{I_{yy}} \leq 30$	one edge to be held in line
2.10.10 (e)	$30 < \dfrac{I_{xx}}{I_{yy}} \leq 40$	beam to be restrained by bridging or other bracing at intervals of not more than 2.4 m
2.10.10 (f)	$40 < \dfrac{I_{xx}}{I_{yy}}$	compression flange should be fully restrained

Table 3.3   Lateral Restraint Requirements

3.4.4   *Example 3.3   Ply-web Roof Beam Design*

A local community centre is to be extended to accommodate two squash courts and changing rooms, as shown in Figures 3.17 (a) and (b). The roof construction is to be of traditional flat roof design comprising felt, insulation and sarking, supported by a series of timber ply-web I-beam sections sitting on block walls. Check the suitability of the proposed.beam section for a typical internal beam (wind loading is not considered).

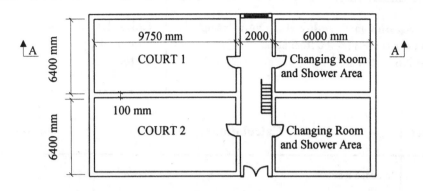

Figure 3.17 (a)

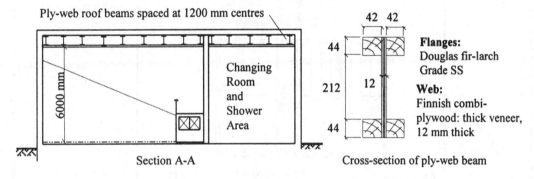

Figure 3.17 (b)

3.4.4.1 Solution to Example 3.3

Contract: Squash Court — Job Ref. No.: Example 3.3	Calcs. By: W.McK.
Part of Structure: Ply-web Roof Beam	Checked by:
Calc. Sheet No: 1 of 6	Date:

References	Calculations	Output
BS 5268 : Part 2 BS 6399 : Part 1	Structural use of timber Code of practice for dead and imposed loads **Loading:** 3 layers bituminous felt $\quad=\quad$ 0.11 kN/m² Fibreboard insulation $\quad=\quad$ 0.2 kN/m² Timber sarking $\quad\quad\quad=\quad$ <u>0.07 kN/m²</u> $\quad\quad\quad\quad\quad\quad\quad=\quad$ 0.38 kN/m² Allowing for self-weight assume Total $\quad=\quad$ 0.4 kN/m²	

Contract: Squash Court Job Ref. No.: Example 3.3	Calcs. By: W.McK.
Part of Structure: Ply-web Roof beam	Checked by:
Calc. Sheet No: 2 of 6	Date:

References	Calculations	Output

References

BS 5628 : Part 2
Table 14

Table 8

Table 43

Calculations

Imposed load $= 0.75$ kN/m^2

Roof area supported by one internal beam $=$ shaded area

1200 mm spacing

shaded area $= 1.2 \times (6400 + 100) = 7.8$ m^2
long-term load $= 0.4 \times 7.8$ $= 3.12$ kN
medium-term loading $= (0.75 + 0.4) \times 7.8$ $= 8.97$ kN

load duration factor $K_3 = 1.0$ for long-term
                              $= 1.25$ for medium-term

$$\frac{\text{medium term}}{K_3} = \frac{8.97}{1.25} = 7.18 \text{ kN} > 3.12 \text{ kN}$$

medium term is critical load case.

design bending moment $= \dfrac{wL}{8} = \dfrac{8.97 \times 6500}{8} = 7.29$ kNm

design shear force $= 0.5 \times 8.97$ $= 4.49$ kN

Grade stresses:
Douglas fir-larch Grade SS
$\sigma_{m,g,||} = 7.5$ N/mm^2 $\sigma_{t,g,||} = 4.5$ N/mm^2
$\sigma_{c,g,||} = 7.9$ N/mm^2 $\sigma_{c,g,\perp} = 2.4$ N/mm^2
$\tau_{g,||} = 0.85$ N/mm^2
$E_{mean} = 11,000$ N/mm^2 $E_{min} = 7500$ N/mm^2

Finnish combi-plywood wood (12 mm thick, 9 plies)
$\sigma_{t,g,\perp} = 16.2$ N/mm^2 $\sigma_{c,g,\perp} = 8.47$ N/mm^2

Contract: Squash Court **Job Ref. No.:** Example 3.3	**Calcs. By: W.McK.**
Part of Structure: Ply-web Roof Beam	**Checked by:**
Calc. Sheet No: 3 of 6	**Date:**

References	Calculations	Output

$\sigma_{b,g}$ = 3.0 N/mm^2 τ_p = 4.43 N/mm^2

$\tau_{roll,g}$ = 0.79 N/mm^2 $E_{b,\perp}$ = 3100 N/mm^2

$E_{c,\perp}$ = $E_{t,\perp}$ = 3750 N/mm^2 $G_\perp$ = 285 N/mm^2

Table 7
Table 43

E_{flange} = 11,000 N/mm^2 E_{web} = 3100 N/mm^2

Using a transformed section, the equivalent thickness of the transformed web is given by

$$t_{transformed} = t_{actual} \times \text{modular ratio } (\alpha)$$

$$= 12 \times \frac{E_{web}}{E_{flange}} \quad \therefore t^* = 12 \times \frac{3100}{11000} = 3.38 \text{ mm}$$

Transformed section properties:

$$A^* = (300 \times 87.38) - (84 \times 212)$$
$$= 8.406 \times 10^3 \text{ mm}^2$$

$$I^*{}_{xx} = \frac{87.38 \times 300^3}{12} - \frac{84 \times 212^3}{12}$$
$$= 129.91 \times 10^6 \text{ mm}^4$$

$$I^*{}_{yy} = \frac{2 \times 44 \times 87.38^3}{12} - \frac{212 \times 3.38^3}{12}$$
$$= 4.89 \times 10^6 \text{ mm}^4$$

(dimensions shown on section: 42, 42, 44, 212, 44, 3.38)

$$Z^*{}_{xx} = \frac{129.91 \times 10^6}{150}$$
$$= 866.1 \times 10^3 \text{ mm}^3$$

$$\frac{I_{xx}}{I_{yy}} = \frac{129.91}{4.8} = 26.6$$

Clause 2.10.10

One edge should be held in line, this will be achieved by the sarking on the roof.

Bending:

$$\sigma_{m,a,||} = \frac{7.29 \times 10^6}{866.1 \times 10^3} = 8.41 \text{ N/mm}^2$$

References	Calculations	Output
	$\sigma_{m,adm,||} = \sigma_{m,g,||} \times K_2 \times K_3 \times K_8$ Assume no load-sharing $\quad \therefore K_8 = 1.0$ medium term loading $\quad \therefore K_2 = 1.25$ $\sigma_{m,adm,||} = 7.5 \times 1.25 = 9.38 \text{ N/mm} > 8.41 \text{ N/mm}^2$	Flanges are adequate in bending
Clause 4.6	*Compression flange of plywood:* $\sigma_{c,a} = \sigma_{t,a} = \dfrac{M}{Z} \times \alpha = 8.41 \times \dfrac{3100}{11000} = 2.37 \text{ N/mm}^2$ $\sigma_{c,adm,\perp} = \sigma_{c,g,\perp} \times K_8 \times K_{36} \qquad$ as before $K_8 = 1.0$	
Clause 4.5	$K_{36} = 1.33 \;\therefore\; \sigma_{c,adm,\perp} = 8.47 \times 1.33 = 11.26 \text{ N/mm}^2$ $\gg 2.37 \text{ N/mm}^2$	
Clause 4.6 See Section 3.4.1.1	*Tension flange of plywood:* $\sigma_{t,a} = 1.54 \text{ N/mm}^2 \qquad \sigma_{t,adm,\perp} = \sigma_{t,g,\perp} \times K_8 \times K_{36}$ $\sigma_{t,adm,\perp} = 16.2 \times 1.33 = 21.5 \text{ N/mm}^2$ $\gg 2.37 \text{ N/mm}^2$ *Panel shear:*	Plywood is adequate in bending
	The panel shear stress is given by: $$\tau_{p,a} = \dfrac{VA\bar{y}}{bI_{NA}}$$ V = maximum shear force = 4.49 kN $A\bar{y}$ = 1st moment of area above the neutral axis $\quad = (84 \times 44 \times 128) + (150 \times 3.38 \times 75)$ $\quad = 511.1 \times 10^3 \text{ mm}^3$ $\tau_{p,a,transf} = \dfrac{4.49 \times 10^3 \times 511.1 \times 10^3}{3.38 \times 129.91 \times 10^6} = 5.23 \text{ N/mm}^2$ $\tau_{p,a,plywood} = \tau_{p,a,transf} \times \alpha = 5.23 \times \dfrac{3100}{11000} = 1.47 \text{ N/mm}^2$ $\tau_{p,adm,plywood} = \tau_{p,g} \times K_{36} = 4.43 \times 1.33 = 5.89 \text{ N/mm}^2$ $> 1.47 \text{ N/mm}^2$	Plywood is adequate in panel shear

Contract: Squash Court Job Ref. No.: Example 3.3	Calcs. By: W.McK.
Part of Structure: Ply-web Roof Beam	Checked by:
Calc. Sheet No: 5 of 6	Date:

References	Calculations	Output

Rolling shear:

The rolling shear stress is given by $\tau_{p,a} = \dfrac{VA\bar{y}}{bI_{NA}}$

V = maximum shear force = 4.49 kN

$A\bar{y}$ = 1st moment of area of the flanges above the neutral axis

= (2 × 44 × 42 × 128)

= 473 × 10^3 mm^3

$\tau_{p,a,transf}$ = $\dfrac{4.49 \times 10^3 \times 473 \times 10^3}{2 \times 44 \times 129.91 \times 10^6}$ = 0.19 N/mm^2

$\tau_{roll,a,plywood}$ = $\tau_{roll,a,transf} \times \alpha$ = 0.19 × $\dfrac{3100}{11000}$ = 0.05 N/mm^2

Table 33

$\tau_{roll,adm,plywood}$ = $\tau_{roll,g} \times K_{36} \times K_{37}$ = 0.79 × 1.33 × 0.5

= 0.53 N/mm^2

Clause 4.6

>> 0.05 N/mm^2

Output: Plywood is adequate in rolling shear

Deflection:

Clause 2.10.7

δ_{adm} = 0.003 × 6500 = 19.5 mm

Clause 4.6

$\delta_{actual} \approx \delta_{bending} + \delta_{shear}$

Section 3.4.2.2.1

$\delta_{bending} \approx \dfrac{5WL^3}{384EI}$

$EI = E_{flange}(I_{flange} + \alpha I_{web})$

$I_{flange} = 4\left\{ \dfrac{42 \times 44^3}{12} + \left(42 \times 44 \times 128^2\right) \right\} = 122.3 \times 10^6$ mm^4

References	Calculations	Output

<table>
<tr><td>

Contract: Squash Court   **Job Ref. No.:** Example 3.3
Part of Structure: Ply-web Roof Beam
Calc. Sheet No: 6 of 6

</td><td>

Calcs. By: W.McK.
Checked by:
Date:

</td></tr>
</table>

	$\alpha I_{web} = \left\{ \dfrac{3100}{11000} \times \dfrac{12 \times 300^3}{12} \right\}$ $= 7.61 \times 10^6 \text{ mm}^4$	
	$EI = 11000 \,(135.4 + 7.61) \times 10^6 = 1429 \times 10^9 \text{ Nmm}^2$	
	$\delta_{bending} = \dfrac{5 \times 8.97 \times 10^3 \times 6500^3}{384 \times 1576 \times 10^9}$ $= 20.4 \text{ mm}$	
Section 3.4.2.2.2	$\delta_{shear} \approx \dfrac{M}{G_{web} A_w}$; $G = 285 \text{ N/mm}^2$;	
Table 43	$\delta_{shear} \approx \dfrac{7.29 \times 10^6}{285 \times (12 \times 300)} = 7.1 \text{ mm}$	Ply-web beam is **inadequate** in deflection A deeper section is required
	$\delta_{actual} \approx 20.4 + 7.1 = 27.5 \text{ mm}$ $\delta_{adm} = 27.5 \text{ mm} > 19.2 \text{ mm}$	
	Note: the shear deflection makes a significant contribution to the total deflection of the beam	

3.4.5   *Example 3.4*   *Access Bridge in Exhibition Centre*

A temporary timber access bridge is required within an exhibition hall, as indicated in Figure 3.18. Details of the proposed cross-section of the structure are indicated in Figures 3.19 (a) and (b). Using this information, check the suitability of the following timber members:

     i)   the boarding, allowing 5 mm for wear,
     ii)   a typical central stringer,
     iii)   a typical cross-beam,
     iv)   a main ply-web box beam.

Boards, stringers and cross-beams are to be strength class C24.
Assume that the structure satisfies Service Class 2 requirements.

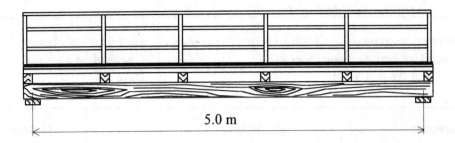

Figure 3.18

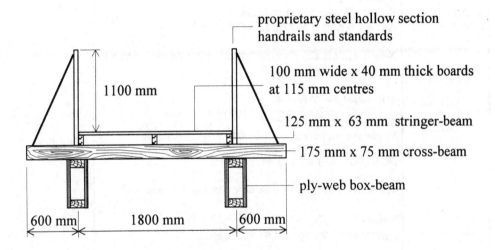

proprietary steel hollow section
handrails and standards

100 mm wide x 40 mm thick boards
at 115 mm centres

125 mm x 63 mm stringer-beam

175 mm x 75 mm cross-beam

ply-web box-beam

1100 mm

600 mm   1800 mm   600 mm

Figure 3.19 (a)

British Grown Douglas fir : Grade GS

1.4 mm veneer sanded Finnish combi
plywood (7 plies), face ply perpendicular
to span

British Grown Douglas fir : Grade   GS

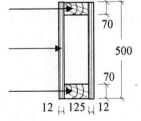

70

500

70

12 125 12

Figure 3.19 (b)

3.4.5.1   Solution to Example 3.4

<table>
<tr>
<td colspan="2">Contract : Footbridge   Job Ref. No. : Example 3.4
Part of Structure :   Beam Elements
Calc. Sheet No. : 1 of 11</td>
<td>Calcs. by : W.McK.
Checked by :
Date :</td>
</tr>
</table>

References	Calculations	Output
BS 5268 : Part 2 BS 6399 : Part 1 BS 5268 : Part 2 Table 7	Structural use of timber Code of practice for dead and imposed loads Loading: Boards, stringers and cross-beams: Average density = 500 kg/m^3 = 4.91 kN/m^3 **Note**: a value is also given for 'characteristic density', which is used when designing joints. Self-weight due to boards: 100 mm x 40 mm Volume/m^2 of plan area = $1.0 \times 0.04 \times \dfrac{100}{115} = 0.035$ m^3 Dead load = 4.91 × 0.035 = 0.17 kN/m^2 Self-weight due to stringer section: 125 mm x 63 mm Volume/m length = $0.125 \times 0.063 = 7.9 \times 10^{-3}$ m^3 Dead load = $7.9 \times 10^{-3} \times 4.91 = 0.04$ kN/m. Self-weight due to cross-beams: 175 mm x 75 mm Volume/m length = $0.175 \times 0.075 = 13.0 \times 10^{-3}$ m^3 Dead load = $13.0 \times 10^{-3} \times 4.91 = 0.06$ kN/m. Assume an allowance for handrails, fitments etc. = 1.0 kN/m^2 Self-weight of ply-web beams: Assume plywood 12 mm thick = 7.14 kg/m^2 = 0.07 kN/m^2	Boarding: 0.17 kN/m^2 Stringers: 0.04 kN/m Cross-beams: 0.06 kN/m Handrails etc.: 1.0 kN/m^2

References	Calculations	Output
	Contract: Footbridge **Job Ref. No.:** Example 3.4 **Part of Structure:** Beam Elements **Calc. Sheet No:** 2 of 11 **Calcs. By: W.McK.** **Checked by:** **Date:**	

References	Calculations	Output
Table 2 Table 7	British grown Douglas fir is strength class C14 for GS grade Average density for C14 timber ≈ 350 kg/m^3 = 3.43 kN/m^3 Volume/m length = $0.125 \times 0.7 \times 1.0 = 88 \times 10^{-3}$ m^3 / flange Self-weight due to flanges = $2 \times 0.088 \times 3.43 = 0.6$ kN/m Self-weight due to webs = $2 \times 0.5 \times 1.0 \times 0.07 = 0.07$ kN/m Dead load = $(0.6 + 0.07) = 0.67$ kN/m	Ply-web beams: 0.67 kN/m
BS 5268 : Part 2 Table 7	Grade Stresses: Class C24 Timber – class 2 $\sigma_{m,g,\|\|} = 7.5$ N/mm^2 , $\sigma_{c,g,\perp} = 2.4$ N/mm^2 (assume wane is not permitted), $\tau_{g,\|\|} = 0.71$ N/mm^2, $E_{mean} = 10800$ N/mm^2 , $E_{min} = 7200$ N/mm^2 Class C14 Timber – class 2 $\sigma_{m,g,\|\|} = 4.1$ N/mm^2, $\sigma_{c,g,\perp} = 2.1$ N/mm^2 (assume wane is not permitted), $\tau_{g,\|\|} = 0.6$ N/mm^2, $E_{mean} = 6800$ N/mm^2 , $E_{min} = 4600$ N/mm^2	
Table 43	Finnish combi-plywood wood (12 mm thick, 9 plies) $\sigma_{t,g,\perp} = 16.2$ N/mm^2 , $\sigma_{c,g,\perp} = 8.47$ N/mm^2 $\sigma_{b,g,} = 3.0$ N/mm^2, $\tau_p = 4.43$ N/mm^2 $\tau_{roll,g} = 0.79$ N/mm^2, $E_{b,\perp} = 3100$ N/mm^2 $E_{c,\perp} = E_{t,\perp} = 3750$ N/mm^2, $G_\perp = 285$ N/mm^2 **Note:** Use dry stresses since structure is inside building **Boarding:** Consider 1 metre width Dead load = 0.17 kN/m Imposed load = 4.0 kN/m or 4.5 kN concentrated load	
BS 6399 : Part 1 Table 7	Three load cases should be considered: (i) maximum bending moment with both spans fully loaded (ii) maximum bending moment with one span fully loaded and the other span with only dead load (iii) maximum moment with concentrated load at mid-span.	

Contract: Footbridge Job Ref. No.: Example 3.4	Calcs. By: W.McK.
Part of Structure: Beam Elements	Checked by:
Calc. Sheet No: 3 of 11	Date:

References	Calculations	Output
	Load case (i) 	

Appendix A
 (this text)
	Maximum bending moment = B.Max = $-0.125\ WL$
	  (occurs over support) $= -0.125 \times (4.17 \times 0.9) \times 0.9$
	                                         $= -0.42$ kNm
	 Load case (ii): maximum span moment
	
		load case (i)
		 B.Max = 0.42 kNm

Appendix A	Continuity moments $M = -(0.125 \times 4.17 \times 0.9) - (0.063 \times 4.0 \times 0.9) = -0.71$ kNm Consider the left-hand span 	

Contract: Footbridge Job Ref. No.: Example 3.4	Calcs. By: W.McK.
Part of Structure: Beam Elements	Checked by:
Calc. Sheet No: 4 of 11	Date:

References	Calculations	Output
	Sum of the moments to the left-hand side: $+\,0.71 + (0.9 \times V) - (4.17 \times 0.9 \times \dfrac{0.9}{2}) = 0$ $\therefore V = 1.1$ kN 1.1 kN part shear force diagram x position of zero shear $= x = \dfrac{1.1}{4.17} = 0.26$ m maximum bending moment = area under shear force diagram B.Max $= 0.5 \times 0.26 \times 1.1 = 0.14$ kNm. load case (iii) 4.5 kN 450 mm 450 mm 900 mm	load case (ii) B.Max = 0.31 kNm
Appendix A	B.Max $= 0.203\,WL = 0.203 \times 4.5 \times 0.9 = 0.82$ kNm Load case (iii) is the critical case *Bending:* allow 5 mm thickness for wear $\qquad Z = \dfrac{bd^2}{6} = \dfrac{100 \times 35^2}{6} = 20.42 \times 10^3$ mm^3 $\qquad$ B.Max per board $= 0.82 \times \dfrac{125}{1000} = 0.1$ kNm $\qquad \sigma_{m,a,||} = \dfrac{0.1 \times 10^6}{20.42 \times 10^3} = 4.9$ N/mm^2 $\qquad \sigma_{m,adm,||} = \sigma_{m,g,||} \times K_2 \times K_3 = 7.5 \times 1.25$ $\qquad\qquad\qquad = 9.38$ N/mm$^2 > 4.9$ N/mm^2	load case (iii) B.Max = 0.82 kNm Adequate in bending
See Chapter 2	*Deflection:* $I = \dfrac{bd^3}{12} = \dfrac{100 \times 35^3}{12} = 357.29 \times 10^3$ mm^4	

Contract: Footbridge	Job Ref. No.: Example 3.4	Calcs. By: W.McK.
Part of Structure: Beam Elements		Checked by:
Calc. Sheet No: 5 of 11		Date:

References	Calculations	Output
Section 2.9.1 Table 2.1	Equivalent UDL $= \dfrac{w_e L^2}{8} = 0.1$ kNm $\qquad w_e = \dfrac{8 \times 0.1}{0.9^2} \approx 1.0$ kN/m $\delta_{actual} \approx \dfrac{5 w_e L^4}{384 EI} = \dfrac{5 \times 1.0 \times 900^4}{384 \times 7200 \times 357.29 \times 10^3} = 3.32$ mm $\delta_{adm} = 0.003 \times$ span $= 0.003 \times 900 = 2.7$ mm < 3.32 mm Despite $\delta_{actual} > \delta_{adm}$ a larger section to limit deflection would be rather onerous since the boards are only 15 mm apart, and the assumed concentrated load applied to one board is excessive and grossly overestimates actual deflection **Adopt 100 mm x 40 mm boarding at 115 mm centres** **Central Stringers:** The load imposed on a central stringer is equal to the central support reaction from the two span boarding, i.e.	Accept calculated deflection
	The maximum value of the reaction 'V' occurs when the full load is applied to both spans of the boarding.	
Appendix A	$\therefore$ load on central stinger $= 1.25 \times 4.17 \times 0.9 = 4.69$ kN/m Assuming stringers to be single-span and simply supported B.Max $= \dfrac{wL^2}{8} = \dfrac{4.69 \times 1.0^2}{8} = 0.59$ kNm *Bending:* $\qquad Z = \dfrac{bd^2}{6} = \dfrac{63 \times 125^2}{6} = 164.1 \times 10^3$ mm^3	

Contract: Footbridge Job Ref. No.: Example 3.4	Calcs. By: W.McK.
Part of Structure: Beam Elements	Checked by:
Calc. Sheet No: 6 of 11	Date:

References	Calculations	Output
	$\sigma_{m,a,\|\|} = \dfrac{0.59 \times 10^6}{169.3 \times 10^3} = 3.6 \text{ N/mm}^2$	
	$\sigma_{m,adm,\|\|} = 9.38 \text{ N/mm}^2 > 3.5 \text{ N/mm}^2$	
	Deflection: $I = \dfrac{bd^3}{12} = \dfrac{63 \times 125^3}{12} = 10.25 \times 10^6 \text{ mm}^4$	
	$\delta_{actual} \approx \dfrac{5wL^4}{384EI} = \dfrac{5 \times 4.69 \times 1000^4}{384 \times 7200 \times 10.25 \times 10^6} = 0.827 \text{ mm}$	
	$\delta_{adm} = 0.003 \times \text{span} = 0.003 \times 1000 = 3.0 \text{ mm} \gg 0.827 \text{ mm}$	Adequate in deflection
	Shear:	
	Maximum shear force $= 4.69 \times 0.5 = 2.35 \text{ kN}$	
	$\tau_{a,\|\|} = \dfrac{1.5 \times 2.35 \times 10^3}{63 \times 125} = 0.45 \text{ N/mm}^2$	
	$\tau_{adm,\|\|} = \tau_{g,\|\|} \times K_3 = 0.71 \times 1.25 \text{ N/mm}^2 = 0.89 \text{ N/mm}^2$ $> 0.45 \text{ N/mm}^2$	Adequate in shear
	Adopt 125 mm x 63 mm for stringers	
BS 6399 : Part 1 Clause 9.1 Table 4 (h)	**Cross-beams:** Two load cases should be considered (i) A horizontal force (F) which is considered to act at a height of 1.1 m above the datum level. $F = 1.0 \text{ kN/m}$ (ii) The vertical loading due to dead and imposed load.	
	In this case the two load cases compensate for each other and should be considered separately.	
	Load case (i):	
	$F = 1.0 \text{ kN}$ 1100 mm 253 mm cross-beam	

References	Calculations	Output
	Contract: Footbridge Job Ref. No.: Example 3.4 Calcs. By: W.McK. Part of Structure: Beam Elements Checked by: Calc. Sheet No: 7 of 11 Date:	

References	Calculations	Output
	Since the vertical standards are spaced at 1.0 m centres Horizontal load/post = 1.0 kN Bending moment due to horizontal load = $1.0 \times (1.1 + 0.253)$ $ = 1.353$ kNm. *Load case (ii):* load due to stringer = end reaction + self-weight $ = 4.69 + (0.04 \times 1.0) = 4.73$ kN (neglect self-weight of cross-beam) 2.37 kN 4.73 kN 2.37 kN 4.73 kN 4.73 kN 1800 mm Maximum bending moment $\approx \dfrac{wL}{4} = \dfrac{4.73 \times 1.8}{4} = 2.13$ kNm Critical load case is due to the vertical loading *Bending:* $$Z = \frac{bd^2}{6} = \frac{75 \times 175^2}{6} = 382.8 \times 10^3 \text{ mm}^3$$ $$\sigma_{m,a,||} = \frac{2.13 \times 10^6}{382.8 \times 10^3} = 5.56 \text{ N/mm}^2$$ $$\sigma_{m,adm,||} = 7.5 \text{ N/mm}^2 > 5.56 \text{ N/mm}^2$$	Adequate in bending

Contract: Footbridge **Job Ref. No.:** Example 3.4		**Calcs. By:** W.McK.
Part of Structure: Beam Elements		**Checked by:**
Calc. Sheet No: 8 of 11		**Date:**

References	Calculations	Output
	Deflection: $I = \dfrac{bd^3}{12} = \dfrac{75 \times 175^3}{12} = 33.5 \times 10^6$ mm^4	

Deflection: $I = \dfrac{bd^3}{12} = \dfrac{75 \times 175^3}{12} = 33.5 \times 10^6$ mm^4

$\delta_{actual} \approx \dfrac{PL^3}{48EI} = \dfrac{4.73 \times 10^3 \times 1800^3}{48 \times 7200 \times 33.5 \times 10^6} = 2.38$ mm

$\delta_{adm} = 0.003 \times$ span $= 0.003 \times 1800 = 5.4$ mm $\gg 2.38$ mm

Shear:
Maximum shear force $= 4.73 \times 0.5 = 2.37$ kN

$\tau_{a,||} = \dfrac{1.5 \times 2.37 \times 10^3}{75 \times 175} = 0.27$ N/mm^2

$\tau_{adm,||} = \tau_{g,||} \times K_3 = 0.71 \times 1.25$ N/mm$^2 = 0.89$ N/mm^2
> 0.27 N/mm^2

Adopt 175 mm x 75 mm for cross-beams

Output: Adequate in shear

Box-Beams:
The box-beam supports cross-beams at 1.0 m centres.
Reaction from each cross-beam $= 4.73$ kN
Self-weight $= 0.67$ kN/m

2.74 kN 4.73 kN 4.73 kN 4.73 kN 4.73 kN 2.74 kN

0.67 kN/m

5 @ 1.0 m centres

13.5 kN   13.5 kN

B.Max $=$ $(13.5 \times 2.5) - (2.74 \times 2.5) - (4.73 \times [0.5 + 1.5])$
$=$ 17.44 kNm
S.Max. $=$ $(13.5 - 2.74) = 10.76$ kN

Bending:
Using a transformed section the equivalent thickness of the transformed web is given by

$t_{transformed} = t_{actual} \times$ modular ratio (α)

$= 12 \times \dfrac{E_{web}}{E_{flange}}$

References	Calculations	Output
Table 7 Table 43	E_{flange} = 6800 N/mm^2 E_{web} = 3100 N/mm^2 t^* = $12 \times \dfrac{3100}{6800}$ = 5.5 mm Transformed section properties: A^* = $(500 \times 136) - (360 \times 125)$ = 23.0×10^3 mm^2 I^*_{xx} = $\dfrac{136 \times 500^3}{12} - \dfrac{125 \times 360^3}{12}$ = 930.67×10^6 mm^4 I^*_{yy} = $\dfrac{500 \times 136^3}{12} - \dfrac{360 \times 125^3}{12}$ = 46.22×10^6 mm^4 Z^*_{xx} = $\dfrac{930.67 \times 10^6}{250}$ = 3.72×10^6 mm^3 $\dfrac{I_{xx}}{I_{yy}}$ = $\dfrac{930.67}{46.22} = 20.14$	
Clause 2.10.10	One edge should be held in line. **Note:** The cross–beams provide lateral restraint to the compression flange of individual box beams at 1.0 m intervals. The beams will be held in line at the ends. *Bending:* $$\sigma_{m,a,||} = \dfrac{17.4 \times 10^6}{3.72 \times 10^6} = 4.68 \text{ N/mm}^2$$ $$\sigma_{m,adm,||} = \sigma_{m,g,||} \times K_2 \times K_3 \times K_8$$ Assume no load-sharing $\therefore K_8 = 1.0$ medium-term loading $\therefore K_2 = 1.25$ $\sigma_{m,adm,||} = 4.1 \times 1.25 = 5.13$ N/mm > 4.95 N/mm^2	Flanges are adequate in bending
Clause 4.6	*Compression flange of plywood:* $$\sigma_{c,a} = \sigma_{t,a} = \dfrac{BM}{Z} \times \alpha = 4.68 \times \dfrac{3100}{6800} = 2.13 \text{ N/mm}^2$$	

References	Calculations	Output
	Contract: Footbridge **Job Ref. No.: Example 3.4** **Calcs. By: W.McK.**	

Contract: Footbridge   **Job Ref. No.: Example 3.4**   **Calcs. By: W.McK.**
Part of Structure: Beam Elements   **Checked by:**
Calc. Sheet No: 10 of 11   **Date:**

References	Calculations	Output
Clause 4.5	$\sigma_{c,adm,\perp} = \sigma_{c,g,\perp} \times K_8 \times K_{36}$ as before $K_8 = 1.0$ $K_{36} = 1.33$ $\therefore$ $\sigma_{c,adm,\perp} = 8.47 \times 1.33 = 11.26 \ \text{N/mm}^2$ $\gg 2.04 \ \text{N/mm}^2$	
Clause 4.6	*Tension flange of plywood:* $\sigma_{t,a} = 2.04 \ \text{N/mm}^2$ $\sigma_{t,adm,\perp} = \sigma_{t,g,\perp} \times K_8 \times K_{36}$ $\sigma_{t,adm,\perp} = 16.2 \times 1.33 = 21.5 \ \text{N/mm}^2$ $\gg 2.04 \ \text{N/mm}^2$	Plywood is adequate in bending

See Section 3.4.1.1	*Panel shear:*
	
	 The panel shear stress is given by $\tau_{p,a} = \dfrac{VA\bar{y}}{bI_{NA}}$
	
	 V = maximum shear force = 10.76 kN
	 $A\bar{y}$ = 1st moment of area above the neutral axis
	     $= (125 \times 70 \times 215) + 2(5.5 \times 250 \times 125)$
	     $= 2.23 \times 10^6 \ \text{mm}^3$
	
	 $\tau_{p,a,transf} = \dfrac{10.76 \times 10^3 \times 2.23 \times 10^6}{2 \times 5.5 \times 930.67 \times 10^6} = 2.34 \ \text{N/mm}^2$
	
	 $\tau_{p,a,plywood} = \tau_{p,a,transf} \times \alpha = 5.5 \times \dfrac{3100}{6800} = 2.51 \ \text{N/mm}^2$
	
	 $\tau_{p,adm,plywood} = \tau_{p,g} \times K_{36} = 4.43 \times 1.33 = 5.89 \ \text{N/mm}^2$
	 $> 2.51 \ \text{N/mm}^2$
	
	 Rolling shear:
	
	 The rolling shear stress is given by $\tau_{p,a} = \dfrac{VA\bar{y}}{bI_{NA}}$
		Plywood is adequate in panel shear

Contract: Footbridge	Job Ref. No.: Example 3.4	Calcs. By: W.McK.
Part of Structure: Beam Elements		Checked by:
Calc. Sheet No: 11 of 11		Date:

References	Calculations	Output
	V = maximum shear force = 10.76 kN $A\bar{y}$ = 1st moment of area of the flanges above the neutral axis = $(125 \times 70 \times 215)$ = 1.88×10^6 mm^3 $\tau_{p,a,transf} = \dfrac{10.76 \times 10^3 \times 1.88 \times 10^6}{2 \times 70 \times 930.67 \times 10^6} = 0.16$ N/mm^2 $\tau_{roll,a,plywood} = \tau_{roll,a,transf} \times \alpha = 0.16 \times \dfrac{3100}{6800} = 0.07$ N/mm^2	
Table 33 Clause 4.6	$\tau_{roll,adm,plywood} = \tau_{roll,g} \times K_{36} \times K_{37} = 0.79 \times 1.33 \times 0.5$ $= 0.53$ N/mm^2 $\gg 0.07$ N/mm^2	Plywood is adequate in rolling shear
Clause 2.10.7 Clause 4.6 Section 3.4.2.2.1	*Deflection:* $\delta_{adm} = 0.003 \times 5000 = 15$ mm $\delta_{actual} \approx \delta_{bending} + \delta_{shear}$ $\delta_{bending} \approx \dfrac{5 w_e L^4}{384 EI}$ w_e = equivalent UDL = $\dfrac{8 B\,max}{l^2} = \dfrac{8 \times 17.44}{5.0^2} = 5.58$ kN/m $EI = E_{flange}(I_{flange} + \alpha I_{web})$ $I_{flange} = 2\left\{\dfrac{125 \times 70^3}{12} + 125 \times 70 \times 215^2\right\} = 816 \times 10^6$ mm^4 $\alpha I_{web} = 2\left\{\dfrac{3100}{6800} \times \dfrac{12 \times 500^3}{12}\right\} = 113.9 \times 10^6$ mm^4 $EI = 6800\,(816 + 113.9) \times 10^6 = 6323.3 \times 10^9$ Nmm^2 $\delta_{bending} = \dfrac{5 \times 5.58 \times 5000^4}{384 \times 6323.3 \times 10^9} = 7.18$ mm	
Section 3.4.2.2.2 Table 43	$\delta_{shear} \approx \dfrac{M}{G_{web} A_w}$; $\quad G_{web} = 28.5$ N/mm^2 ; $\delta_{shear} \approx \dfrac{17.44 \times 10^6}{285 \times (2 \times 12 \times 500)} = 5.1$ mm $\delta_{actual} \approx 7.18 + 5.1 = 12.3$ mm $\delta_{adm} = 15$ mm > 12.3 mm	Box-beam is adequate in deflection

3.5 Stressed-Skin Panels

A typical cross-section of a stressed-skin panel is shown in Figure 3.20. The construction consists of solid longitudinal members (webs/ribs/stringers) and normally plywood skins, connected to form a composite structural section. The skins may consist of other material such as particle board or fibre board and the connecting mechanism may be glue, nails, screws or proprietary mechanical fasteners.

The composite section acts as a series of T-beams if only one side is covered with a skin or a series of I - beams if there are skins on both sides.

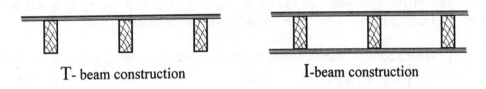

T- beam construction   I-beam construction

Figure 3.20

The primary objective of stressed-skin panels is to make structural use of the skin in addition to the ribs. In traditional construction using standard timber floors, the joists carry the full load without assistance from the flooring. The efficient use of materials using stressed-skin panels results in smaller quantities of timber being required, a reduction in weight to be handled and an improvement in efficiency of construction.

The most common uses for stressed panels are for prefabricated roof or floor panels in timber frame construction. In addition, they can be used to resist compression, bending and racking forces when used as wall units.

Stressed-skin panels are prefabricated and transported to site for erection. Generally roof and floor panels are 1.25 m to 2.5 m wide and between 5 m and 6 m long. Panels used as walls are normally about 2.5 m high with a maximum length of 10 m.

The ribs of panels are normally solid sawn timber but can be made from other alternatives such as wood-based panels, glulam or prefabricated I-section. In roofs and floors sawn timber ribs vary in width between 38 mm and 63 mm and between 150 mm and 300 mm in depth. Similarly for wall panels, the corresponding dimensions are between 38 mm and 80 mm for the width and 80 mm and 200 mm for the depth. The rib spacing varies between 300 mm and 625 mm depending on the type and size of sheeting adopted for the flanges.

The flanges of panels are usually between 10 mm and 19 mm thick. Generally the face grain of Douglas fir plywood flanges runs parallel to the ribs and the permissible stress parallel to the face grain is used when assessing the composite strength. In some Finnish plywood sheets, the face grain runs in the short direction and more economic and efficient design may result from this face grain running perpendicular to the ribs. This arrangement improves the ability of the plywood to span between the ribs, allowing a greater rib spacing, and in addition reduces the number of joints required in the length of the panel. In this case the stress perpendicular to the face grain is used when evaluating the composite strength of the panel.

The effect of shear deformation is complex and reduces the contribution of the flange to the bending strength and bending stiffness of the composite unit. In design this is usually dealt with by considering an effective width of flange, similar to the practice adopted in the design of reinforced concrete beam/slab floor systems. A detailed discussion of the effects of shear deformation and its influence on the behaviour of the flange is beyond the scope of this text and further reference should be made to the *Timber Designers' Manual* (13), and *STEP1:* and *STEP2: Structural Timber Education Programme* (14, 15).

3.5.1   Example 3.5   Stressed-Skin Floor Panel

A stressed-skin flat roof panel as shown in Figure 3.21 is required to span 4.0 m and support the loads indicated. Check the suitability of the proposed section.

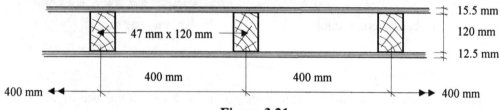

Figure 3.21

Top flange: Canadian Douglas fir : unsanded (5 ply) / face grain parallel to the ribs
Bottom flange: Canadian Douglas fir : unsanded (4 ply)
Ribs: Whitewood Class C24

Dead load   (excluding self-weight)   : 0.6 kN/m^2
Imposed load: 0.75 kN/m^2

3.5.1.1   Solution to Example 3.5

Contract : **Flat Roof** Job Ref. No. : **Example 3.5** Part of Structure : **Stressed-Skin Panel** Calc. Sheet No. : **1 of 8**		Calcs. by : **W.McK.** Checked by : Date :
References	**Calculations**	**Output**
BS 5268 : Part 2 Table 7 Table 27	Structural Use of Timber Timber Designers' Manual Assume the density of the ribs ≈ 420 kg/m^3 Self-weight of ribs = $(0.047 \times 0.12 \times 4.12)$ = 0.02 kN/m *Consider 1.0 m width of flange* **Top flange:** minimum thickness = 15.5 mm mass/unit area = 8.9 kg/m^2	

References	Calculations	Output

Contract : Flat Roof   **Job Ref. No. :** Example 3.5
Part of Structure : Stressed-Skin Panel
Calc. Sheet No. : 2 of 8

Calcs. by : W.McK.
Checked by :
Date :

Self-weight $\quad\quad = \quad 0.087\ \mathrm{kN/m^2}$

Area $\quad\quad A \quad = \quad 15.5 \times 10^3\ \mathrm{mm^2/m}$ width

Modulus $\quad\quad Z \quad = \quad 40.0 \times 10^3\ \mathrm{mm^3/m}$ width

Second moment of area $\quad I \quad = \quad 310.3 \times 10^3\ \mathrm{mm^4/m}$ width

Bottom flange:

minimum thickness $\quad = \quad 12.5\ \mathrm{mm}$

mass/unit area $\quad = \quad 7.2\ \mathrm{kg/m^2}$

Self-weight $\quad = \quad 0.071\ \mathrm{kN/m^2}$

Area $\quad\quad A \quad = \quad 12.5 \times 10^3\ \mathrm{mm^2/m}$ width

Modulus $\quad\quad Z \quad = \quad 26 \times 10^3\ \mathrm{mm^3/m}$ width

Second moment of area $\quad I \quad = \quad 162.8 \times 10^3\ \mathrm{mm^4/m}$ width

Grade Stresses:

Table 7
Table 39

Web: C24

$\sigma_{m,g,||} \quad = \quad 7.5\ \mathrm{N/mm^2} \quad\quad\quad \sigma_{t,g,,||} = \quad 4.5\ \mathrm{N/mm^2}$

$\sigma_{c,g,,||} \quad = \quad 7.9\ \mathrm{N/mm^2} \quad\quad\quad \sigma_{c,g,\perp} = \quad 2.4\ \mathrm{N/mm^2}$

$\tau_{g,||} \quad = \quad 0.71\ \mathrm{N/mm^2}$

$E_{m,||} \quad = \quad 10{,}800\ \mathrm{N/mm^2} \quad\quad E_{min} = \quad 7{,}200\ \mathrm{N/mm^2}$

Top flange:

$\sigma_{m,g,||} \quad = \quad 12.9\ \mathrm{N/mm^2} \quad\quad\quad \sigma_{m,g,\perp} = \quad 4.73\ \mathrm{N/mm^2}$

$\sigma_{b,g} \quad = \quad 2.16\ \mathrm{N/mm^2} \quad\quad\quad \tau_{r,g} = \quad 0.51\ \mathrm{N/mm^2}$

$\tau_{transv,g,||} \quad = \quad 0.65\ \mathrm{N/mm^2} \quad\quad \tau_{transv,g,\perp} = \quad 0.33\ \mathrm{N/mm^2}$

$\tau_{p,g} \quad = \quad 1.77\ \mathrm{N/mm^2} \quad\quad\quad G = \quad 255\ \mathrm{N/mm^2}$

$E_{m,||} \quad = \quad 4965\ \mathrm{N/mm^2} \quad\quad E_{m,\perp} = \quad 1055\ \mathrm{N/mm^2}$

Bottom flange:

$\sigma_{m,g,||} \quad = \quad 10.9\ \mathrm{N/mm^2} \quad\quad\quad \sigma_{m,g,\perp} = \quad 3.45\ \mathrm{N/mm^2}$

$\sigma_{b,g} \quad = \quad 2.16\ \mathrm{N/mm^2} \quad\quad\quad \tau_{r,g} = \quad 0.39\ \mathrm{N/mm^2}$

$\tau_{transv,g,||} \quad = \quad 0.47\ \mathrm{N/mm^2} \quad\quad \tau_{transv,g,\perp} = \quad 0.73\ \mathrm{N/mm^2}$

$\tau_{p,g} \quad = \quad 1.72\ \mathrm{N/mm^2} \quad\quad\quad G = \quad 260\ \mathrm{N/mm^2}$

$E_{m,||} \quad = \quad 5490\ \mathrm{N/mm^2} \quad\quad E_{m,\perp} = \quad 615\ \mathrm{N/mm^2}$

Since the face grain is parallel to the span of the ribs, the stresses perpendicular to the grain should be used to determine the strength of the panel between the ribs.

Contract : Flat Roof Job Ref. No. : Example 3.5 Part of Structure : Stressed-Skin Panel Calc. Sheet No. : 3 of 8	Calcs. by : W.McK. Checked by : Date :

References	Calculations	Output
Clause 2.9	Modification factors: load-sharing does not apply to the panels spanning between the ribs $\therefore$ K_8 = 1.0	

Table 33	Load duration factor K_{36} applies to both stresses and modulus
	
	long-term stress K_{36} = 1.0
	          modulus K_{36} = 1.0
	medium-term stress K_{36} = 1.33
	          modulus K_{36} = 1.54	

Clause 4.6	At the outermost rib and plywood flange the rolling shear stress should be multiplied by K_{38} which equals 0.5 **Loading:** long-term loading = (0.6 + 0.087 + 0.071) = 0.76 kN/m^2 medium-term loading = (0.76 + 0.75) = 1.51 kN/m^2 $\dfrac{\text{Medium term}}{K_{36}}$ = $\dfrac{1.51}{1.33}$ = 1.13 N/mm^2 > long-term Design for medium term loading 1.51 kN/m^2 rib supports spaced at 400 mm centres Consider 1.0 m width of flange **Bending:** Maximum applied bending moment $\approx 0.107\ wL^2$ B.Max $\approx$ $0.107 \times 1.51 \times 0.42^2$ = 0.03 kNm $\sigma_{m,a,\perp}$ = $\dfrac{0.03 \times 10^6}{40 \times 10^3}$ = 0.75 N/mm^2 $\sigma_{m,adm,\perp}$ = $\sigma_{m,g,\perp} \times K_8 \times K_{36}$ = 4.73 × 1.33 = 6.29 N/mm^2 >> 0.75 N/mm^2	Top flange is adequate in bending

Contract : Flat Roof Job Ref. No. : Example 3.5	Calcs. by : W.McK.
Part of Structure : Stressed-Skin Panel	Checked by :
Calc. Sheet No. : 4 of 8	Date :

References	Calculations	Output
Timber Designers'Manual (section 10.3.2)	The top flange is in compression and should be checked for compression **Buckling:** $$W_{cr} = \frac{eK_{cr}}{(L_s L)^2}$$ e $= (120 + 7.75 + 6.25) = 134$ mm, $K_{cr} = 192$ $L_s = 400 - 47 = 353$ mm, $L = 4.0$ m $W_{cr} = \dfrac{0.134 \times 192}{(0.353 \times 4.0)^2}$ $= 12.9$ kN/m^2 > 1.51 kN/m^2	Top flange is adequate in buckling
Timber Designers'Manual (Table 10.2)	**Deflection:** Assume $\delta_{actual} \approx \dfrac{wL^4}{154EI}$ $E = E_{m,\perp} \times K_{36} = 1055 \times 1.54 = 1624$ N/mm^2 $\delta_{actual} \approx \dfrac{1.51 \times 353^4}{154 \times 1624 \times 310.3 \times 10^3} = 0.3$ mm $\delta_{adm} = 0.003 \times \text{span} = 0.003 \times 353 = 1.06$ mm > 0.3 mm **Composite Panel:** The composite panel spans 4.0 m. Consider a width equal to 400 mm comprising one web and a width of flange on each side equal to 200 mm 	

References	Calculations	Output

Contract : Flat Roof   **Job Ref. No. :** Example 3.5   **Calcs. by :** W.McK.
Part of Structure : Stressed-Skin Panel   **Checked by :**
Calc. Sheet No. : 5 of 8   **Date :**

Loading:

long-term loading $=$ $0.76 + 0.02$ $=$ 0.78 kN/m^2
medium-term loading $=$ $(0.78 + 0.75)$ $=$ 1.53 kN/m^2
As before the design for medium term is the critical load case.

load carried by a 400 mm width $=$ $1.53 \times 0.4 \times 4.0$
   $=$ 2.45 kN

Design bending moment $=$ $\dfrac{WL}{8} = \dfrac{2.45 \times 4}{8}$ $=$ 1.23 kNm

Design shear force $=$ 0.5×2.45 $=$ 1.23 kN

Transformed section properties:

Top flange: α $=$ $\dfrac{E_{\text{flange}}}{E_{\text{web}}}$ $=$ $\dfrac{4965}{10800}$ $=$ 0.46

$b_{\text{transformed}}$ $=$ 400×0.46 $=$ 184 mm

Bottom flange: α $=$ $\dfrac{E_{\text{flange}}}{E_{\text{web}}}$ $=$ $\dfrac{5490}{10800}$ $=$ 0.508

$b_{\text{transformed}}$ $=$ 400×0.508 $=$ 203.2 mm

$\bar{y} = \dfrac{[(184 \times 15.5 \times 140.25) + (47 \times 120 \times 72.5) + (203.2 \times 12.5 \times 6.25)]}{[(184 \times 15.5) + (47 \times 120) + (203.2 \times 12.5)]}$

$\bar{y}$ $=$ 74.76 mm

$y_{\text{top}} =$ $148 - 74.76 = 73.24 \text{ mm}$

References	Calculations	Output
	Contract : Flat Roof **Job Ref. No. :** Example 3.5 **Part of Structure :** Stressed-Skin Panel **Calc. Sheet No. :** 6 of 8	**Calcs. by :** W.McK. **Checked by :** **Date :**	

References	Calculations	Output
	$I_{xx} = \dfrac{184 \times 15.5^3}{12} + (184 \times 15.5 \times 65.49^2) + \dfrac{47 \times 120^3}{12}$ $\quad + (47 \times 120 \times 2.26^2) + \dfrac{203.2 \times 12.5^3}{12} + (203.2 \times 12.5 \times 68.51^2)$ $\quad = 31.04 \times 10^6 \text{ mm}^4$ **Top flange:** $Z_{xx} = \dfrac{31.04 \times 10^6}{(148 - 74.76)} = 423.81 \times 10^3 \text{ mm}^3$ **Bottom Flange:** $Z_{xx} = \dfrac{31.04 \times 10^6}{74.76} = 415.19 \times 10^3 \text{ mm}^3$ **Top of the web:** $Z_{xx} = \dfrac{31.04 \times 10^6}{(132.5 - 74.76)} = 537.58 \times 10^3 \text{ mm}^3$ **Bottom of the Web:** $Z_{xx} = \dfrac{31.04 \times 10^6}{(74.76 - 12.5)} = 498.55 \times 10^3 \text{ mm}^3$ $EI_{xx} = E_{web}[(I_{web} + (\alpha I)_{\text{top flange}} + (\alpha I)_{\text{bottom flange}}]$ $\quad = 10800 \times 10^6 \times [6.8 + (0.46 \times 12.29) + (0.508 \times 11.95)]$ $\quad = 200.06 \times 10^9 \text{ Nmm}^2$	
See Figure 3.23	$\dfrac{\text{span}}{\text{clear spacing}} = \dfrac{L}{L_s} = \dfrac{4000}{(400 - 47)} = 11.33$	
Clause 2.9	**Bending:** There are normally more than four members in each panel supporting a common load and consequently the load-sharing factor K_8 applies and is equal to 1.1	

References	Calculations	Output
	Contract : Flat Roof **Job Ref. No. :** Example 3.5 **Part of Structure :** Stressed-Skin Panel **Calc. Sheet No. :** 7 of 8	**Calcs. by :** W.McK. **Checked by :** **Date :**

References	Calculations	Output
	Top flange: $\sigma_{c,adm,\parallel}$ $=$ $\sigma_{c,g,\parallel}$ $\times K_8 \times K_{36}$ $\quad\quad = 8.13 \times 1.1 \times 1.33 = 11.89 \text{ N/mm}^2$ $\sigma_{c,a,\parallel}$ $= \alpha \dfrac{\text{Bending Moment}}{Z}$ $\quad\quad = 0.46 \times \dfrac{1.23\times10^6}{423.81\times10^3} = 1.33 \text{ N/mm}^2$ $\quad\quad\quad\quad\quad\quad\quad\quad\quad \ll 11.89 \text{ N/mm}^2$ **Bottom Flange:** $\sigma_{t,adm,\parallel}$ $=$ $\sigma_{t,g,\parallel}$ $\times K_8 \times K_{36}$ $\quad\quad = 5.37 \times 1.1 \times 1.33 = 7.86 \text{ N/mm}^2$ $\sigma_{t,a,\parallel}$ $= 0.508 \times \dfrac{1.23\times10^6}{415.19\times10^3} = 1.5 \text{ N/mm}^2$ $\quad\quad\quad\quad\quad\quad\quad\quad\quad < 7.86 \text{ N/mm}^2$ **Web:** Top $\sigma_{m,adm,\parallel}$ $=$ $\sigma_{m,g,\parallel}$ $\times K_3 \times K_8$ $\quad\quad = 7.5 \times 1.25 \times 1.1 = 10.31 \text{ N/mm}^2$ $\sigma_{m,a,\parallel}$ $= \dfrac{1.23\times10^6}{537.58\times10^3} = 2.29 \text{ N/mm}^2$ $\quad\quad\quad\quad\quad\quad\quad < 10.31 \text{ N/mm}^2$ Bottom $\sigma_{m,a,\parallel}$ $= \dfrac{1.23\times10^6}{498.55\times10^3} = 2.47 \text{ N/mm}^2$ $\quad\quad\quad\quad\quad\quad\quad < 10.31 \text{ N/mm}^2$ **Deflection:** δ_{actual} $\approx \dfrac{5Wl^3}{384EI} = \dfrac{5\times2.45\times10^3\times4000^3}{384\times200.06\times10^9} = 10.21 \text{ mm}$ $\dfrac{\delta_{actual}}{K_c} = \dfrac{10.21}{0.97} = 10.53 \text{ mm}$ $\delta_{adm} = 0.003 \times 4000 = 12 \text{ mm} > 10.53 \text{ mm}$	Top flange is adequate in compression and tension Bottom flange is adequate in compression and tension Web is adequate in compression and tension Composite section is adequate in deflection

References	Calculations	Output
	Contract : Flat Roof **Job Ref. No. :** Example 3.5 **Part of Structure :** Stressed-Skin Panel **Calc. Sheet No. :** 8 of 8	**Calcs. by :** W.McK. **Checked by :** **Date :**

References	Calculations	Output
	Shear: Maximum shear stress occurs at the neutral axis $\tau_{a,\|\|} = \dfrac{QA\bar{y}}{Ib}$ $A\bar{y} = (184 \times 15.5 \times 65.49) + (57.74 \times 47 \times 28.87)$ $\quad = 265.12 \times 10^3 \text{ mm}^3$ $\tau_{a,\|\|} = \dfrac{1.23 \times 10^3 \times 265.12 \times 10^3}{31.04 \times 10^6 \times 47} = 0.22 \text{ N/mm}^2$ $\tau_{adm,\|\|} = 0.7 \times 1.25 \times 1.1 = 0.96 \quad > \quad 0.22 \text{ N/mm}^2$ **Rolling Shear:** Top flange/web connection $A\bar{y} = (184 \times 15.5 \times 65.49) = 186.78 \times 10^3 \text{ mm}^3$ $I \approx \dfrac{EI}{E_{web}} = \dfrac{200.06 \times 10^9}{10800} = 18.52 \times 10^6 \text{ mm}^4$ $\tau_{a,\|\|} = \dfrac{1.23 \times 10^3 \times 186.78 \times 10^3}{18.52 \times 10^6 \times 47} = 0.26 \text{ N/mm}^2$ $\tau_{adm,\|\|} = \tau_{r,g} \times K_8 \times K_{36} \times K_{37}$ $\quad = 0.7 \times 1.1 \times 1.33 \times 0.5 = 0.51 \text{ N/mm}^2 \quad > 0.26 \text{ N/mm}^2$ Bottom flange/web connection $A\bar{y} = (203.2 \times 12.5 \times 68.51) = 174.02 \times 10^3 \text{ mm}^3$ $\tau_{a,\|\|} = \dfrac{1.23 \times 10^3 \times 174.02 \times 10^3}{18.52 \times 10^6 \times 47} = 0.25 \text{ N/mm}^2$ $\quad\quad < \quad 0.37 \text{ N/mm}^2$	Composite section is adequate in shear Composite section is adequate in rolling shear

3.6 Glued Laminated Beams (Glulam)

The concept of using laminated timber as indicated in Figure 3.1(d) has been used for many years. In the early 19th century mechanically laminated timber structures were utilised throughout Europe. The development of synthetic resin adhesives in the 20th century presented the opportunity for extensive development of production techniques.

One of the fastest growing and most successful structural material industries in the UK is that related to the use of glulam. Traditionally until the 1970's and with the exception of specialist uses such as in aircraft and marine components, glulam was purpose made for a limited number of types of structure such as swimming pools, churches or footbridges. The availability of standard glulam components such as straight, curved or cambered members has been made possible by the introduction of improved, modern high-volume production plants. This has resulted in an ever expanding range of uses, e.g. timber lintel beams in domestic housing, large portal frames in conference and leisure centres, to structures such as the 162 m diameter dome of the Tacoma Sports and Convention Centre in Washington State, USA.

Glulam has many advantages such as:

♦ members can be straight or curved in profile and uniform or variable in cross-section,

♦ the strength:weight ratio is high, enabling the dead load due to the superstructure to be kept to a minimum with a consequent saving in foundation construction,

♦ factory production allows a high standard of material quality to be achieved,

♦ timbers of large cross-section have a superior performance in fire than alternatives such as concrete and steel,

♦ when treated with appropriate preservatives, softwood laminated timber is very durable in wet exposure situations; in addition it also has a high resistance to chemical attack and aggressive/polluted environments,

♦ there is no need for expansion joints because of the low coefficient of thermal expansion,

♦ defects such as knots are restricted to the thickness of one lamination and their effects on overall structural behaviour is significantly reduced,

♦ large spans are possible within the constraints of transportation to site.

An indication of the range of structures for which glulam is suitable is given in Figures 3.22 (a) and (b).

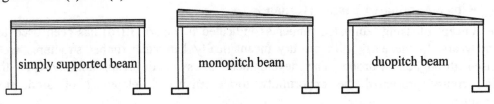

simply supported beam   monopitch beam   duopitch beam

Figure 3.22 (a)

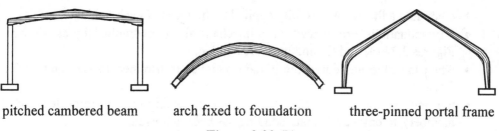

pitched cambered beam   arch fixed to foundation   three-pinned portal frame

Figure 3.22 (b)

3.6.1 *Manufacture of Glulam*

Glulam members are fabricated by gluing together accurately prepared timber laminations in which the grain is in the longitudinal direction. *BS 5628 : Part 2, Clause 3.2* states that *'Members may be horizontally laminated from two strength classes, provided that the strength classes are not more than three classes apart in table 7 (i.e. C24 and C16 may be horizontally laminated, but C24 and C14 may not), and the members are fabricated so that not less than 25% of the depth of both the top and the bottom of the members is of the superior strength class.*

This is illustrated in the examples shown in Figure 3.23:

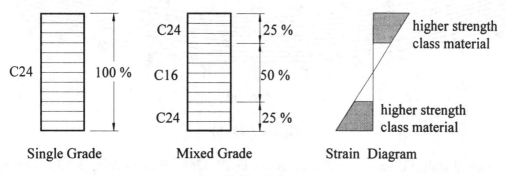

Single Grade   Mixed Grade   Strain Diagram

Figure 3.23

When using mixed grade laminations it is evident that the higher strength laminations are used to resist the larger bending stresses in the outer fibres of the cross-section.

3.6.1.1 *Sequence of production operations*

A typical sequence of operations for the production of glulam is as follows:

- ♦ selection of stress grade laminations,
- ♦ the laminations are dried in a kiln to achieve a moisture content of approximately 12% to ensure a maximum bond strength and glulam stability,
- ♦ individual laminations are finger-jointed to produce a continuous lamination of the appropriate stress grade (see Section 3.5.1.2),
- ♦ each finger-jointed laminate is accurately planed to the required thickness and cut to the required length,

♦ a bonding adhesive is carefully applied to the faces of each laminate,
♦ all laminations are placed in a mechanical or hydraulic jig as shown in Figures 3.24 (a) and (b) and pressure applied,
♦ when the glue has cured the glulam member is trimmed to size and surfaces finished,
♦ the bond strength is checked by mechanical testing (e.g. bending tests on the member), to ensure adequate bonding has been achieved.

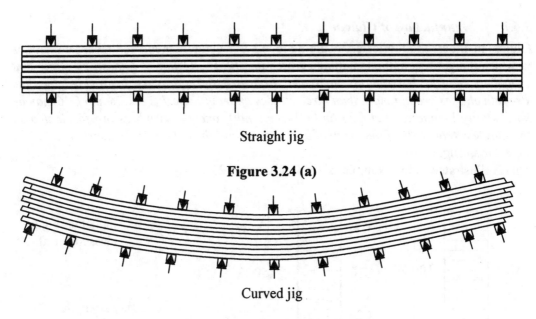

Straight jig

Figure 3.24 (a)

Curved jig

Figure 3.24 (b)

For curved glulam beams the radius permitted by *BS 5268 : Part 2 Clause 3.5.3.1* is given by:

$$\frac{r}{t} \geq \frac{E_{mean}}{70}$$

where:
r   radius of curvature,
t   thickness of laminate,
E_{mean} mean modulus of elasticity of the superior grade timber used.
This applies to both softwoods and hardwoods.

3.6.1.2   Finger-Joints

The length of glulam members frequently exceeds the length of commercially available solid timber, resulting in the need to finger-joint together individual planks to make laminations of the required length.
A typical finger-joint is shown in Figure 3.25:

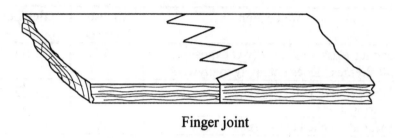

Finger joint

Figure 3.25

The finger-joint is cut into the end-grain of each plank and the planks are pressed together after applying adhesive.

In Clause 6.10.2 of the BS it is stated that "Finger joints should be manufactured in accordance with BS EN 385 1995."

3.6.1.3 Adhesives

The most widely used adhesives are the phenol-resorcinol-formaldehyde (PRF) type. The adhesive, which is a liquid, is used with a 'hardener' containing formaldehyde and various inert fillers. Pure resorcinal, which is expensive, is usually replaced with alternative cheaper chemicals (phenols), which also react with formaldehyde. The chemical bond formed during this reaction is a carbon-to-carbon type which is very strong and durable.

The resulting adhesives are fully water, boil and weather resistant. In addition, PRF adhesives do not decompose or ignite in a fire and delamination will not occur under normal circumstances. The chemical 'pH' value is approximately 7 (i.e. neutral) and hence alkaline or acidic damage/corrosion will not occur in either the timber or any metal components.

3.6.1.4 Surface finishes

Finished glulam beams are normally planed on their sides to remove any residual adhesive which has been squeezed out of their joints during manufacture. Modern planing machinery usually provides a finish of sufficient quality that subsequent sanding is unnecessary.

3.6.1.5 Preservation treatment

The preservative treatment to glulam members tends to be applied to the finished product rather than individual laminations prior to gluing. The preservatives discussed in Chapter 1, Section 1.5 apply to glulam members and should comply with the requirements of *BS 5268 : Part 5* as indicated in *Clause 7.7.1 of BS 5268 : Part 2.*

3.6.1.6 Modification factors

The modification factors which apply to glued laminated beams are summarised in Table 3.4. The provisions for axially loaded members and joints are given in Chapters 4 and 6 respectively.

Factors	Application	Clause Number	Value/Location
K_2	service class 3 sections (wet exposure) : all stresses. Does not apply to plywood	2.6.2	Table 13
K_3	load duration : all stresses	2.8	Table 14
K_4	bearing stress	2.10.2	Table 15
K_5	shear at notched ends : shear stress	2.10.4	Equations given
K_6	bending stresses : form factor	2.10.5	Equations given
K_7	bending stresses : depth factor	2.10.6	Equations given
K_8	load-sharing : all stresses	2.9	1.1
K_{15}	bending parallel to grain	3.2	Table 21
K_{16}	tension parallel to grain	3.2	Table 21
K_{17}	compression parallel to grain	3.2	Table 21
K_{18}	compression perpendicular to grain	3.2	Table 21
K_{19}	shear parallel to grain	3.2	Table 21
K_{20}	modulus of elasticity	3.2	Table 21
K_{27}	bending, tension, & shear parallel to grain	3.3	Table 22
K_{28}	modulus of elasticity & compression parallel to grain	3.3	Table 22
K_{29}	compression perpendicular to grain	3.3	Table 22
K_{30}	*end joints in horizontal glulam*	*3.4*	*Table 23*
K_{31}	*end joints in horizontal glulam*	*3.4*	*Table 23*
K_{32}	*end joints in horizontal glulam*	*3.4*	*Table 23*
K_{33}	curved glulam members : bending, tension & compression all parallel to grain	3.5.3.2	Equations given
K_{34}	curved glulam members : calculated bending stresses	3.5.3.2	Equations given
K_{35}	calculated radial stresses in pitched cambered glulam beams	3.5.4.2	Equations given

Note: K_{15} to K_{20} apply to horizontally laminated beams
K_{27} to K_{29} apply to vertically laminated beams
K_{30} to K_{32} apply to individually designed glued end joints in horizontally glued laminated members

Table 3.4   Modification Factors for Glulam Beams

3.6.2   *Vertically Laminated Beams*

Vertically laminated beams in which the applied load is parallel to the laminate joints usually occur in elements such as laminated columns subjected to both axial and flexural loads. They are dealt with in Chapter 5 – *Members subject to combined axial and flexural loads.*

3.6.3   *Horizontally Laminated Beams*

Horizontally laminated beams are beams in which the laminations are parallel to the neutral plane. The loading is applied in a direction perpendicular to the plane of the laminations.

The admissible stresses are determined by modifying the grade stresses. There are two possibilities to consider:

♦ where the strength class is specified, and,
♦ where a specific grade and species are specified.

Strength Class specified
The grade stresses are determined from *Table 7* and modified using factors K_{15} to K_{20} given in *Table 21* for individual strength classes and number of laminations. This is in addition to the requirements of *Clauses 2.6.2, 2.8, 2.9 and 2.10.*

Grade and Species specified
The grade stresses are determined from *Tables 8 to 12* for the appropriate grade and species. These values are modified using the factors K_{15} to K_{20} in *Table 21* assuming a strength class appropriate to the grade and species as given in *Tables 2 to 6*. This is in addition to the requirements of *Clauses 2.62, 2.8, 2.9 and 2.10.*

In addition to the modification factors indicated in Table 3.4, where members are laminated from two strength classes the grade stresses for the superior lamination are used and those relating to bending, tension and compression parallel to the grain should be multiplied by 0.95.

The design of glulam beams follows the same pattern as solid rectangular beams where shear, bending, bearing and deflection are the main criteria to be considered. The following stress criteria should be satisfied:

shear stress:
$$\tau_{a,||} \leq \tau_{g,||} \times K_2 \times K_3 \times K_5 \times K_8 \times K_{19}$$
where:
  $\tau_{a,||}$ = maximum applied horizontal shear stress
  $\tau_{g,||}$ = grade stress parallel to the grain
  $K_2, K_3, K_5, K_8, K_{19}$ are modification factors used where appropriate

bending stress:
$$\sigma_{m,a,||} \leq \sigma_{m,g,||} \times K_2 \times K_3 \times K_6 \times K_7 \times K_8 \times K_{15} \times K_{33}$$
where:
  $\sigma_{m,a,||}$ = maximum applied bending stress
  $\sigma_{m,g,||}$ = grade stress parallel to the grain
  $K_2, K_3, K_5, K_6, K_7, K_8, K_{15}, K_{33}$ are modification factors used where appropriate

Note: In the case of curved glulam members, equations are given to determine the maximum radial and bending stresses.

radial stress:
$$\sigma_{r,a} \leq \sigma_{t,g,\perp} \times K_2 \times K_3 \times K_8$$
where:

$\sigma_{r,a}$ = maximum radial stress, calculated as given in Clauses 3.5.3.3 and 3.5.4.2

$\sigma_{r,g,\perp}$ = grade tension stress perpendicular to the grain, calculated in accordance with Clause 2.7, i.e. equal to $0.33 \times \tau_{g,||}$

K_2, K_3, K_5, K_8, are modification factors used where appropriate

bearing stress:
$$\sigma_{c,a,\perp} \leq \sigma_{c,g,\perp} \times K_2 \times K_3 \times K_8 \times K_{18}$$
where:

$\sigma_{c,a,\perp}$ = maximum applied bearing stress

$\sigma_{c,g,\perp}$ = grade stress perpendicular to the grain

K_2, K_3, K_8, K_{18}, are modification factors used where appropriate

In addition to satisfying stress criteria, the deflection due to bending and shear should be considered, i.e.
$$\delta_{actual} \leq 0.003 \times span$$

The manufacture of glulam beams lends itself to introducing an initial pre-camber to offset the deflection due to dead and permanent loads. Where advantage is taken of this the calculated deflection due to live or intermittent imposed load only should not exceed $0.003 \times$ span.

3.6.4   Example 3.6   Glulam Roof Beam Design

An exhibition hall is to be designed with 10 m span glued laminated timber beams at 3.0 m centres supporting the roof structure. The roofing is to be 63 mm tongue and groove boarding which is exposed on the underside and covered on the top side with insulation, felt and chippings.

Check the suitability of the proposed section for the glulam beam indicated in Figure 3.26.

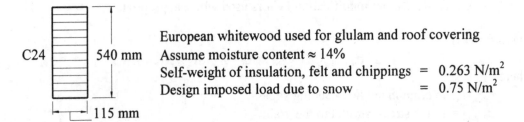

European whitewood used for glulam and roof covering
Assume moisture content $\approx$ 14%
Self-weight of insulation, felt and chippings = 0.263 N/m²
Design imposed load due to snow = 0.75 N/m²

Figure 3.26

3.6.4.1   Solution to Example 3.6

References	Calculations	Output
	Contract : Exhibition Hall **Job Ref. No. :** Example 3.6 **Part of Structure :** Roof beam **Calc. Sheet No. :** 1 of 3 **Calcs. by :** W.McK. **Checked by :** **Date :**	

References	Calculations	Output
BS 5268 : Part 2	Structural use of timber	
Table 7	**Loading:** Class C24 timber average density = 420 kg/m³ Assume 500 kg/m³ to allow for adhesive etc. = 5.0 kN/m³ Self-weight of beam = $(115 \times 0.54 \times 5.0)$ = 0.31 kN/m Self-weight of decking = (4.2×0.063) = 0.26 kN/m² Self-weight of insulation, felt and chippings = 0.263kN/m² Design dead load = $[(0.26 + 0.263) \times 3.0] + 0.31$ = 1.88 kN/m Design imposed load = (0.75×3.0) = 2.25 kN/m Total design load = $(1.88 + 2.25)$ = 4.13 kN/m The beam will be manufactured from class C24 whitewood throughout with 12 horizontal laminations each 45 mm thick. **Grade stresses:** $\sigma_{m,g,\|}$ = 7.5 N/mm² $\sigma_{t,g,\|}$ = 4.5 N/mm² $\sigma_{c,g,\|}$ = 7.9 N/mm² $\sigma_{c,g,\perp}$ = 2.4 N/mm² $\tau_{g,\|}$ = 0.71 N/mm² E_{mean} = 10,800 N/mm² E_{min} = 7,200 N/mm² **Section properties:** Area = 115×540 = 62.1×10^3 mm² I_{xx} = $\dfrac{115 \times 540^3}{12}$ = 1509×10^6 mm⁴ Z_{xx} = $\dfrac{115 \times 540^2}{6}$ = 5.58×10^6 mm³ D/B = $\dfrac{540}{115}$ = 4.7	
Table 16	$4 \; < \; D/B \; < \; 5$ The ends should be held in position and the compression edge held in line, as by direct connection of sheathing, deck or joists.	Lateral restraint is adequate
Clause 2.8 Table 14	long-term loading = 1.88 kN/m medium-term loading = $\dfrac{4.13}{1.25}$ = 3.3 kN/m > 1.88 kN/m medium-term loading is the worst design load case	

References	Calculations	Output
	Bending:	

Bending:

Maximum applied bending moment $= \dfrac{4.13 \times 10^2}{8}$

$$= 51.63 \text{ kNm}$$

$$\sigma_{m,a,\|} = \frac{51.63 \times 10^6}{5.58 \times 10^6} = 9.25 \text{ N/mm}^2$$

$$\sigma_{m,adm,\|} = \sigma_{m,g,\|} \times K_2 \times K_3 \times K_6 \times K_7 \times K_8 \times K_{15}$$

Clause 1.6.4   Moisture content $< 20°C$ ∴   Service class 1

Table 13 $K_2 = 1.0$

Table 14   Medium-term loading $K_3 = 1.25$

Clause 2.10.5   Form factor $K_6 = 1.0$

Clause 2.10.6   Depth factor $K_7 = 0.81 \times \dfrac{\left(h^2 + 92{,}300\right)}{\left(h^2 + 56{,}800\right)}$

$$K_7 = 0.81 \times \frac{\left(540^2 + 92{,}300\right)}{\left(540^2 + 56{,}800\right)} = 0.893$$

Clause 2.9   Since beam centres > 600 mm load-sharing (K_8) does not apply

Table 21   Strength class C24,   number of laminations   =   12

$$K_{15} = 1.43 + \left(1.48 - 1.43\right) \times \frac{2}{5} = 1.45$$

Note: Interpolation is permitted for intermediate number of laminations

$$\sigma_{m,adm,\|} = 7.5 \times 1.0 \times 1.25 \times 1.0 \times 0.893 \times 1.45$$
$$= 12.14 \text{ N/mm}^2 > \sigma_{m,a,\|} \ (9.25 \text{ N/mm}^2)$$

Shear:

Maximum applied shear force   = 4.13×5.0 =   20.65 kN

$$\tau_{a,\|} = 1.5 \times \text{average } \tau_{a,\|}$$

$$= \frac{1.5 \times 20.65 \times 10^3}{62.1 \times 10^3} = 0.5 \text{ N/mm}^2$$

$$\tau_{adm,\|} = \tau_{g,\|} \times K_2 \times K_3 \times K_5 \times K_8 \times K_{19}$$

As before $K_2 = 1.0$, $K_3 = 1.25$

References	Calculations	Output
	Contract : Exhibition Hall **Job Ref. No. : Example 3.6** **Calcs. by : W.McK.** Part of Structure : Roof beam **Checked by :** Calc. Sheet No. : 3 of 3 **Date :**	

References	Calculations	Output
Table 21	K_5 for notched ends and K_8 do not apply in this case. $K_{19} = 2.34$ $\tau_{adm,\|\|} = 0.71 \times 1.25 \times 2.34 = 2.07 \, \text{N/mm}^2 \gg \tau_{a.\|\|}$	Beam is adequate in shear
	Deflection:	
Table 21	$\delta_{actual} = \delta_{bending} + \delta_{shear}$ The mean modulus should be multiplied by $K_{20} = 1.07$ $E = E_{mean} \times K_{20} = 10800 \times 1.07 = 11556 \, \text{N/mm}^2$ $\delta_{actual} = \dfrac{5wL^4}{384EI} + \dfrac{M}{AG}$ The value of the shear modulus is normally assumed to be equal to $E/16$ $\therefore \ G = \dfrac{11556}{16} = 722 \, \text{N/mm}^2$ $\delta_{actual} = \dfrac{5 \times 4.13 \times (10000)^4}{384 \times 11556 \times 1509 \times 10^6} + \dfrac{5.163 \times 10^6}{115 \times 540 \times 722}$ $\qquad = 30.8 + 0.12 = 31 \, \text{mm}$ It is evident that the shear deflection is considerably less than that due to bending and can be ignored. The shear deflection may be more significant in short span beams	
Clause 2.10.7	$\delta_{adm} = 0.003 \times \text{span} = 0.003 \times 10000 = 30.0 \, \text{mm}$	
Clause 3.5.2	Provide camber to offset the dead load deflection Dead load $= 1.88 \, \text{kN/m}$ Dead load deflection $\approx 31 \times \dfrac{1.88}{4.13} = 14.1 \, \text{mm}$ $\delta_{actual,imposed} = 31 - 14.1 = 16.9 \, \text{mm} < \delta_{adm}$	Beam is adequate in deflection with a 15 mm pre-camber to offset dead load deflection
	Bearing:	
Clause 2.10.2	$\sigma_{b,adm} = \sigma_{c,g,\perp} \times K_2 \times K_3 \times K_4 \times K_8 \times K_{18}$ As before $K_2 = 1.0$, $K_3 = 1.25$, K_8 does not apply	
Table 21	$K_{18} = 1.55 \qquad$ Neglect K_4 $\sigma_{b,adm} = 2.4 \times 1.25 \times 1.55 = 4.65 \, \text{N/mm}^2$ Minimum bearing length required $= \dfrac{20.65 \times 10^3}{4.65 \times 115} = 39 \, \text{mm}$	Provide a minimum bearing length of 50 mm at the ends

3.7   Review Problems

3.1   Determine the admissible bending stress for a solid timber beam
       200 mm deep x 50 mm wide in which the average moisture content is
       not expected to exceed 20%, the loading is assumed to be medium-
       term. The beam is one of a series of beams at 450 mm centres
       supporting a floor system capable of transverse load distribution.
       Assume the timber to be of Strength Class C18.
       ($\sigma_{m,adm,||}$ = 8.37 N/mm^2 see Section 3.3.2 and Section 2.1)

3.2   Determine the maximum bending moment which can be supported by
       the beam above.
       (M = 2.79 kNm   see Section 3.3.2)

3.3   Determine the maximum long-term shear force which can be
       supported by the beam above.
       (F = 4.91 kN   see Section 3.3.1)

3.4   Identify the modification factors required to allow for the effect of a
       notched end on the shear strength of a beam.
       (see Section 3.3.6.1)

3.5   Under which circumstances is the 'mean' modulus of elasticity **not**
       used to calculate deflection in a load sharing system.
       (see Section 2.2)

3.6   Describe how the possibility of lateral torsional buckling in solid and
       laminated flexural members is avoided.
       (see Section 3.3.5)

3.7   Explain the difference between panel shear and rolling shear in ply-
       web beams.
       (see Section 3.4.1)

3.8   Explain the purpose of web stiffeners in ply-web beams.
       (see Section 3.4.1.3)

3.9   Identify the types of deflection which should be calculated when
       designing ply-web beams.
       (see Section 3.4.2.2)

4. Axially Loaded Members

Objective: *to illustrate the design of axially loaded members considering single tension and compression frame elements, single and spaced columns.*

4.1 Introduction

The design of axially loaded members considers any member where the applied loading induces either axial tension or axial compression. Members subject to axial forces frequently occur in bracing systems, roof trusses or lattice girders.

Frequently, in structural frames, sections are subjected to combined axial and bending effects, which may be caused by eccentric connections, wind loading or rigid-frame action. The design of such members is discussed and illustrated in Chapter 5. In BS 5268 : Part 2 : 1996, the design of compression members is considered in Clause 2.11 and the design of tension members in Clause 2.12. In both cases the service class, duration of loading and load sharing modification factors apply. In addition, for compression members allowance must be made for the slenderness of the section (see section 4.3.1), and in the case of tension members a width factor is also considered. The relevant modification factors which apply to axially loaded members are summarized in Table 4.1.

Factors	Application	Clause Number	Value/Location
K_2	service class 3 sections (wet exposure): all stresses	2.6.2	Table 13
K_3	load duration: all stresses	2.8	Table 14
K_8	load-sharing: all stresses	2.9	1.1
K_9	modulus of elasticity	2.10.11 / 2.11.5	Table 17
K_{12}	slenderness of columns	2.11.5	Table 19
K_{13}	spaced columns: effective length	2.11.10	Table 20
K_{14}	width factor: tensile stresses	2.12.2	Equations given
K_{28}	minimum modulus of elasticity: **compression parallel** to the grain in **vertically laminated** glulam members	2.11.5	Table 22
K_{29}	minimum modulus of elasticity: **compression perpendicular** to the grain in **vertically laminated** glulam members	2.11.5	Table 22

Table 4.1   Modification Factors – axially loaded members

4.2   Design of Tension Members (Clause 2.12)

The design of tension members is based on the effective area of the cross-section allowing for a reduction due to notches, bolts, dowels, screw holes or any mechanical fastener inserted in the member. Since the grade stresses given in Table 7 of the code apply to material assigned to a strength class and having a width of 300 mm (the **greater** transverse dimension '*h*'), a modification factor 'K_{14}' must be used. The value to be used for K_{14} is given in Clause 2.12.2 as:

solid timber members   where $h \leq 72$ mm $K_4 = 1.17$

solid and glulam members   where $h \geq 72$ mm $K_4 = (300/h)^{0.11}$

The tension capacity of a section is given by:

$$P_t = [\sigma_{t,g,||} \times K_2 \times K_3 \times K_8 \times K_{14}] \times [\text{effective cross-sectional area}]$$

where:
$\sigma_{t,g,||}$ is the grade stress
$K_2, K_3, K_8,$ and K_{14} are modification factors
effective cross-sectional area is the cross-sectional area after allowances have been made as described above.

4.2.1   Example 4.1   Collar Tie Member

A collar tie roof construction comprises two rafters and a collar tie (100 mm x 50 mm), connected to the rafters by M8 steel bolts as shown in Figure 4.1. Assuming the wall does not provide any lateral restraint to the toe of the rafter, check the suitability of the collar tie.

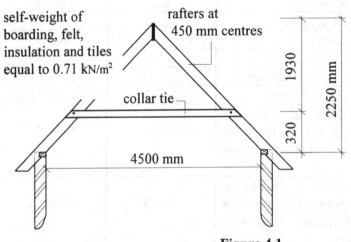

self-weight of boarding, felt, insulation and tiles equal to 0.71 kN/m²

rafters at 450 mm centres

1930

320

2250 mm

collar tie:
Douglas fir   GS grade
Connected to rafter
using 8 mm steel bolts

collar tie

4500 mm

Figure 4.1

4.2.1.1 Solution to Example 4.1

Contract : Collar Tie Roof **Job Ref. No. :** Example 4.1	**Calcs. by : W.McK.**	
Part of Structure : Collar Tie	**Checked by :**	
Calc. Sheet No. : 1 of 2	**Date :**	

References	Calculations	Output

BS 5268 : Part 2
BS 6399 : Part 1
 	
BS 6399 : Part 1
  Clause 6.2
 	
Clause 6.6.1
 	
  Table 2
  Table 7
 	
Clause 2.6.2
	Structural use of timber
	Code of Practice for dead and imposed loads
	
	$\begin{array}{lllll}\text{Dead load / frame} & = & 0.71 \times 0.45 & = & 0.32 \text{ kN/m}\\ \text{Imposed load / frame} & = & 0.75 \times 0.45 & = & 0.34 \text{ kN/m}\\ \text{long-term load} & = & 0.32 \text{ kN/m}\\ \text{medium-term load} & = & (0.32 + 0.34) & = & 0.66 \text{ kN/m}\end{array}$
	
	$\dfrac{0.66}{1.25} = 0.53 \text{ kN/m} >$ long-term loading,
	
	$\therefore$ check for medium-term loading
	
	Σ Moments about the apex $\qquad\qquad = \quad 0$
	$(1.49 \times 2.25) - (0.66 \times 2.25 \times 1.125) - (1.93 \times F_t) = \quad 0$
	$\qquad\qquad\qquad\qquad\qquad\qquad\qquad F_t \;=\; 0.87 \text{ kN}$
	
	$\sigma_{t,a,||} \;=\; \dfrac{F_t}{\text{Effective Area}}$
	Effective area $=$ gross area $-$ projected area of bolt hole
	$\qquad\qquad\quad = \;(100 \times 50) - (10 \times 50) = \; 4500 \text{ mm}^2$
	Note: the bolt hole is 2 mm larger than the bolt diameter
	
	$\sigma_{t,a,||} \;=\; \dfrac{0.87 \times 10^3}{4500} = \; 0.19 \text{ N/mm}^2$
	
	$\sigma_{t,adm,||} \;=\; \sigma_{t,g,||} \times K_2 \times K_3 \times K_8 \times K_{14}$
	Douglas fir Grade GS is strength Class C14
	Tension parallel to grain $\quad \sigma_{t,g,||} = 2.5 \text{ N/mm}^2$
	
	K_2 – wet exposure does not apply in this case	

References	Calculations	Output
Contract : Collar Tie Roof **Job Ref. No. :** Example 4.1		**Calcs. by :** W.McK.
Part of Structure : Collar Tie		**Checked by :**
Calc. Sheet No. : 2 of 2		**Date :**

References	Calculations	Output
Clause 2.8 Clause 2.9 Clause 2.12.2	K_3 – load duration Medium-term $K_3 = 1.25$ K_8 – load sharing stresses does not apply in this case K_{14} – width of section $h \; > 72$ mm $K_{14} = \left(\dfrac{300}{100}\right)^{0.11} \quad = \quad 1.128$ $\sigma_{t,adm,\parallel} = 2.5 \times 1.25 \times 1.128 = 3.53$ N/mm^2 $\gg 0.19$ N/mm^2 There is considerable reserve of strength in the collar tie.	Collar tie is adequate

4.3 Design of Compression Members (Clause 2.11)

The design of compression members is more complex than that of tension members and encompasses the design of structural elements referred to as columns, stanchions or struts. The term struts is usually used when referring to members in lattice/truss frameworks, whilst the other two generally refer to vertical or inclined members supporting floors and/or roofs in structural frames.

As with tension members in many cases they are subjected to both axial and bending effects. This chapter deals with those members, which are subjected to concentric axial loading.

The dominant mode of failure to be considered when designing struts is axial buckling. Buckling failure is caused by secondary bending effects induced by factors such as:

- ◆ The inherent eccentricity of applied loads due to asymmetric connection details.
- ◆ Imperfections present in the cross-section and/or profile of a member throughout its length. The allowable deviation from straightness when using either visual or machine grading (i.e. bow not greater than 20 mm lateral displacement over a length of 2.0 m) is inadequate when considering compression members. More severe restrictions such as *L/300* for structural timber and *L/500* for glulam sections should be considered.
- ◆ Non-uniformity of material properties throughout a member.

The effects of these characteristics are to introduce initial curvature, secondary bending and consequently premature failure by buckling before the stress in the material reaches the failure value. The stress at which failure will occur is influenced by several variables, e.g.

- the cross-sectional shape of the member,
- the slenderness of the member,
- the permissible stress of the material,

A practical and realistic assessment of the critical slenderness of a strut is the most important criterion in determining the compressive strength.

4.3.1 Slenderness

Slenderness is evaluated using **either**:

(i) $\quad \lambda = \dfrac{L_e}{i}$

where:
λ is the slenderness ratio,
L_e is the effective length with respect to the axis of buckling being considered,
i is the radius of gyration with respect to the axis of buckling being considered.

or for a rectangular section the alternative given in (ii) can be used:

(ii) $\quad \lambda = \dfrac{L_e}{b}$

where:
λ and L_e are as above and
b is the lesser transverse dimension of the member being considered.

Note: For a rectangular section of breadth b and depth d

$$i = \sqrt{\frac{I}{A}} = \sqrt{\frac{db^3}{12}} = \frac{b}{2\sqrt{3}}$$

e.g.   when $\lambda = 20$ $\therefore \dfrac{L_e}{i} = 20$ $\therefore \dfrac{L_e \times 2\sqrt{3}}{b} = 20 \therefore \dfrac{L_e}{b} = 5.77$

In BS 5268 : Part 2 values for both $\dfrac{L_e}{i}$ and $\dfrac{L_e}{b}$ are given in Table 19. In most cases rectangular sections are used in timber design, therefore the slenderness can be evaluated using $\dfrac{L_e}{b}$. Limiting values of slenderness are given in the code to reduce the possibility of premature failure in long struts, and to ensure an acceptable degree of robustness in a member. These limits, which are given in Clause 2.11.4, are shown in Table 4.2 of this chapter.

4.3.1.1   *Effective Length*

The effective length is considered to be the actual length of the member between points of restraint multiplied by a coefficient to allow for effects such as stiffening due to end connections of the frame of which the member is a part. Appropriate values for the coefficients are given in Table 18 of the code and illustrated in Figure 4.2. Alternatively the effective length can be considered to be '*the distance between adjacent points of zero bending between which the member is in single curvature*' as indicated in Clause 2.11.3.

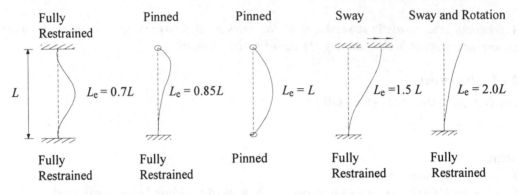

Figure 4.2   Effective Lengths (L_e)

Type of member	$\lambda_{maximum}$	L_e/b
(a) any compression member carrying dead and imposed loads other than loads resulting from wind; (b) any compression member, however loaded, which by its deformation will adversely affect the stress in another member carrying dead and imposed loads other than wind	180	52
(c) any member normally subject to tension or combined tension and bending arising from dead and imposed loads, but subject to a reversal of axial stress solely from the effect of wind; (d) any compression member carrying self-weight and wind loads only (e.g. wind bracing)	250	72.3

Table 4.2

When considering members in triangulated frameworks (other than trussed rafters which are considered in BS 5268 : Part 3 : 1985), with **continuous compression members**, e.g. the top chord of a lattice girder, the effective length may be taken as:

♦ between 0.85 × distance '*l*' between the node points   and
                  1.0 × distance '*l*' between the node points
    for buckling in the plane of the framework   and

♦ between 0.85 × actual distance between effective lateral restraints   and
    1.0 × actual distance between effective lateral restraints
for buckling perpendicular to the plane of the framework.

The value used depends on the degree of fixity and the distribution of load between the node points.

When considering **non-continuous compression members** such as web elements within a framework (i.e. uprights and diagonals in compression), the effective length is influenced by the type of end connection. A single bolt or connector which permits rotation at the ends of the member is assumed to be a pin and the effective length should be taken as 1.0 × length between the bolts or connectors. Where glued gusset plates are used, then partial restraint exists. The effective length in both the plane of the frame and perpendicular to the plane of the frame should be taken as 0.9 × the actual distance between the points of intersection of the lines passing through the centroids of the members connected. These requirements are given in Clause 2.11.11 of the code.

All other cases should be assessed and the appropriate factor from Table 18 used to determine the effective length.

The compression capacity of a section is given by:

$$P_c = [\sigma_{c,g,||} \times K_2 \times K_3 \times K_8 \times K_{12}] \times [K_{17} \text{ or } K_{18}] \times [\text{effective cross-sectional area}]$$

where:

$\sigma_{c,g,||}$ is the grade stress
$K_2, K_3, K_8, K_{12}, K_{17}$ and K_{18} are modification factors
effective cross-sectional area is the cross-sectional area after allowances have been made for open holes, notches etc. If a bolt is inserted into a hole with only nominal clearance, then no deduction is required.

The K_{12} factor applies when the slenderness of a member is greater than 5. The values of K_{12} are given in Table 19 and require the value of slenderness (L_e/i or L_e/b), and $E/\sigma_{c,||}$.

The value of E to be used is the minimum value. If appropriate, the E_{min} value can be modified by K_9 from Table 17 for members comprising two or more pieces connected together in parallel and acting together to support the loads. In the case of vertically laminated members the E_{min} value can be multiplied by K_{28} from Table 22. For horizontally laminated members the mean modulus modified by K_{20} from Table 21 should be used. The value of $\sigma_{c.g.||}$ should be modified using only K_2 for moisture content and K_3 for load duration. The size factor for compression members does not apply since the grade compression stresses given in Tables 7 to 12 apply to all solid timber members and laminations graded in accordance with BS 4978, BS 5756 or BS EN 519.

A consequence of the inclusion of the K_3 factor in determining K_{12} is that all relevant loading conditions should be considered separately, since K_{12} and subsequently $\sigma_{c,adm,||}$ is different in each case.

4.3.2   *Example 4.2*   *Concentrically Loaded Column*

A symmetrically loaded internal column is required to support four beams as shown in Figure 4.3. The top and bottom can be considered to be held in position but not in direction. A lateral restraint is provided at the mid-height as indicated. Assuming Service Class 2, check the suitability of a 75 mm x 155 mm, strength class C18 section to resist a long-term load of 8.0 kN and a medium-term load of 24.0 kN.

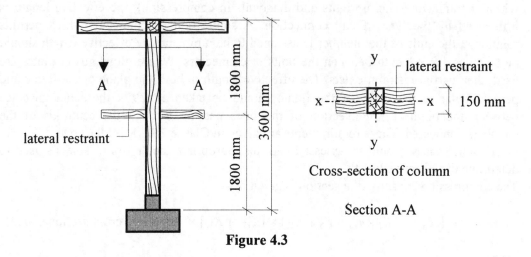

Figure 4.3

4.3.2.1   *Solution to Example 4.2*

Contract : Struts Job Ref. No. : Example 4.2	Calcs. by : W.McK.
Part of Structure : **Axially Loaded Column**	Checked by :
Calc. Sheet No. : 1 of 3	Date :

References	Calculations	Output
BS 5268 : Part 2	Structural Use of Timber	
Table 7	Strength Class C18 $\sigma_{c,g,\parallel} = 7.1 \text{ N/mm}^2$, $E_{min} = 6000 \text{ N/mm}^2$	
Table 14	K_2 (wet exposure), and K_8 (load sharing), do not apply long-term loading $K_3 = 1.0$ medium-term loading $K_3 = 1.25$	
Clause 2.11.3 Table 18 Clause 2.11.4	**Slenderness:** x-x axis $L_{exx} = 1.0 \times 3600 = 3600 \text{ mm}$ $\dfrac{L_{exx}}{b} = \dfrac{3600}{150} = 24 < 52$	

Contract : Struts	Job Ref. No. : Example 4.2	Calcs. by : W.McK.
Part of Structure : Axially Loaded Column		Checked by :
Calc. Sheet No. : 2 of 3		Date :

References	Calculations	Output
Clause 2.11.4	y-y axis $\quad L_{eyy} \quad = \quad 1.0 \times 1800 = \quad 1800$ mm $$\frac{L_{eyy}}{b} \; = \; \frac{1800}{75} \; = \; 24 \; < \; 52$$ **critical slenderness = 24**	
Clause 2.11.5 Table 19	**long-term:** $E/\sigma_{c,\|\|}$ is determined using E_{min} and $\sigma_{c,\|\|} = \sigma_{c,g,\|\|} \times K_3$ $E_{min} \; = \; 6000 \text{ N/mm}^2$ $\sigma_{c,\|\|} \; = \; 7.1 \times 1.0 \; = \; 7.1 \text{ N/mm}^2$ $E/\sigma_{c,\|\|} = \dfrac{6000}{7.1} \; = \; 845; \quad \lambda = 24$ The value of K_{12} can be determined by interpolation from Table 19:	

Extract from Table 19

L_e/b \ $E/\sigma_{c,\|\|}$	23.1	26.0
800	0.497	0.43
900	0.522	0.456

A conservative, approximate answer can be found
using the lowest value corresponding with the lowest $E/\sigma c_{,\|\|}$
and highest λ value i.e. in this case 0.43. If the
section is adequate with this value then it will also be
adequate with a more accurate determination of K_{12}

$\sigma_{c,adm,\|\|} \quad = \quad \sigma_{c,g,\|\|} \times K_3 \times K_{12}$

$\sigma_{c,adm,\|\|} \quad \approx \quad 7.1 \times 1.0 \times 0.43 = \quad 3.05 \text{ N/mm}^2$

$\sigma_{c,a,\|\|} \; = \; \dfrac{F_c}{\text{Effective Area}}$

Effective area $=$ gross area $=$ $(150 \times 75) =$ 11250 mm^2

$\sigma_{c,a,\|\|} \; = \; \dfrac{8 \times 10^3}{11250} \; = \; 0.71 \text{ N/mm}^2 \; < \; 3.05 \text{ N/mm}^2$

long-term capacity is adequate

medium-term:

(Table 19)

$E/\sigma_{c,\|\|}$ is determined using E_{min} and $\sigma_{c,\|\|} = \sigma_{c,g,\|\|} \times K_3$

$E_{min} \; = \; 6000 \text{ N/mm}^2$

References	Calculations	Output

Contract : Struts   **Job Ref. No. :** Example 4.2   **Calcs. by :** W.McK.
Part of Structure :   Axially Loaded Column   **Checked by :**
Calc. Sheet No. :   3 of 3   **Date :**

$\sigma_{c,||} = 7.1 \times 1.25 = 8.88 \text{ N/mm}^2$

$E/\sigma_{c,||} = \dfrac{6000}{8.88} = 675.7; \qquad \lambda = 24$

The value of K_{12} can be determined by interpolation from Table 19 or as above use an approximate value. If necessary a more precise value can be determined.

Extract from Table 19

L_e/b $E/\sigma_{c,||}$	23.1	26.0
600	0.43	0.363
700	0.467	0.399

$K_{12} \approx 0.363$

$\sigma_{c,adm,||} = \sigma_{c,g,||} \times K_3 \times K_{12}$

$\sigma_{c,adm,||} \approx 7.1 \times 1.25 \times 0.363 = 3.22 \text{ N/mm}^2$

$\sigma_{c,a,||} = \dfrac{F_c}{\text{Effective Area}}$

Effective area = gross area = $(150 \times 75) = 11250 \text{ mm}^2$

$\sigma_{c,a,||} = \dfrac{24 \times 10^3}{11250} = 2.1 \text{ N/mm}^2 < 3.22 \text{ N/mm}^2$

Output: medium-term capacity is adequate

4.3.3   Example 4.3   Covered Walkway

A covered walkway is to be constructed comprising a series of timber columns and timber beams with a glazed roof as shown in Figure 4.4. Check the suitability of the proposed timber section for a typical internal column.

Data:

Timber post: British grown Douglas fir   =   Grade GS

Dead load including self-weight of glazing panels   = 0.32 kN/m^2

Imposed load   = 0.75 kN/m^2

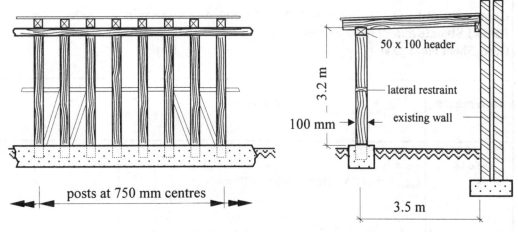

Figure 4.4

4.3.3.1   Solution to Example 4.3

References	Calculations	Output
	Contract : Walkway **Job Ref. No. :** Example 4.3 **Calcs. by :** W.McK. **Part of Structure :** Typical Internal Column **Checked by :** **Calc. Sheet No. :** 1 of 4 **Date :**	

References	Calculations	Output
BS 5268 : Part 2	Structural use of timber	
	dead load / post $\quad = 0.5 \times (0.32 \times 0.75 \times 3.5) \quad = \quad 0.42$ kN	
	imposed load / post $= 0.5 \times (0.75 \times 0.75 \times 3.5) \quad = \quad 0.98$ kN	
	long-term load $\quad\quad\quad = \quad 0.42$ kN	
	medium-term load $\ = (0.42 + 0.98) \quad\quad\quad\quad = \quad 1.4$ kN	
	Load-sharing does not occur since posts are > 610 mm apart	
	Check long-term and medium-term loading separately since	
	K_{12} values are different.	
Table 8	British grown Douglas fir grade GS	
	$\sigma_{c,g,\parallel} = 5.2$ N/mm^2, $\quad E_{min} = 6000$ N/mm^2	
	K_2 (wet exposure), and K_8 (load sharing), do not apply	
Table 14	long-term loading $\quad\quad K_3 = 1.0$	
	medium-term loading $\quad K_3 = 1.25$	
Clause 1.6.4	This structure is Service Class 3	
Clause 2.6.2	E and stress values should be multiplied by K_2 from Table 13	

Contract : **Walkway**   **Job Ref. No. : Example 4.3**   **Calcs. by : W.McK.**

Contract : Walkway   **Job Ref. No. : Example 4.3**   **Calcs. by : W.McK.**
Part of Structure : Typical Internal Column   **Checked by :**
Calc. Sheet No. : 2 of 4   **Date :**

References	Calculations	Output
Clause 2.11.3 Table 18	**Slenderness:** **x-x axis** L_{exx} = $0.85 \times (3200 - 50)$ = 2678 mm	
Clause 2.11.4	$\dfrac{L_{exx}}{b}$ = $\dfrac{2678}{100}$ = 26.8 < 52	
	y-y axis L_{eyy} = $\dfrac{1.0 \times (3200 - 50)}{2}$ = 1575 mm or L_{eyy} = $\dfrac{0.85 \times (3200 - 50)}{2}$ = 1339 mm	
Clause 2.11.4	$\dfrac{L_{eyy}}{b}$ = $\dfrac{1575}{50}$ = 31.5 < 52 **critical slenderness = 31.5**	
Clause 2.11.5 Table 19 Table 13	**long-term:** $E/\sigma_{c,\parallel}$ is determined using $E_{min} \times K_2$ and E = 6000×0.8 = 4800 N/mm^2 $\sigma_{c,\parallel}$ = $\sigma_{c,g,\parallel} \times K_3$ $\sigma_{c,\parallel}$ = 5.2×1.0 = 5.2 N/mm^2 $E/\sigma_{c,\parallel}$ = $\dfrac{4800}{5.2}$ = 923; $\lambda = 31.5$ The value of K_{12} can be determined by interpolation from Table 19:	

Extract from Table 19

L_e/b $\diagdown$ $E/\sigma_{c,\parallel}$	28.9	34.7
900	0.397	0.304
1000	0.420	0.325

As in Example 4.2 a conservative, approximate answer can be
found using the lowest value corresponding with the highest
$E/\sigma_{c,\parallel}$ and λ value, i.e. in this case 0.304. If the
section is adequate with this value then it will also be
adequate with a more accurate determination of K_{12}

References	Calculations	Output

Contract : Walkway   **Job Ref. No. :** Example 4.3   **Calcs. by :** W.McK.
Part of Structure : Typical Internal Column   **Checked by :**
Calc. Sheet No. : 3 of 4   **Date :**

$\sigma_{c,adm,||} = \sigma_{c,g,||} \times K_3 \times K_{12}$

$\sigma_{c,adm,||} \approx 5.2 \times 1.0 \times 0.304 = 1.58 \text{ N/mm}^2$

$\sigma_{c,a,||} = \dfrac{F_c}{\text{Effective Area}}$

Effective area $=$ gross area $= (100 \times 50) = 5000 \text{ mm}^2$

$\sigma_{c,a,||} = \dfrac{0.42 \times 10^3}{5000} = 0.08 \text{ N/mm}^2 \quad < \quad 1.58 \text{ N/mm}^2$

Output: long-term capacity is adequate

medium-term:

Table 19
Table 13

$E/\sigma_{c,||}$ is determined using $E_{min} \times K_2$ and

$E = 6000 \times 0.8 = 4800 \text{ N/mm}^2$

$\sigma_{c,||} = \sigma_{c,g,||} \times K_3$

$\sigma_{c,||} = 5.2 \times 1.25 = 6.5 \text{ N/mm}^2$

$E/\sigma_{c,||} = \dfrac{4800}{6.5} = 738; \quad \lambda = 31.5$

From Table 19 use an approximate value of K_{12}, if necessary a more precise value can be determined.

Extract from Table 19

L_e/b $\diagdown$ $E/\sigma_{c,||}$	28.9	34.7
700	0.341	0.254
800	0.371	0.280

$K_{12} \approx 0.254$

$\sigma_{c,adm,||} = \sigma_{c,g,||} \times K_3 \times K_{12}$

$\sigma_{c,adm,||} \approx 5.2 \times 1.25 \times 0.254 = 1.65 \text{ N/mm}^2$

$\sigma_{c,a,||} = \dfrac{F_c}{\text{Effective Area}}$

Effective area $=$ gross area $= (100 \times 50) = 5000 \text{ mm}^2$

$\sigma_{c,a,||} = \dfrac{1.4 \times 10^3}{5000} = 0.28 \text{ N/mm}^2 \quad < \quad 1.82 \text{ N/mm}^2$

Output: medium-term capacity is adequate

Contract : **Walkway** **Job Ref. No. : Example 4.3**	Calcs. by : **W.McK.**
Part of Structure : **Typical Internal Column**	Checked by :
Calc. Sheet No. : **4** of **4**	Date :

References	Calculations	Output
Clause 2.10.2	**Bearing stress:** Check the bearing stress in the header at the top of the post. Consider medium term (by inspection this is more critical than the long-term load case) $\sigma_{c,adm,\perp} = \sigma_{c,g,\perp} \times K_2 \times K_3 \times K_4 \times K_8 \times K_{12}$	
Table 8 Table 13 Table 15 Table 14 Table 19	$\sigma_{c,g,\perp} = 2.1 \text{ N/mm}^2$ $K_2 = 0.6$ K_3 load sharing does not apply $K_4 = 1.1$ (the length of bearing is 100 mm) $K_8 = 1.25$ (medium-term loading) $K_{12} = 0.28$ $\sigma_{c,adm,\perp} = 2.1 \times 0.6 \times 1.1 \times 1.25 \times 0.28 = 0.48 \text{ N/mm}^2$ $\sigma_{c,a,\perp} = \dfrac{1.4 \times 10^3}{(50 \times 100)} = 0.28 \text{ N/mm}^2 = \sigma_{c,adm,\perp}$ The calculated stress is equal to the permissible; this can either be accepted or the timber used for the header changed to a higher grade.	

4.3.4   *Spaced Columns*   *(Clause 2.11.8)*

Spaced columns comprise at least two equal shafts connected and spaced apart by end and intermediate packing blocks, as shown in Figure 4.5. The columns behave compositely to resist an applied axial load. Composite members such as this occur either as individual columns in a building or as members in a lattice girder.

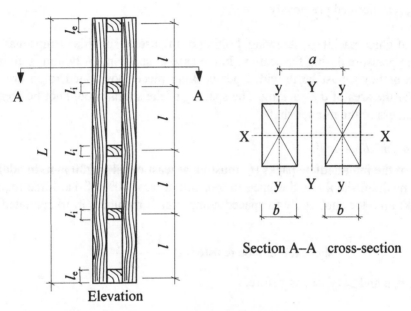

Elevation

Section A–A   cross-section

Figure 4.5

where:

L = overall length of the composite column,
l_e = thickness of the end packing pieces,
l_i = thickness of the intermediate packing pieces,
l = spacing of the packing pieces,
a = the distance between the centre-lines of adjacent shafts,
b = the thickness of a single shaft

The shafts may be solid timber or glued laminated timber sections. The dimensions and spacings of the packing pieces (which are required to limit the effective length of the individual shafts) are specified in Clause 2.11.9.1.1 for mechanically fastened units and Clause 2.11.9.1.2 for glued connections.

4.3.4.1   *End packs*

$l_e \geq 6b$

$\geq$ length required to accommodate a connecting medium (e.g. nails, screws, connectors or glue) between the abutting face of the packing and one adjacent shaft capable of resisting a shear force equal to the value given in equation (1); this does not apply to spaced compression members in triangulated frames.

$$\frac{1.3Ab\sigma_{c,a,||}}{na} \qquad\qquad \text{equation (1)}$$

where:

A is the **total** cross-sectional area of the column   (i.e. n × area of one shaft),

n the number of shafts,

b, a and $\sigma_{c,a,||}$ as defined previously

In the case of glued packings, screwing, bolting or the use of suitable clamps may provide the clamping pressure during fabrication. In the case of screwing or bolting a minimum of four screws or bolts must be provided per packing piece, positioned to ensure an even pressure over the area of the packing. The spacing of the shafts should not be greater than 3 × the thickness of the thinner shaft.

4.3.4.2   *Intermediate packs*

The length of the intermediate packs (l_i) must be at least equal to 230 mm. In addition the connecting medium should be designed to transmit at least 50% of that force required for an end pack; this does not apply to spaced compression members in triangulated frames, i.e.

$$\text{shear force to be resisted} \geq \frac{1.3Ab\sigma_{c,a,||}}{2na}$$

where A, b, n, a and $\sigma_{c,a,||}$ are as before.

In cases where $L \leq 30b$ only *one* intermediate packing is required. The slenderness of an individual shaft between the packing pieces should be such that:

$$\left(\frac{L_e}{i}\right)_{\text{individual shaft}} \leq 70 \qquad\qquad\qquad \text{and}$$

$$\leq 0.7 \times \left(\frac{L_e}{i}\right)_{\text{whole column}}$$

where L_e is the length between the centroids of the groups of mechanical connectors or glue areas in adjacent packings ('l' in Figure 4.5).

The maximum axial load, which can be supported by a spaced column, is given in Clause 2.1.11.10 as the least of the following:

- *bending about the* X-X *axis*   Axial capacity = (total column area) × ($\sigma_{c,adm,||}$).
- *bending about the* Y-Y *axis*   Axial capacity = (total column area) × ($\sigma_{c,adm,||}$), where the effective length L_{eyy} is assessed in accordance with table 18 and multiplied by the modification factor K_{13} from table 20. The modification factor K_{13} allows for different connecting media for the packing pieces and the ratio of the shaft thickness to the spacing of the shafts.
- *individual shaft buckling*   Axial capacity = (n × area of one shaft) × ($\sigma_{c,adm,||}$), where the effective length L_e is equal to the spacing of the packing pieces and the 'i' value is for y-y axis of a single shaft.

4.3.5 Example 4.4 Spaced Glulam Column

An internal spaced column in an exhibition centre is required to support long-term and medium-term loads of 80 kN and 140 kN respectively. Check the suitability of the proposed section indicated in Figure 4.6.

Data:

Timber : Imported redwood Grade SS

Assume Service Class 2

The column comprises two shafts each of four laminations with glued packing pieces, assume the strength of the glue to be 0.71 N/mm^2

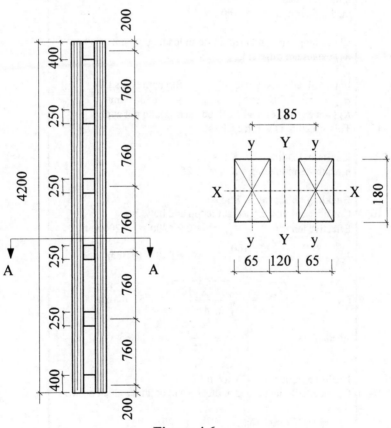

Figure 4.6

4.3.5.1   Solution to Example 4.4

References	Calculations	Output
Contract : Conf. Centre **Job Ref. No. :** Example 4.4		**Calcs. by : W.McK.**
Part of Structure : Spaced Glulam Column		**Checked by :**
Calc. Sheet No. : 1 of 4		**Date :**

References	Calculations	Output
BS 5268 : Part 2	Structural use of timber	
	long-term load = 80 kN medium-term load = 140 kN	
	Check long-term and medium-term loading separately since K_{12} values are different.	
Table 2 Table 7 Clause 1.6.4	Imported redwood grade SS; Strength Class C24 $\sigma_{c.g.\parallel}$ = 7.9 N/mm^2, E_{mean} = 10800 N/mm^2 K_2 (wet exposure), and K_8 (load sharing), do not apply This structure is Service Class 2	
Table 14	long-term loading K_3 = 1.0 medium-term loading K_3 = 1.25	
	Buckling about the X-X axis:	
Clause 2.11.10(a) Table 18	Consider column pinned at the top and bottom Effective length L_{exx}= 1.0 × 4200 = 4200 mm	
	I_{xx} = $2 \times \left(\dfrac{65 \times 180^3}{12} \right)$ = 63.18 × 10^6 mm^4	
	i_{xx} = $\sqrt{\dfrac{I_{xx}}{A}}$ = $\sqrt{\dfrac{63.18 \times 10^6}{23.4 \times 10^3}}$ = 51.96 mm	
	slenderness = $\dfrac{L_{exx}}{i_{xx}}$ = $\dfrac{4200}{51.96}$ = 80.83	
	Buckling about the Y-Y axis:	
Clause 2.11.10(c)	Consider column pinned at the top and bottom / glued packers	
Table 20	$\dfrac{\text{space between shafts}}{\text{thickness of thinner member}}$ = $\dfrac{120}{65}$ = 1.85 $\therefore K_3 = 1.27$ Effective length L_{exx}= 1.27 × 4200 = 5334 mm	
	I_{yy} $=2 \times \left\{ \dfrac{180 \times 65^3}{12} + \left(180 \times 65 \times 92.5^2 \right) \right\}$ $= 208.46 \times 10^6$ mm^4	
	i_{yy} = $\sqrt{\dfrac{I_{yy}}{A}}$ = $\sqrt{\dfrac{208.46 \times 10^6}{23.4 \times 10^3}}$ = 94.39 mm	

Contract : Conf. Centre Job Ref. No. : Example 4.4	Calcs. by : W.McK.
Part of Structure : Spaced Glulam Column	**Checked by :**
Calc. Sheet No. : 2 of 4	**Date :**

References	Calculations	Output
	slenderness $= \dfrac{L_{eyy}}{i_{yy}} = \dfrac{5334}{94.39} = 56.51$	
	Buckling of a single shaft about the y-y axis:	
Clause 2.11.10(b)	L_{eyy} = centres of packers = 760 mm	
see Section 4.3.1	For a rectangular section $i_{yy} = \dfrac{b}{2\sqrt{3}} = 18.76$ mm	
	slenderness $= \dfrac{L_{eyy}}{i_{yy}} = \dfrac{760}{18.76} = 40.51$	
Clause 2.11.9.2	$\dfrac{L_{eyy}}{i_{yy}} \leq 70$ and $\leq 0.7 \times$ slenderness of whole column	
	$40.51 < 70$ and $< 0.7 \times 80.83 = 56.58$	
Clause 2.11.4	**Critical Slenderness Ratio= 80.83 < 180**	
	Long-term: $\sigma_{c,adm,||} = \sigma_{c,g,||} \times K_2 \times K_3 \times K_8 \times K_{12} \times K_{28}$	
Table 22	Column is vertically laminated member $K_{28} = 1.24$	
Clause 3.6	Use $E_{mean} \times K_{28} = 10800 \times 1.24 = 13392$ N/mm^2	
	$\sigma_{c,||} = 7.9 \times 1.0 = 7.9$ N/mm^2 $E/\sigma_{c,||} = \dfrac{13392}{7.9} = 1695$	

Extract from Table 19

L_e/i $E/\sigma_{c,||}$	80	90
1600	0.611	0.559
1700	0.618	0.567

values corresponding to slenderness ratio = 80.83

$$0.611 - \left\{ \frac{(0.611-0.559)\times 0.83}{10} \right\} = 0.607$$

$$0.618 - \left\{ \frac{(0.618-0.567)\times 0.83}{10} \right\} = 0.614$$

Contract : Conf. Centre Job Ref. No. : Example 4.4	Calcs. by : W.McK.
Part of Structure : Spaced Glulam Column	Checked by :
Calc. Sheet No. : 3 of 4	Date :

References	Calculations	Output

Calculations:

L_e/i	80.83
$E/\sigma_{c,\parallel}$	
1600	0.607
1700	0.614

values corresponding to $E/\sigma_{c,\parallel} = $ 1695

$$K_{12} = 0.607 + \left\{ \frac{(0.614 - 0.607) \times 95}{100} \right\} = 0.614$$

$$\sigma_{c,adm,\parallel} = \sigma_{c,g,\parallel} \times K_3 \times K_{12} \times K_{28}$$
$$= 7.9 \times 1.0 \times 0.614 \times 1.24 = 6.01 \text{ N/mm}^2$$

long-term load capacity $= (23.4 \times 10^3 \times 6.01)/10^3$
$= 140.6 \text{ kN} \quad > 80 \text{ kN}$

medium-term:
$$\sigma_{c,adm,\parallel} = \sigma_{c,g,\parallel} \times K_3 \times K_{12} \times K_{28}$$

References: Table 22

Column is vertically laminated member $K_{28} = 1.24$

References: Clause 3.6

Use $E_{mean} \times K_{28} = 13392 \text{ N/mm}^2$

$\sigma_{c,\parallel} = 7.9 \times 1.25 = 9.88 \text{ N/mm}^2 \quad E/\sigma_{c,\parallel} = \dfrac{13392}{9.88} = 1355$

Extract from Table 19

L_e/i	80	90
$E/\sigma_{c,\parallel}$		
1300	0.584	0.527
1400	0.595	0.539

values corresponding to slenderness = 80.83

$$0.584 - \left\{ \frac{(0.584 - 0.527) \times 0.83}{10} \right\} = 0.579$$

$$0.595 - \left\{ \frac{(0.595 - 0.539) \times 0.83}{10} \right\} = 0.590$$

L_e/i	80.83
$E/\sigma_{c,\parallel}$	
1300	0.579
1400	0.590

Output:
Long-Term Capacity is adequate

References	Calculations	Output

Contract : Conf. Centre   **Job Ref. No. :** Example 4.4   **Calcs. by :** W.McK.
Part of Structure :   Spaced Glulam Column   **Checked by :**
Calc. Sheet No. : 4 of 4   **Date :**

References	Calculations	Output
	values corresponding to $E/\sigma_{c,||} = 1355$ $$K_{12} = 0.579 + \left\{\frac{(0.590-0.579)\times 55}{100}\right\} = 0.585$$ $\sigma_{c,adm,||} = \sigma_{c,g,||} \times K_3 \times K_{12} \times K_{28}$ $\quad\quad = 7.9 \times 1.25 \times 0.585 \times 1.24 = 7.16 \text{ N/mm}^2$ medium-term load capacity $= (23.4 \times 10^3 \times 7.16)/10^3$ $\quad\quad\quad\quad\quad\quad\quad = 167.5 \text{ kN} \quad > \quad 140 \text{ kN}$	Medium-term Capacity is adequate
	Check spacing of shafts and packer dimensions	
Clause 2.11.8	clear space between individual shafts $\leq 3 \times$ thickness of shaft $\therefore \quad 120 \quad\quad\quad\quad\quad \leq (3 \times 65) = 195$	Spacing of shafts is adequate
Clause 2.11.9.1	Shear force to be resisted $= \dfrac{1.3Ab\sigma_{c,a,||}}{na} = \dfrac{1.3Ab(P/A)}{na}$ $$= \dfrac{1.3bP}{na} = \dfrac{1.3\times 65\times 140}{2\times 120}$$ $\quad\quad\quad\quad\quad = 49.3 \text{ kN}$ Surface area of end pack in contact with shaft $= (400 \times 180)$ $\quad\quad\quad\quad\quad\quad\quad\quad\quad\quad\quad\quad\quad\quad = 72 \times 10^3 \text{ mm}^2$ Shear capacity of glued surface $= \dfrac{72\times 10^3 \times 0.71}{10^3} = 51.12 \text{ kN}$ $\quad\quad\quad\quad\quad\quad\quad\quad\quad\quad > 49.3 \text{ kN}$	Contact area of end packs is adequate
Clause 2.11.9.1.2	Length of pack along axis of column $\geq 6 \times$ thickness of shaft $\quad\quad\quad\quad 400 \quad\quad\quad\quad \geq (6 \times 65) = 390 \text{ mm}$	Length of end packs is adequate
Clause 2.11.9.2	Length of intermediate packs $\geq 230 \text{ mm}$ $\therefore \quad 250 \quad\quad\quad\quad\quad \geq 230 \text{ mm}$ Shear force to be resisted $= 0.5\times\left(\dfrac{1.3bP}{na}\right)$ $\quad\quad\quad\quad = 0.5 \times 49.3 = 24.65 \text{ kN}$ Surface area of end pack in contact with shaft $= (250 \times 180)$ $\quad\quad\quad\quad\quad\quad\quad\quad\quad\quad\quad\quad\quad\quad = 45 \times 10^3 \text{ mm}^2$ Shear capacity of glued surface $= \dfrac{45\times 10^3 \times 0.71}{10^3} = 31.95 \text{ kN}$	Length of intermediate packs is adequate

Contact area of end packs is adequate |

4.4   Parallel-Chord Lattice Beams

For flat and mono-pitch roofs of 6 m to 10 m span, ply-web or glulam beams are popular but there are cases, particularly larger spans, in which parallel lattice beams would be the choice either for architectural, functional or manufacturing reasons. A lattice beam is ideally suited to accommodate large diameter service pipes/ducts within the depth of the beam. One possible disadvantage is that the large forces which are induced in the web members necessitate heavier joints at the nodes. The section sizes may need to be increased to accommodate the connections. Economically designed lattice beams are deeper than either glulam or ply-web beams having an effective depth (*H*) of approximately 1/10 to 1/8 of the span.

A typical construction consists of a top and bottom chord with internal members such as the Pratt (or N) Truss or Warren Truss shown in Figure 4.7.

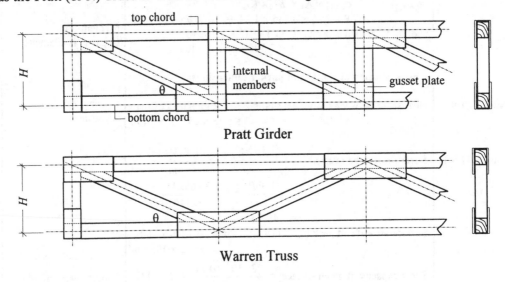

Figure 4.7

There are numerous other possible member configurations which can be used. It is preferable to keep the number of joints to a minimum to reduce fabrication costs and the deflection due to joint slip, except in the case of glued girders. Generally the inclination of the sloping web members is greater than or equal to 30°.

The internal members are frequently the same size throughout the span and the same width as the main chords. This arrangement simplifies the manufacturing of the girder. They usually have a low slenderness ratio and compression members are unlikely to have any significant reduction in strength. A consequence of this is that the internal configuration is more dependent on manufacturing requirements or appearance than design strength.

Trusses in which all members are single and in the same plane (see Figure 4.7) are known as mono-chord trusses. The gusset plates can be manufactured from plywood (glued or nailed), thin steel plates (nailed, screwed or bolted), single-sided tooth plates or shear-plate connectors or pre-punched metal-plate fasteners, and normally occur on each side of the truss. All the members of the lattice girders are usually surfaced on all sides irrespective of the gussets used.

In double chord trusses the chords and/or some internal members are fabricated using two sections for individual members, as indicated in Figure 4.8. The chords and internal members are normally connected using split-rings or tooth-plates. The use of single connector units rather than multiple dowel-type fasteners more closely reflects the assumption of pinned joints in the analysis to determine the member forces. The deformation of such trusses is influenced by joint slip and will be more significant than will occur when using glued joints.

The design of section sizes for truss members may need to be increased to accommodate the particular type of fastener used when detailed connection design is carried out.

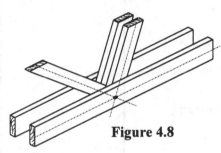

Figure 4.8

Double compression members in triangulated frames can be designed with or without spacers, depending on the level of lateral restraint provided by additional structural members such as purlins. If spacers are not used each component part is considered to support a proportion of the load and designed accordingly as a strut; when spacers are used the combined member can be designed in the same manner as a spaced column.

4.4.1 Example 4.5 Lattice Girder

A series of warren trusses as indicated in Figure 4.9 are spaced at 1.2 m centres and support the roof of a small workshop. Check the suitability of the proposed section for the diagonal members of the truss. (**Note:** the top chord is subject to secondary bending effects which are dealt with in Chapter 5.)

Data:
Timber   Whitewood Strength Class C24
Gusset plates   Finnish, birch-faced plywood glued/nailed to each side of single members.
Dead load   = 1.2 kN/m^2 , Imposed load   = 0.75 kN/m^2

top chord
50 mm x 175 mm

diagonals
50 mm x 75 mm

bottom chord
50 mm x 100 mm

800 mm

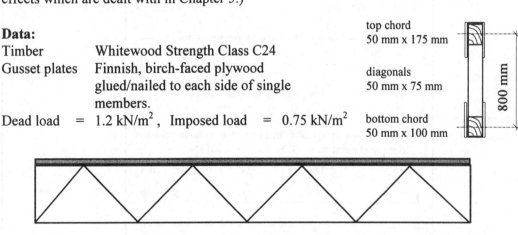

4 bays @ 2.0 m each = 8.0 m

Figure 4.9

4.4.1.1   Solution to Example 4.5

References	Calculations	Output
Contract : Workshop **Job Ref. No. :** Example 4.4 **Calcs. by :** W.McK. **Part of Structure :** Lattice Girder Diagonals **Checked by :** **Calc. Sheet No. :** 1 of 4 **Date :**		

References	Calculations	Output
BS 5268 : Part 2	Structural use of timber	
	long-term load = 1.2 kN/m^2 medium-term load = 0.75 kN/m^2	
Table 7	$\sigma_{c.g.\|\|}$ = 7.9 N/mm^2, E_{min} = 6000 N/mm^2 $\sigma_{t,g,\|\|}$ = 4.5 N/mm^2	
Clause 1.6.4 Clause 2.6.2 Clause 2.9 Table 14	This structure is Service Class 2 K_2 (wet exposure), and K_8 (load sharing), do not apply long-term loading K_3 = 1.0 medium-term loading K_3 = 1.25	
	Section properties: Since all members are glued allow for surface reduction e.g. 3 mm in both directions Diagonals: 50 mm x 75 mm ∴ assume 47 mm x 97 mm Cross-sectional area A = (47 × 97) = 3384 mm^2 Assume a UNIT load/metre and determine member forces.	
See Chapter 2 Section 2.11.2	Consider the load to be distributed to each internal panel point. ∴ load/panel point = 1.0 × 2.0 = 2.0 kN	

Contract : Workshop **Job Ref. No. :** Example 4.4	**Calcs. by :** W.McK.
Part of Structure : Lattice Girder Diagonals	**Checked by :**
Calc. Sheet No. : 2 of 4	**Date :**

References	Calculations	Output

Note: The distributed nature of the load on the top chord induces a bending moment in addition to an axial load. This is dealt with in Chapter 5.

Consider Section x-x

Length of the diagonal $= \sqrt{\left(0.8^2 + 1.0^2\right)}$

$\qquad\qquad\qquad\qquad = 1.281$ m

$\sin\theta \;=\; \dfrac{0.8}{1.281} = 0.625$

Resolve the vertical forces

$\Sigma F_y = 4.0 - 0.5 + F_1 \sin\theta = \;0 \quad F_1 \;=\; -\dfrac{3.5}{0.625} = -5.6$ kN

$\qquad\qquad\qquad\qquad\qquad\qquad\qquad\qquad$ Compression

Consider Section y-y

$\sin\theta \;=\; \dfrac{0.8}{1.281} = 0.625$

Resolve the vertical forces

$\Sigma F_y = 4.0 - 0.5 - 1.5 - F_2 \sin\theta \qquad = \;0$

$\qquad\qquad\qquad F_2 \;=\; +\dfrac{2.0}{0.625} \quad = \;+3.2$ kN

$\qquad\qquad\qquad\qquad\qquad\qquad\qquad\qquad\qquad$ Tension

Forces in members due to UNIT load/m length
Compression diagonal = 5.6 units
Tension diagonal   = 3.2 units

Compression Diagonal:

Clause 2.11.11(b) Since glued gusset plates have been used the effective length of the diagonal should be taken as 0.9 × actual distance between the assumed intersection points.

Contract : **Workshop** **Job Ref. No. : Example 4.4**	**Calcs. by : W.McK.**
Part of Structure : Lattice Girder Diagonals	**Checked by :**
Calc. Sheet No. : 3 of 4	**Date :**

References	Calculations	Output
	Effective length $= 0.9 \times 1.281 = 1.153$ m	
Clause 2.11.3	**Slenderness:**	
Clause 2.11.4	x-x axis $\dfrac{L_{exx}}{h} = \dfrac{1153}{72} = 16 \quad < \quad 52$	
Clause 2.11.4	y-y axis $\dfrac{L_{eyy}}{b} = \dfrac{1153}{47} = 24.5 \quad < \quad 52$	
	critical slenderness = 24.5	
Clause 2.11.5 Table 19	***long-term:*** $E/\sigma_{c,\|\|}$ is determined using E_{min} and $\sigma_{c,\|\|} = \sigma_{c,g,\|\|} \times K_3$ $E_{min} = 7200$ N/mm^2 $\sigma_{c,\|\|} = 7.9 \times 1.0 = 7.9$ N/mm^2 $E/\sigma_{c,\|\|} = \dfrac{7200}{7.9} = 911.4; \qquad \lambda = 24.5$	
Table 19	The value of K_{12} can be determined by interpolation from Table 19:	
	<div align="center">Extract from Table 19</div>	

L_e/b $E/\sigma_{c,\|\|}$	23.1	26.0
900	0.522	0.456
1000	0.542	0.478

References	Calculations	Output
	Assume lowest value $\therefore \; K_{12} \approx 0.456$ $\sigma_{c,adm,\|\|} = \sigma_{c,g,\|\|} \times K_3 \times K_{12}$ $\sigma_{c,adm,\|\|} \approx 7.9 \times 1.0 \times 0.456 = 3.6$ N/mm^2 long-term load/m = unit load $\times$ actual force/m $\qquad\qquad\qquad = 1.2 \times 1.2 = 1.44$ kN/m long-term load $= 5.6 \times 1.44 = 8.06$ kN $\sigma_{c,a,\|\|} = \dfrac{F_c}{\text{Effective Area}} = \dfrac{8.06 \times 10^3}{4559} = 1.77$ N/mm^2 $\qquad\qquad\qquad\qquad\qquad < \; 3.6$ N/mm^2	long-term capacity is adequate
	(**Note:** there is no need to evaluate a precise value for K_{12}) ***medium-term:*** $E/\sigma_{c,\|\|}$ is determined using E_{min} and $\sigma_{c,\|\|} = \sigma_{c,g,\|\|} \times K_3$	

Contract : Workshop Job Ref. No. : Example 4.4	Calcs. by : W.McK.
Part of Structure : Lattice Girder Diagonals	Checked by :
Calc. Sheet No. : 4 of 4	Date :

References	Calculations	Output
	$\sigma_{c,||} = 7.9 \times 1.25 = 9.88 \text{ N/mm}^2$ $E/\sigma_{c,||} = \dfrac{7200}{9.88} = 729; \qquad \lambda = 24$	
Table 19	Extract from Table 19 <table><tr><td>L_e/b $E/\sigma_{c,||}$</td><td>23.1</td><td>26.0</td></tr><tr><td>700</td><td>0.467</td><td>0.399</td></tr><tr><td>800</td><td>0.497</td><td>0.430</td></tr></table> $K_{12} \approx 0.399$ $\sigma_{c,adm,||} = \sigma_{c,g,||} \times K_3 \times K_{12}$ $\sigma_{c,adm,||} \approx 7.9 \times 1.25 \times 0.399 = 3.94 \text{ N/mm}^2$ medium-term load $= 5.6 \times 2.34 = 13.10 \text{ kN}$ $\sigma_{c,a,||} = \dfrac{F_c}{\text{Effective Area}} = \sigma_{c,a,||} = \dfrac{13.1 \times 10^3}{4559} = 2.87 \text{ N/mm}^2$ $< 3.94 \text{ N/mm}^2$	medium-term capacity is adequate
Table 7 Clause 2.12.2	**Tension Diagonal:** $\sigma_{t,adm,||} = \sigma_{t,g,||} \times K_3 \times K_{14}$ $\sigma_{t,g,||} = 4.5 \text{ N/mm}^2$ K_{14} – width of section $\qquad h = 72 \text{ mm} \qquad K_{14} = 1.17$ *long-term:* $\sigma_{t,adm,||} = 4.5 \times 1.0 \times 1.17 = 5.26 \text{ N/mm}^2$ long-term load $= 3.2 \times 1.44 = 4.61 \text{ kN}$ $\sigma_{c,a,||} = \dfrac{4.61 \times 10^3}{4559} = 1.01 \text{ N/mm}^2 < 5.26 \text{ N/mm}^2$	long-term capacity is adequate
	medium term: $\sigma_{t,adm,||} = 4.5 \times 1.25 \times 1.17 = 6.58 \text{ N/mm}^2$ medium-term load $= 3.2 \times 2.34 = 7.49 \text{ kN}$ $\sigma_{c,a,||} = \dfrac{7.49 \times 10^3}{4559} = 1.64 \text{ N/mm}^2 < 6.58 \text{ N/mm}^2$	medium-term capacity is adequate

4.5   Review Problems

4.1   Discuss factors which may induce buckling and influence the failure
       load of members subject to axial compression.
       (see Section 4.3)

4.2   Explain the terms: effective length and slenderness ratio.
       (see Section 4.3.1)

4.3   Explain the purpose of packs in spaced columns.
       (see Section 4.3.6)

4.4   Compare the stress/strain characteristics of timber subject to tensile or
       compressive stress parallel to the grain and perpendicular to the grain.
       (see Section 2.1)

5. Members Subject to Combined Axial and Flexural Loads

> **Objective:** *to illustrate the design of members subject to combined bending and axial loads including lattice girder elements and portal frame members.*

5.1 Introduction

Many structural elements such as beams and truss members are subjected to a single dominant effect, i.e. applied bending or axial stresses. Secondary effects which also occur are often insignificant and can be neglected. There are, however, numerous elements in which the combined effects of bending and axial stresses must be considered, e.g. rigid-jointed frames such as portals, chords in lattice girders with applied loading between the node points, and columns with eccentrically applied loading. The behaviour of such members is dependent on the interaction characteristics of the individual components of load. Generally, members resisting combined bending and tension are easier to design than those resisting combined bending and compression. This is due to the susceptibility of the latter to associated buckling effects. Interaction equations are given for both cases in BS 5268 : Part 2 : 1996.

The relevant modification factors which apply to members subject to combined loading are those which apply to the individual types, i.e. axially loaded and flexural members, and are summarized in Table 5.1.

Factors	Application	Clause Number	Value/Location
K_2	service class 3 sections (wet exposure): all stresses	2.6.2	Table 13
K_3	load duration: all stresses	2.8	Table 14
K_8	load-sharing: all stresses	2.9	1.1
K_9	modulus of elasticity	2.10.11 – 2.11.5	Table 17
K_{12}	slenderness of columns	2.11.5	Table 19
K_{13}	spaced columns: effective length	2.11.10	Table 20
K_{14}	width factor: tensile stresses	2.12.2	Equations given
$K_{15} - K_{20}$	horizontally laminated members	3.2	Table 21
$K_{28} - K_{29}$	vertically laminated members	3.3	Table 22
K_{33} & K_{34}	curved laminated members	3.5.3	Equations given
K_{35}	pitched cambered laminated members	3.5.4	Equations given

Table 5.1   Modification Factors

5.2 Combined Bending and Axial Tension   (Clause 2.12.3)

The interaction equation for members subject to combined bending and axial tension is given in Clause 2.12.3 as:

$$\frac{\sigma_{m,a,||}}{\sigma_{m,adm,||}} + \frac{\sigma_{t,a,||}}{\sigma_{t,adm,||}} \leq 1.0$$

where:

$\sigma_{m,a,||}$ is the applied bending stress,
$\sigma_{m,adm,||}$ is the permissible bending stress,
$\sigma_{t,a,||}$ is the applied tension stress,
$\sigma_{t,adm,||}$ is the permissible tension stress.

The values of $\sigma_{m,adm,||}$ and $\sigma_{t,adm,||}$ are evaluated using the modification factors where appropriate as described in Chapters 3 and 4. The value of $\sigma_{m,a,||}$ should represent the maximum value of the bending stress in the cross-section. In some instances bending will occur about both the x-x and y-y axes simultaneously, in which case:

$$\sigma_{m,a,||} = (\sigma_{m,ax,||} + \sigma_{m,ay,||})$$

where:

$\sigma_{m,ax,||}$ is the maximum bending stress due to bending about the x-x axis of the section,
$\sigma_{m,ay,||}$ is the maximum bending stress due to bending about the y-y axis of the section.

The expression given in the code is a linear interaction formula and could have been written using separate terms for bending about the x-x and y-y axes as:

$$\frac{\sigma_{m,ax,||}}{\sigma_{m,adm,||}} + \frac{\sigma_{m,ay,||}}{\sigma_{m,adm,||}} + \frac{\sigma_{t,a,||}}{\sigma_{t,adm,||}} \leq 1.0$$

This equation can be represented graphically as a linear interaction surface as shown in Figure 5.1. Any point located within or on the boundaries of the axes and interaction surface represents a combination of applied axial stress and bending stresses which satisfy the interaction equation.

Note: In glulam members the value of $\sigma_{m,adm,||}$ about the x-x axis and $\sigma_{m,adm,||}$ about the y-y axis may differ.

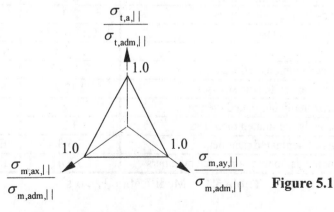

Figure 5.1

5.2.1   Example 5.1   Pitched Roof Truss – Ceiling Tie

An existing pitched roof truss is required to support an additional load on the main tie, as indicated in Figure 5.2. Assuming all loading given to be medium-term, check the suitability of the section used for the main tie.

Data:
Timber   Strength Class TR26
Medium term axial loading in main tie before additional load = 10 kN
Main tie 50 mm x 125 mm section

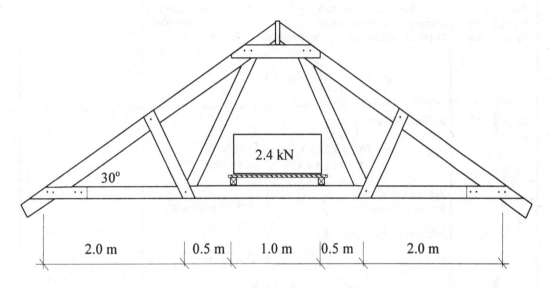

Figure 5.2

5.2.1.1   Solution to Example 5.1

<table>
<tr>
<td colspan="2">Contract : Roof Truss   Job Ref. No. : Example 5.1
Part of Structure :   Main Tie
Calc. Sheet No. : 1 of 4</td>
<td>Calcs. by : W.McK.
Checked by :
Date :</td>
</tr>
<tr>
<td>References</td>
<td>Calculations</td>
<td>Output</td>
</tr>
<tr>
<td>BS 5268 : Part 2
Clause 2.6.2
Table 7</td>
<td>Structural use of timber
Service Class 2 K_2 is not required
Strength Class   TR26
$\sigma_{m,g,||}$ = 10.0 N/mm^2, $\sigma_{t,g,||}$ = 6.0 N/mm^2</td>
<td></td>
</tr>
</table>

References	Calculations	Output
	Contract : Roof Truss **Job Ref. No. :** Example 5.1 **Calcs. by :** W.McK. **Part of Structure :** Main Tie **Checked by :** **Calc. Sheet No. :** 2 of 4 **Date :**	

References	Calculations	Output
Table 14 Clause 2.9 Clause 2.10.5 Clause 2.10.6	Duration of load is medium-term $K_3 = 1.25$ Load sharing does not exist K_8 is not required Rectangular section is used K_6 is not required Depth of section factor is required since $72 < h < 300$ $$\therefore K_7 = \left(\frac{300}{125}\right)^{0.11} = 1.1$$	
Clause 2.12.2	similarly for tension loads $K_{14} = 1.1$ $\sigma_{m,g,\parallel} \quad = \quad 10.0 \times 1.25 \times 1.1 \quad = \quad 13.75 \text{ N/mm}^2$ $\sigma_{t,g,\parallel} \quad = \quad 6.0 \times 1.25 \times 1.1 \quad = \quad 8.25 \text{ N/mm}^2$ **Section Properties:** Effective cross-section $= \quad 50 \times 125 \ = \ 6250 \text{ mm}^2$ Effective section modulus $= \quad \dfrac{50 \times 125^2}{6}$ $= \quad 130.21 \times 10^3 \text{ mm}^3$ existing axial tie load $= \quad 10 \text{ kN}$ medium-term load on tie $= \quad 2.4 \text{ kN}$ this load induces both axial and bending load effects in the main tie The additional **axial** load on the tie is determined assuming the load applied between nodes to be distributed statically to each of the adjacent nodes	

Contract : Roof Truss Job Ref. No. : Example 5.1	Calcs. by : W.McK.
Part of Structure : Main Tie	Checked by :
Calc. Sheet No. : 3 of 4	Date :

References	Calculations	Output

Σ Moments about 'o' $= 0$

$(1.2 \times 3.0) - (1.2 \times 0.5) - (F_t \times 1.732) = 0$

$$F_t = 1.73 \text{ kN}$$

Total axial load in the tie =   10 + 1.73   =   11.73 kN

The secondary bending moment can be estimated by assuming the main tie to be a three span beam as shown and evaluating the maximum bending moment.

A more approximate estimate of the bending moment can be made assuming the central span to be simply supported.

$1.2 \times 0.5 = 0.6 \text{ kNm}$

References	Calculations	Output

Contract : Roof Truss   **Job Ref. No. :** Example 5.1
Part of Structure : Main Tie
Calc. Sheet No. : 4 of 4

Calcs. by : W.McK.
Checked by :
Date :

This will overestimate the bending moment since it does not allow for the continuity of the tie. If the section is adequate for the simply supported moment then a more precise value will not be required.

Assume the bending moment ≈ 0.6 kNm

Axial stress:

$$\sigma_{t,a,||} = \frac{F_t}{\text{Effective Area}} = \frac{11.73 \times 10^3}{6250} = 1.88 \text{ N/mm}^2$$

Bending stress:

$$\sigma_{m,a,||} = \frac{\text{Bending moment}}{\text{Section modulus}} = \frac{0.6 \times 10^6}{130.21 \times 10^3} = 4.61 \text{ N/mm}^2$$

Combined tension and bending:

Clause 2.1.2.3

$$\frac{\sigma_{m,a,||}}{\sigma_{m,adm,||}} + \frac{\sigma_{t,a,||}}{\sigma_{t,adm,||}} \leq 1.0$$

$$\frac{4.61}{13.75} + \frac{1.88}{8.25} = 0.56 \leq 1.0$$

The ceiling tie can be reduced in size, however only one load case has been considered here and in addition the design of the connections may require a larger section size than is necessary for the combined axial and bending stresses.

5.3   Combined Bending and Axial Compression   (Clause 2.11.6)

As indicated in Chapter 4, Section 4.3, in slender members subjected to axial compressive loads there is a tendency for lateral instability to occur. This type of failure is called buckling and is reflected in the modification factor K_{12} which is used to reduce the permissible compressive stress in a member.

When combined bending and axial compressive stresses occur simultaneously in a section there is an increased tendency for buckling failure to occur. The axial load and its associated secondary bending effect, in addition to the bending effect induced by the applied lateral load, is shown in Figure 5.3.

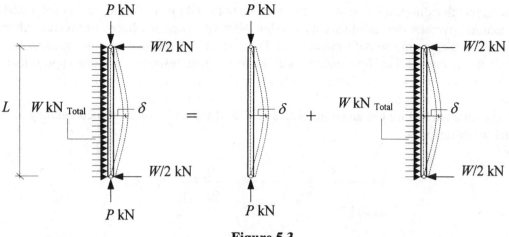

Figure 5.3

δ is the total deflection due to imperfections as described in Section 4.3 of Chapter 4, in addition to bending deflection due to the applied lateral load.

$$\text{Total bending moment} = (P \times \delta) + \left(\frac{WL}{8}\right)$$

The interaction diagram for combined bending and compression is more complex than that for combined tension and bending. For stocky members (i.e. slenderness ratio values λ lower than approximately 30), a non-linear relationship exists between axial stresses and bending stresses. For members with a high slenderness ratio a linear approximation is more realistic, as shown in Figure 5.4.

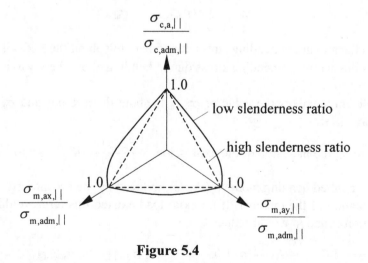

Figure 5.4

The non-linear behaviour in members with low slenderness ratios is a consequence of the higher values of compressive stress required to induce failure. Unlike timber subjected to tension which exhibits a linear stress-strain curve until failure is reached, timber subjected to compressive stresses exhibits considerable plasticity (i.e. non-linear behaviour) after the initial elastic linear deformation. At high values of slenderness the stresses are relatively low when buckling occurs and hence a linear response is more appropriate, whilst at low values of slenderness relatively high values of stress occur at failure and hence a non-linear approximation is more realistic (see Section 2.1).

The interaction formula given in Clause 2.11.6 of the code for combined bending and axial compression is:

$$\frac{\sigma_{m,a,||}}{\sigma_{m,adm,||}\left(1-\dfrac{1.5\sigma_{c,a,||}}{\sigma_e}\times K_{12}\right)} + \frac{\sigma_{c,a,||}}{\sigma_{c,adm,||}} \leq 1.0$$

where:

$\sigma_{m,a,\|\|}$	is the applied bending stress,
$\sigma_{m,adm,\|\|}$	is the permissible bending stress,
$\sigma_{c,a,\|\|}$	is the applied tension stress,
$\sigma_{c,adm,\|\|}$	is the permissible tension stress,
σ_e	is the Euler critical stress $= \dfrac{\pi^2 EI}{L^2}$

The values of $\sigma_{m,adm,||}$ and $\sigma_{c,adm,||}$ are determined using the modification factors where appropriate as described in Chapters 3 and 4. The value of $\sigma_{m,a,||}$ should represent the maximum value of the bending stress in the cross-section. In some instances bending will occur about both the x-x and y-y axes simultaneously, in which case:

$$\sigma_{m,a,||} = (\sigma_{m,ax,||} + \sigma_{m,ay,||})$$

where:

$\sigma_{m,ax,\|\|}$	is the maximum bending stress due to bending about the x-x axis of the section,
$\sigma_{m,ay,\|\|}$	is the maximum bending stress due to bending about the y-y axis of the section.

Note: In glulam members the value of $\sigma_{m,adm,||}$ about the x-x axis and $\sigma_{m,adm,||}$ about the y-y axis may differ.

In the first term, the inclusion of the expression $\dfrac{1.5\sigma_{c,a,||}}{\sigma_e}\times K_{12}$ is to allow for the 'additional' applied bending moment ($P \times \delta$), induced by the eccentricity of the axial load after deformation of the member. If no axial load existed this term would equal zero and the interaction equation would reduce to:

$$\frac{\sigma_{m,a,||}}{\sigma_{m,adm,||}} \leq 1.0 \qquad \text{i.e.} \quad \sigma_{m,a,||} \leq \sigma_{m,adm,||}$$

which is the same as that required for a member subject to bending only.

5.3.1   Example 5.2   Lattice Girder – Top Chord

A lattice girder supports a series of roof purlins as shown in Figure 5.5. Using the data provided, check the suitability of the proposed section for:

i)   the top chord of the girder,
ii) the left hand column.

Data:
Top chord to be a continuous member	2/50 mm x 225 mm double section
Column section to be	250 mm x 250 mm
Whitewood strength class C24 to be used throughout	

Loading:
Dead load	0.6 kN/m²
Imposed load	0.75 kN/m²
Wind loading	as indicated in Figure 5.5
All loading is assumed to be medium term	

Spacing of frames	4.0 m
Spacing of purlins	600 mm

All purlins may be assumed to be adequately fastened to the top chord and carried back to other bracing or support systems.

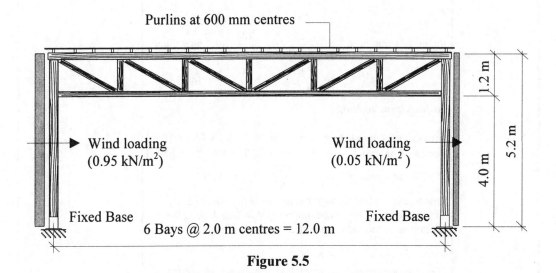

Purlins at 600 mm centres

Wind loading (0.95 kN/m²)

Wind loading (0.05 kN/m²)

Fixed Base

Fixed Base

6 Bays @ 2.0 m centres = 12.0 m

1.2 m

5.2 m

4.0 m

Figure 5.5

5.3.1.1   Solution to Example 5.2

Contract : Lattice Girder Job Ref. No. : Example 5.2	Calcs. by : W.McK.
Part of Structure : Top Chord	Checked by :
Calc. Sheet No. : 1 of 10	Date :

References	Calculations	Output
BS 5268 : Part 2 Clause 2.6.2 Table 7	Structural use of timber Service Class 2 $\qquad K_2$ is not required Strength Class C24 $\sigma_{m,g,\parallel} = 7.5\ \text{N/mm}^2$, $\qquad \sigma_{c,g,\parallel} = 7.9\ \text{N/mm}^2$ $E_{min} = 7{,}200\ \text{N/mm}^2$	
Table 14 Clause 2.9 Clause 2.10.5 Clause 2.10.6	Duration of load is medium-term $\qquad K_3 = 1.25$ Load sharing does not exist $\qquad K_8$ is not required Rectangular section is used $\qquad K_6$ is not required Depth of section factor is required since $\quad 72 < h < 300$ $$\therefore\ K_7 = \left(\frac{300}{225}\right)^{0.11} = 1.03$$ **Section Properties:** Effective cross-section $\qquad = 50 \times 225 = 11250\ \text{mm}^2$ Effective section modulus $\qquad = \dfrac{50 \times 225^2}{6}$ $\qquad = 421.87 \times 10^3\ \text{mm}^3$ Radius of gyration $i_{xx} = \dfrac{d}{2\sqrt{3}} = \dfrac{225}{2\sqrt{3}} = 64.95\ \text{mm}$ $i_{yy} = \dfrac{b}{2\sqrt{3}} = \dfrac{50}{2\sqrt{3}} = 14.43\ \text{mm}$ **medium term loading:** Area of roof supported by each girder $= 12.0 \times 4.0 = 48\ \text{m}^2$ Total load on girder $\quad = (0.6 + 0.75) \times 48 = 64.8\ \text{kN}$ Load at each node point $\quad = \dfrac{64.8}{6} = 10.8\ \text{kN}$ This load is applied through the purlins at 600 mm centres, and can be considered to be uniformly distributed along the continuous chord inducing both axial and bending effects. 64.8 kN 	

References	Calculations	Output
	Contract : Lattice Girder **Job Ref. No. :** Example 5.2 **Calcs. by : W.McK.**	

Contract : Lattice Girder   **Job Ref. No. :** Example 5.2   **Calcs. by : W.McK.**
Part of Structure :   Top Chord   **Checked by :**
Calc. Sheet No. : 2 of 10   **Date :**

References	Calculations	Output
	Equivalent loading system:	
Appendix A (this text)	5.4 kN 10.8 kN 10.8 kN 10.8 kN 10.8 kN 10.8 kN 5.4 kN	

Equivalent loading system:

5.4 kN 10.8 kN 10.8 kN 10.8 kN 10.8 kN 10.8 kN 5.4 kN

X

X

Axial Effects

+

0.107*W*

Bending Effects

Maximum bending moment = 0.107*W*
where '*W*' is the total load between two nodes = 10.8 kN
(Alternatively simplify using $wL^2/8$)
The maximum axial load in the top chord occurs at mid-span at
Section X-X as shown.

5.4 kN 10.8 kN 10.8 kN

1.2 m

O

32.4 kN   2.0 m | 2.0 m | 2.0 m |

Σ Moments about 'O' = 0
$(32.4 \times 6) - (5.4 \times 6) - (10.8 \times 4) - (10.8 \times 2) + (F_c \times 1.2) = 0$
$$F_c = -81.0 \text{ kN (Compression)}$$

Maximum bending moment = $0.107 \times 10.8 = 1.156$ kNm

The top chord can be designed as two separate members
each supporting 50% of the axial load and moment or as a
spaced column supporting the full load.

References	Calculations	Output
	Contract : Lattice Girder **Job Ref. No. :** Example 5.2 **Calcs. by :** W.McK. **Part of Structure :** Top Chord **Checked by :** **Calc. Sheet No. :** 3 of 10 **Date :**	

References	Calculations	Output
	'Consider each section as a separate member'	
	Axial load / member $= 0.5 \times 81.0 = 40.5$ kN	
	Bending moment / member $= 0.5 \times 1.156 = 0.58$ kNm	
	$\sigma_{m,a,\parallel} = \dfrac{0.58 \times 10^6}{421.87 \times 10^3} = 1.37$ N/mm^2	
	$\sigma_{c,a,\parallel} = \dfrac{40.5 \times 10^3}{11.25 \times 10^3} = 3.6$ N/mm^2	
	$\sigma_{m,adm,\parallel} = \sigma_{m,g,\parallel} \times K_3 \times K_7$ $= (7.5 \times 1.25 \times 1.03) = 9.65$ N/mm^2	
Clause 2.11.5	$E_{min} = 7200$ N/mm^2,	
	$\sigma_{c,\parallel} = \sigma_{c,g,\parallel} \times K_3$ $= (7.9 \times 1.25) = 9.8$ N/mm^2	
	$E/\sigma_{c,\parallel} = \dfrac{7200}{9.87} = 729.4$	
Clause 2.11.11	Effective length in the plane of the framework (i.e. about the x-x axis)	
	$L_{exx} = 0.85 \times 2000 = 1700$ mm, $i_{xx} = 64.95$ mm	
	$\lambda_{xx} = \dfrac{L_{exx}}{i_{xx}} = \dfrac{1700}{64.95} = 26.17$	
	Effective length in the plane of the framework (i.e. about the y-y axis)	
	$L_{eyy} = 600$ (spacing of the purlins), $i_{yy} = 14.43$ mm	
	$\lambda_{yy} = \dfrac{L_{eyy}}{i_{yy}} = \dfrac{600}{14.43} = 41.58$	
Table 19	Extract from Table 19	

$E/\sigma_{c,\parallel}$ \ L_e/i	40	50
700	0.784	0.711
800	0.792	0.724

Contract : Lattice Girder Job Ref. No. : Example 5.2	Calcs. by : W.McK.
Part of Structure : Top Chord	Checked by :
Calc. Sheet No. : 4 of 10	Date :

References	Calculations	Output
	values corresponding to slenderness ratio = 41.58	

values corresponding to slenderness ratio = 41.58

$$0.784 - \left\{ \frac{(0.784 - 0.711) \times 1.58}{10} \right\} = 0.772$$

$$0.792 - \left\{ \frac{(0.792 - 0.724) \times 1.58}{10} \right\} = 0.781$$

$E/\sigma_{c,||}$ \ L_e/i	41.58
700	0.772
800	0.781

values corresponding to $E/\sigma_{c,||} = $ 729.4

$$K_{12} = 0.772 + \left\{ \frac{(0.781 - 0.772) \times 29.4}{100} \right\} = 0.775$$

$$\sigma_{c,adm,||} = \sigma_{c,g,||} \times K_3 \times K_{12}$$
$$= 7.5 \times 1.25 \times 0.775 = 7.27 \text{ N/mm}^2$$

Clause 2.11.6

$$\frac{\sigma_{m,a,||}}{\sigma_{m,adm,||} \left(1 - \frac{1.5\sigma_{c,a,||}}{\sigma_e} \times K_{12} \right)} + \frac{\sigma_{c,a,||}}{\sigma_{c,adm,||}} = \leq 1$$

where σ_e is the Euler critical stress $= \dfrac{\pi^2 E}{(L_e / i)^2} = \dfrac{\pi^2 E}{\lambda^2}$

$$\sigma_e = \frac{\pi^2 \times 7200}{41.58^2} = 41.1 \text{ N/mm}^2$$

$$\frac{1.5\sigma_{c,a,||}}{\sigma_e} \times K_{12} = \frac{1.5 \times 3.6 \times 0.775}{41.1} = 0.102$$

Interaction Equation:

$$\frac{1.37}{9.67(1 - 0.102)} + \frac{3.6}{7.27} = 0.65 \leq 1$$

Output: Section is adequate

Note: As before only one load case has been considered and the connection details may influence the section size.

Contract : Lattice Girder Job Ref. No. : Example 5.2	Calcs. by : W.McK.
Part of Structure : Column	Checked by :
Calc. Sheet No. : 5 of 10	Date :

References	Calculations	Output

Column Section
Section Properties:

Area A $=$ 250×250 $=$ $62.5 \times 10^3 \text{ mm}^2$

Section modulus Z $=$ $\dfrac{250 \times 250^2}{6}$ $=$ $2604 \times 10^3 \text{ mm}^3$

Radius of gyration i_{xx} $=$ i_{yy} $=$ $\dfrac{250}{2\sqrt{3}}$ $=$ 72.17 mm

Timber Designer's Manual (13)

Frames with fixed bases and in which sway occurs have a point of contraflexure in the columns. The position of this can be estimated using the equations given in the *Timber Designer's Manual*

$$h_c \approx \frac{h}{2}\left(\frac{h+2H}{2h+H}\right)$$

h_c is the assumed height of the point of contraflexure (i.e. zero moment) above the fixed base. This assumption is sufficiently accurate for design purposes even when the loading on each column is not equal.

spacing of frames $=$ 4.0 m
loading on column AB $=$ 0.95×4.0 $=$ 3.8 kN/m
loading on column DC $=$ 0.1×4.0 $=$ 0.4 kN/m

$$h_c = \frac{h}{2}\left(\frac{h+2H}{2h+H}\right) = \frac{4.0}{2}\left(\frac{4.0+(2\times5.2)}{8+5.2}\right) = 2.18 \text{ m}$$

References	Calculations	Output

Contract : Lattice Girder   **Job Ref. No. :** Example 5.2
Part of Structure :   Column
Calc. Sheet No. : 6 of 10

Calcs. by : W.McK.
Checked by :
Date :

Consider a horizontal section through the point of contraflexure

64.8 kN (total)

B   C

3.02 m

3.8 kN/m   1.82 m   0.4 kN/m

S   P1   S   P2

12.0 m

V₁   V₂

$\Sigma F_x = 0$

$(3.8 \times 3.02) + (0.4 \times 3.02) - 2S \quad = \quad 0 \qquad \therefore S = 6.34 \text{ kN}$

$\Sigma M_{P1} = 0$

$(64.8 \times 6) + \dfrac{3.8 \times 3.02 \times 3.02}{2} + \dfrac{0.4 \times 3.02 \times 3.02}{2} - 12V_R = 0$

$\therefore V_2 = 34.0 \text{ kN}$

$\Sigma F_y = 0$

$V_A - 64.8 + 34.0 \quad = \quad 0 \qquad\qquad \therefore V_1 = 30.8 \text{ kN}$

Bending moment at C $\quad = \quad -(6.34 \times 1.82) + \dfrac{0.4 \times 1.82 \times 1.82}{2}$

$= \quad -10.87 \text{ kNm}$

Bending moment at B $\quad = \quad +(6.34 \times 1.82) - \dfrac{3.8 \times 1.82 \times 1.82}{2}$

$= \quad +5.25 \text{ kNm}$

Consider column AB below the point of contraflexure to determine the value of the horizontal reaction and bending moment at the base

Contract : Lattice Girder Job Ref. No. : Example 5.2 Part of Structure : Column Calc. Sheet No. : 7 of 10	Calcs. by : W.McK. Checked by : Date :

References	Calculations	Output

6.34 kN

3.8 kN/m

2.18 m

M_A H_A

A

30.8 kN

$\Sigma F_x = 0$

$(3.8 \times 2.18) + 6.34 - H_A \quad = \quad 0 \qquad \therefore H_A = 14.62$ kN

$\Sigma M_A = 0$

$- M_A + \dfrac{3.8 \times 2.18 \times 2.18}{2} + (6.34 \times 2.18) = 0$

$\therefore M_A = 22.85$ kNm

Consider column CD below the point of contraflexure   to
determine the value of the horizontal reaction and bending
moment at the base

6.34 kN

0.4 kN/m

2.18 m

M_D H_D

D

34.0 kN

$\Sigma F_x = 0$

$(0.4 \times 2.18) + 6.34 - H_D \quad = \quad 0 \qquad \therefore H_D = 7.21$ kN

$\Sigma M_D = 0$

$- M_D + \dfrac{0.4 \times 2.18 \times 2.18}{2} + (6.34 \times 2.18) = 0$

$\therefore M_D = 14.77$ kNm

References	Calculations	Output

5.25 kNm   10.87 kNm

22.85 kNm   14.77 kNm

Bending Moment Diagrams for columns AB and CD

Column AB is the critical one.

Maximum bending moment = 22.85 kNm
Maximum axial loading = 30.8 kN

$$\sigma_{m,a,||} = \frac{22.85 \times 10^6}{2.604 \times 10^6} = 8.77 \text{ N/mm}^2$$

$$\sigma_{c,a,||} = \frac{30.8 \times 10^3}{62.5 \times 10^3} = 0.49 \text{ N/mm}^2$$

1.82 m

4.0 m

2.18 m

Slenderness:
The value used for this is open to debate; different engineers have different interpretations for effective lengths.

$L_{exx} = 2 \times 2.18 = 4.36$ m $i_{xx} = 72.17$ mm
$L_{eyy} = 0.85 \times 4.0 = 3.4$ m $i_{yy} = 72.17$ mm

$\lambda_{xx} = \dfrac{4360}{72.17} = 60.4$ $\lambda_{yy} = \dfrac{3400}{72.17} = 47.11 < 180$

$E/\sigma_{c,||} = 729.4$ as before and $\lambda_{\text{critical}} = 60.4$

Contract : Lattice Girder Job Ref. No. : Example 5.2	Calcs. by : W.McK.
Part of Structure : Column	Checked by :
Calc. Sheet No. : 9 of 10	Date :

References	Calculations	Output

Table 19

Extract from Table 19

L_e/i $E/\sigma_{c,\|\|}$	60	70
700	0.629	0.545
800	0.649	0.572

values corresponding to slenderness ratio = 60.4

$$0.629 - \left\{\frac{(0.629 - 0.545)\times 0.4}{10}\right\} \quad = \quad 0.626$$

$$0.649 - \left\{\frac{(0.649 - 0.572)\times 0.4}{10}\right\} \quad = \quad 0.646$$

L_e/i $E/\sigma_{c,\|\|}$	60.4
700	0.626
800	0.646

values corresponding to $E/\sigma_{c,\|\|} = $ 729.4

$$K_{12} \quad = \quad 0.626 + \left\{\frac{(0.646 - 0.626)\times 29.4}{100}\right\} \quad = \quad 0.634$$

$\sigma_{c,adm,\|\|} \quad = \quad \sigma_{c,g,\|\|} \times K_3 \times K_{12}$
$\quad\quad\quad = \quad 7.5 \times 1.25 \times 0.634 \;\; = 5.94 \text{ N/mm}^2$

Clause 2.11.6

$$\frac{\sigma_{m,a,\|\|}}{\sigma_{m,adm,\|\|}\left(1 - \dfrac{1.5\sigma_{c,a,\|\|}}{\sigma_e}\times K_{12}\right)} + \frac{\sigma_{c,a,\|\|}}{\sigma_{c,adm,\|\|}} \quad = \quad \le \; 1$$

where σ_e is the Euler critical stress $= \dfrac{\pi^2 E}{(L_e/i)^2} \quad = \dfrac{\pi^2 E}{\lambda^2}$

$$\sigma_e \quad = \quad \frac{\pi^2 \times 7200}{60.4^2} \quad = \quad 19.48 \text{ N/mm}^2$$

$$\frac{1.5\sigma_{c,a,\|\|}}{\sigma_e}\times K_{12} \quad = \quad \frac{1.5\times 0.49\times 0.634}{19.48} \quad = \quad 0.025$$

References	Calculations	Output
	Interaction Equation: $$\frac{8.77}{9.65(1-0.025)} + \frac{0.49}{5.94} = 1.01 > 1$$ This column is slightly overstressed. The strength class of the selected timber can be changed e.g. to C27 which would satisfy the interaction equation.	Section is overstressed

Contract : Lattice Girder   **Job Ref. No. :** Example 5.2   **Calcs. by :** W.McK.
Part of Structure : Column   **Checked by :**
Calc. Sheet No. : 10 of 10   **Date :**

5.3.2   Example 5.3   Laminated Portal Frame

A church building is to be constructed using a series of three-pinned, pitched roof portal frames as shown in Figure 5.6. Assuming all loading to be medium-term loading check the suitability of the glued laminated frame members to resist the combined axial and bending effects.

Data:

Centres of frames	3.0 m
Dead loads (based on slope areas)	
Timber boarding	$0.45 \ kN/m^2$
Insulation, felt etc.	$0.5 \ kN/m^2$
Slates	$0.25 \ kN/m^2$
Imposed loads (based on plan area)	$0.75 \ kN/m^2$

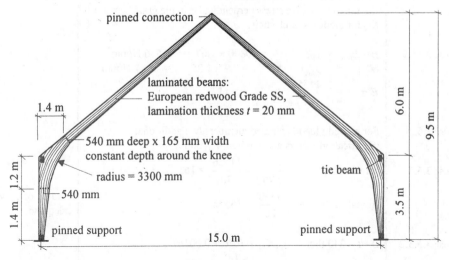

Figure 5.6

5.3.2.1   Solution to Example 5.3

References	Calculations	Output

Contract : Church Hall   **Job Ref. No. :** Example 5.3   **Calcs. by :** W.McK.
Part of Structure : Portal Frame   **Checked by :**
Calc. Sheet No. : 1 of 6   **Date :**

References	Calculations	Output
BS 5268 : Part 2	Structural use of timber *Timber Designers' Manual*	
Clause 2.6.2 Table 2 Table 7	Service Class 2 K_2 is not required European redwood Grade SS: Strength Class C24 Strength Class C24 $\sigma_{m,g,\parallel} = 7.5 \text{ N/mm}^2$, $\sigma_{c,g,\parallel} = 7.9 \text{ N/mm}^2$ $E_{mean} = 10{,}800 \text{ N/mm}^2$ $\sigma_{c,g,\perp} = 2.4 \text{ N/mm}^2$	
Table 14 Clause 2.9 Clause 2.10.5 Clause 2.10.6	Duration of load is medium-term $K_3 = 1.25$ Load sharing does not exist K_8 is not required Rectangular section is used K_6 is not required Depth of section factor is required since $h > 300$ $\therefore K_7 = 0.81\left(\dfrac{h^2 + 92{,}300}{h^2 + 56{,}800}\right) = 0.81\left(\dfrac{540^2 + 92{,}300}{540^2 + 56{,}800}\right) = 0.89$	
Clause 3.2	Number of laminations $= \dfrac{540}{20} = 27 > 20$	
Table 21	K_{15} for bending stress parallel to the grain $= 1.52$ K_{17} for compressive stress parallel to the grain $= 1.04$ K_{18} for compressive stress perpendicular to the grain $= 1.04$ K_{20} for modulus of elasticity $= 1.07$	
Clause 2.11.5	$E = E_{mean} \times K_{20}$ $= 10800 \times 1.07 = 11556 \text{ N/mm}^2$ $\sigma_{c,\parallel} = \sigma_{c,g,\parallel} \times K_3$ $= 7.9 \times 1.25$ $= 9.87 \text{ N/mm}^2$ $E/\sigma_{c,\parallel} = \dfrac{11556}{9.87}$ $= 1171$	
Clause 3.5.3	For curved glued laminated members two additional modification factors are required; K_{33} and K_{34}	
Clause 3.5.3.1	Minimum $r/t = \dfrac{E_{mean}}{70} = \dfrac{11556}{70} = 165$	
	Actual $r/t = \dfrac{3300}{20} = 165 \text{ m}$	Radius of curvature is adequate
Clause 3.5.3.2	If $r/t < 240$ then $K_{33} = 0.76 + 0.001 r/t$ ≤ 1.0 $K_{33} = 0.76 + (0.001 \times 165) = 0.93 \quad \leq 1.0$	

Contract : Church Hall Job Ref. No. : Example 5.3	Calcs. by : W.McK.
Part of Structure : Portal Frame	Checked by :
Calc. Sheet No. : 2 of 6	Date :

References	Calculations	Output

References:

Figure 4

BS 5268 : Part 2

Calculations:

r_{mean} $= r + 0.5h$ $= 3300 + (0.5 \times 540) = 3570$ mm

$\dfrac{r_{mean}}{h}$ $= \dfrac{3570}{540}$ $= 6.6 < 1.0$

K_{34} $= 1 + 0.5\left(\dfrac{h}{r_{mean}}\right) = 1 + 0.5\left(\dfrac{540}{3570}\right)$ $= 1.07$

$\sigma_{m,adm,||}$ $= \sigma_{m,g,||} \times K_3 \times K_7 \times K_{15} \times K_{33}$
           $= 7.5 \times 1.25 \times 0.89 \times 1.52 \times 0.93 = 11.79$ N/mm^2

$\sigma_{c,adm,||}$ $= \sigma_{c,g,||} \times K_3 \times K_{12} \times K_{17} \times K_{33}$
           $= 7.9 \times 1.25 \times 1.04 \times 0.93 \times K_{12} = 9.55 K_{12}$ N/mm^2

K_{12} is evaluated later using Table 19

Section Properties: **540 mm x 165 mm section**

Effective cross-section $= 540 \times 165 = 89100$ mm^2

Effective section modulus $= \dfrac{165 \times 540^2}{6}$

                            $= 8019 \times 10^3$ mm^3

Radius of gyration i_{xx} $= \dfrac{d}{2\sqrt{3}}$ $= \dfrac{540}{2\sqrt{3}}$ $= 155.88$ mm

             i_{yy} $= \dfrac{b}{2\sqrt{3}}$ $= \dfrac{165}{2\sqrt{3}}$ $= 47.63$ mm

medium term loading:

Dead load $= (0.45 + 0.5 + 0.25) = 1.2$ kN/m^2 (slope area)

Slope of the roof $= \tan^{-1}\left(\dfrac{6}{7.5}\right) = 38.66°$

Dead load based on plan area $= \dfrac{1.2}{\cos 38.66°}$ $= 1.54$ kN/m^2

Imposed load $= 0.75$ kN/m^2 (plan area)

Design load $= (1.54 + 0.75) = 2.29$ kN/m^2

Portal frames are spaced at 3.0 m centres

Load / frame $= 2.29 \times 3.0$ $= 6.87$ kN/m

References	Calculations	Output

Contract : Church Hall   **Job Ref. No. :** Example 5.3   **Calcs. by :** W.McK.
Part of Structure : Portal Frame   **Checked by :**
Calc. Sheet No. : 3 of 6   **Date :**

$\Sigma M_A = 0$

$(6.87 \times 15.0 \times 7.5) - 15.0 \times V_E = 0 \quad \therefore V_E = 51.53 \text{ kN}$

$\Sigma F_y = 0$

$V_A - (6.87 \times 15.0) + V_E \qquad = 0 \quad \therefore V_A = 51.53 \text{ kN}$

Consider a section of the frame through the pin at the ridge.

$\Sigma M_C = 0$

$(51.53 \times 7.5) - 9.5 H_A - \left(6.87 \times \dfrac{7.5^2}{2}\right) = 0 \qquad H_A = 20.34 \text{ kN}$

Contract : Church Hall Job Ref. No. : Example 5.3	Calcs. by : W.McK.
Part of Structure : Portal Frame	Checked by :
Calc. Sheet No. : 4 of 6	Date :

References	Calculations	Output
	$\Sigma F_x = 0$ $H_A - H_E = 0$ $\therefore$ $H_E = 20.34$ kN	

$$\text{Bending moment at B} = -(20.34 \times 3.5) = -71.19 \text{ kNm}$$

Maximum bending moment   = 71.19 kNm
Maximum axial loading   = 51.53 kN

Clause 3.5.3.2

$$\sigma_{m,a,||} = K_{34} \times \frac{\text{Bending Moment}}{Z_{xx}} = 1.07 \times \frac{71.19 \times 10^6}{8.019 \times 10^6}$$

$$= 9.5 \text{ N/mm}^2$$

$$\sigma_{c,a,||} = \frac{51.53 \times 10^3}{89.1 \times 10^3} = 0.58 \text{ N/mm}^2$$

References	Calculations	Output

Contract : Church Hall **Job Ref. No. :** Example 5.3
Part of Structure : Portal Frame
Calc. Sheet No. : 5 of 6

Calcs. by : W.McK.
Checked by :
Date :

Slenderness:

$L_{exx} = 0.85 \times 3500 = 2975$ mm $i_{xx} = 155.88$ mm

$\lambda_{xx} = \dfrac{2975}{155.88} = 19.09 < 180$

Restraint to the y-y axis of the column is provided by the brickwork walls of the building.

$E/\sigma_{c,||} = 1171;$ $\lambda_{critical} = 19.09$

Table 19

Extract from Table 19

$E/\sigma_{c,||}$　L_e/i	10	20
1100	0.952	0.905
1200	0.952	0.905

$K_{12} \approx 0.910$

$\sigma_{c,adm,||} = \sigma_{c,g,||} \times K_3 \times K_{12}$
$= 9.55 \times 0.91 = 8.69$ N/mm^2

Clause 2.11.6

$$\dfrac{\sigma_{m,a,||}}{\sigma_{m,adm,||}\left(1 - \dfrac{1.5\sigma_{c,a,||}}{\sigma_e} \times K_{12}\right)} + \dfrac{\sigma_{c,a,||}}{\sigma_{c,adm,||}} = \leq 1$$

where σ_e is the Euler critical stress $= \dfrac{\pi^2 E}{(L_e/i)^2} = \dfrac{\pi^2 E}{\lambda^2}$

$\sigma_e = \dfrac{\pi^2 \times 11}{19.09^2} = 312.9$ N/mm^2

$\dfrac{1.5\sigma_{c,a,||}}{\sigma_e} \times K_{12} = \dfrac{1.5 \times 0.58 \times 0.91}{312.9} = 0.0025$

Interaction Equation:

$$\dfrac{9.5}{14.58(1 - 0.0025)} + \dfrac{0.58}{8.69} = 0.72 \leq 1$$

Clause 3.5.3.3

The radial stresses must be checked at the corners B and D

Combined stress condition is satisfied

References	Calculations	Output
Contract : Church Hall **Job Ref. No. :** Example 5.3 **Part of Structure :** Portal Frame **Calc. Sheet No. :** 6 of 6		**Calcs. by : W.McK.** **Checked by :** **Date :**

References	Calculations	Output
	Applied radial stress $\sigma_r = \dfrac{3M}{2bhr_{mean}} = \dfrac{3 \times 71.19 \times 10^6}{2 \times 165 \times 540 \times 3570} = 0.34 \text{ N/mm}^2$ The negative bending moment at the knee tends to decrease the radius of curvature and the radial stress will be in compression perpendicular to the grain, therefore: $\begin{aligned}\sigma_r &\leq 1.33 \times \sigma_{c,g,\perp} \times K_3 \times K_{18}\\ &= 1.33 \times 2.4 \times 1.25 \times 1.55 = 6.18 \text{ N/mm}^2\end{aligned}$ Further checks such as bearing, shear and other load cases should also be made for suitability.	Radial stress condition is satisfied

5.4   Review Problems

5.1   Explain the differences between the interaction diagram for combined tension and bending and that for combined compression and bending. (see Sections 5.2 and 5.4)

5.2   Explain how the additional bending moment due to initial eccentricity of the member is allowed for in the design for combined compression and bending.

6. Mechanical Fasteners

Objective: *to discuss, and illustrate the design of, the various types of mechanical fasteners, i.e. nails, screws, bolts and dowels, tooth-plate, split-ring and shear-plate connectors and glue, which are used in structural timber.*

6.1 Introduction

As a structural material, timber has been used for many hundreds of years. Traditionally the transfer of forces from one structural member to another was achieved by the construction of carpentry joints such as lap joints, cogging joints, framed joints and tenon joints as indicated in Figure 6.1. In many instances the physical contact or friction between members was relied upon to transfer the forces between them.

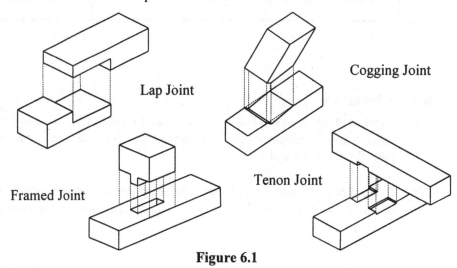

Figure 6.1

The use of mechanical fasteners is now firmly established as an essential part of modern economic design in timber. There are numerous types of fastener available; those considered in BS 5268 : Part 2 are:

- ♦ nailed joints   (Clause 6.4)
- ♦ screwed joints   (Clause 6.5)
- ♦ bolted and dowelled joints   (Clause 6.6)
- ♦ toothed-plate connector joints (Clause 6.7)

Factors	Application	Clause Number	Value/Location
K_2	service class 3 sections:(wet exposure)	2.6.2	Table 13
K_8	load-sharing: all stresses	2.9	1.1
K_{43}	nails driven into end grain	6.4.4.1	0.7
K_{44}	improved nail lateral loads	6.4.4.4	1.2
K_{45}	threaded part of annular ringed shank and helical shank nails	6.4.4.4	1.5
K_{46}	steel plate to timber joint	6.4.5.2	1.25
K_{48}	duration of loading – *nailed* joint	6.4.9	Given in clause
K_{49}	moisture content – *nailed* joint	6.4.9	Given in clause
K_{50}	number of *nails* in each line	6.4.9	Given in clause
K_{52}	duration of loading – *screwed* joint	6.5.7	Given in clause
K_{53}	moisture content – *screwed* joint	6.5.7	Given in clause
K_{54}	number of *screws* in each line	6.5.7	Given in clause
K_{56}	moisture content – *bolted* joint	6.6.6	Given in clause
K_{57}	number of *bolts* in each line	6.6.6	Given in clause
K_{58}	duration of loading – *toothed-plate connector* joint	6.7.6	Given in clause
K_{59}	moisture content – *toothed-plate connector* joint	6.7.6	Given in clause
K_{60}	end distance / edge distance / spacing of *toothed-plate connectors*	6.7.6	Table 79
K_{61}	number of *toothed-plate connectors* in each line	6.7.6	Equation
K_{62}	duration of loading – *split-ring connector* joint	6.8.5	Given in clause
K_{63}	moisture content – *split-ring connector* joint	6.8.5	Given in clause
K_{64}	end distance / edge distance / spacing of *split-ring connectors*	6.8.5	Tables 87,89,90
K_{65}	number of *split-ring connectors* in each line	6.8.5	Equation
K_{66}	duration of loading – *shear-plate connector* joint	6.9.6	Given in clause
K_{67}	moisture content – *shear-plate connector* joint	6.9.6	Given in clause
K_{68}	end distance / edge distance / spacing of *shear-plate connectors*	6.9.6	Tables 87,89,90
K_{69}	number of *shear-plate connectors* in each line	6.9.6	Equation
K_{70}	permissible shear stress for *glue-line*	6.10.1.3	0.9
K_C	end distance – connectors	6.7.6	Table 79,89
K_S	spacing – connectors	6.7.6	Tables 81,82,87
K_D	edge distance – connectors	6.9.6	Table 90

Table 6.1 Modification Factors

- ♦ split-ring connector joints   (Clause 6.8)
- ♦ shear-plate connector joints   (Clause 6.9)
- ♦ glued joints   (Clause 6.10)

A large number of modification factors are associated with the use of mechanical fasteners: these have been summarised in Table 6.1.

There are many proprietary types of fastener, such as punched metal plate fasteners with or without integral teeth, and splice plates (Figure 6.2), which are also used but are not included in the code.

Punched metal plate   Pre-formed splice plate

Figure 6.2

Many factors may influence the use of a particular type of fastener, e.g.

- ♦ method of assembly,
- ♦ connection details,
- ♦ purpose of connection,
- ♦ loading,
- ♦ permissible stresses,
- ♦ aesthetics.

Normally there are several methods of connection for any given joint which could provide an efficient structural solution. The choice will generally be dictated by consideration of cost, availability of skills, suitable fabrication equipment and desired finish required by the client. Glued joints generally require more rigorous conditions of application and control than mechanical fasteners.

The following is a summary of the types of fastener referred to in BS 5268 : Part 2 and their application in construction.

6.2 Nails   (Figure 6.3)

The most commonly used type of nails are (a)*'round plain wire'* nails. Two variations of this type are (b) *'clout nails'*, (often referred to as slate, felt or plasterboard nails), which are simply large versions with a larger diameter head, and (c) *'lost head nails'* in which the head is very small. The introduction of *'improved nails'* such as (d) *'square twisted'*, and (e) *'helically threaded and annular ringed shank nails'* with increased lateral and withdrawal resistance has proved very useful; particularly for fixing sheet materials to roofs and floors where 'popping' is often a problem with plain round nails.

Pneumatically driven nails, (f), when manufactured from suitably hardened and tempered steel, enable relatively straightforward fixing of timber to materials such as concrete, brickwork and stone.

Pre-drilling of holes may be required to avoid splitting and to enable use with dense hardwoods such as greenheart and keruing timbers. The pre-drilled holes should not be greater than $0.8 \times$ nail diameter.

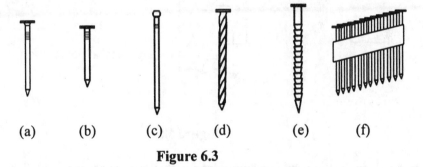

(a)   (b)   (c)   (d)   (e)   (f)

Figure 6.3

Nails are used for either locating timber e.g. a stud to a wall plate as in Figure 6.4(a), or for transferring forces such as the shear force and bending moment at a knee joint in a portal frame joint as shown in Figure 6.4(b).

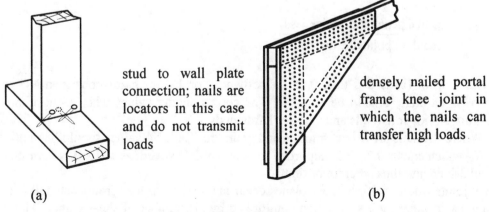

stud to wall plate connection; nails are locators in this case and do not transmit loads

densely nailed portal frame knee joint in which the nails can transfer high loads

(a)

(b)

Figure 6.4

The basic single-shear lateral loads and withdrawal loads for nails in timber-to-timber joints are given in Tables 54 and 55 respectively. The basic single-shear lateral loads for plywood-to-timber, tempered hardboard-to-timber and particle board-to-timber joints are given in Tables 56, 57 and 58.

The design of nailed joints is dependent on a number of factors, two of which are the *headside thickness* and the *pointside thickness* as shown in Figure 6.5:

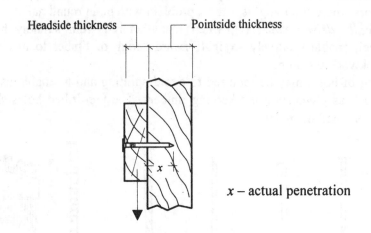

Figure 6.5

Standard values for the headside and pointside thicknesses are given in Table 54. In cases where the actual headside or pointside thickness is less than the standard Table 54 values the basic load is multiplied by the smaller of the following two ratios, (a) and (b):

(a) $\dfrac{\text{actual headside thickness}}{\text{standard headside thickness}}$, and

(b) $\dfrac{\text{actual penetration thickness}}{\text{standard pointside thickness}}$

If either (a) or (b) is less than 0.66 for softwoods or 1.0 for hardwoods then **NO load-carrying capacity** should be assumed. The corresponding values when using improved nails are 0.5 for softwoods and 0.75 for hardwoods.

Where the nails are driven into the end grain, the Table 54 values should be multiplied by K_{43} which equals 0.7. It is important to note that **NO withdrawal load** is permitted by a nail driven into the end grain of timber.

In joints where multiple shear planes occur the total shear load from each nail is equal to the basic value for a single plane multiplied by the number of shear planes. There are additional criteria relating to the timber thicknesses as indicated in Figure 6.6.

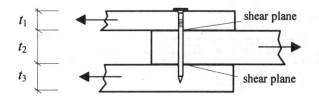

t_1
t_2
t_3

shear plane

shear plane

Figure 6.6

Multiple shear load/nail $=$ (2 × basic shear load) provided that:
$$t_2 \geq 0.85 \times \text{standard thickness (Table 54)}$$

When $t_1 <$ standard thickness   or
        $t_3 <$ standard thickness   or
        $t_2 < 0.85 \times$ standard thickness
Multiple shear load/nail equals the smaller of:
       (2 × basic shear load) × ratio (a)   and
       (2 × basic shear load) × ratio (b)
where ratio (a) and ratio (b) are as before.

The permissible load for a joint is determined by modifying the calculated basic load to allow for duration of loading (K_{48}), moisture content (K_{49}) and the number of nails in each line (K_{50}). Each of the modification factors K_{48}, K_{49} and K_{50} is defined in Clause 6.4.9.

It is necessary to ensure that adequate end and edge distances and spacing between nails is provided to avoid undue splitting. Minimum values are given in Table 53 for all nailed joints. When using Douglas fir the Table 53 values should be multiplied by 0.8.

6.2.1   *Example 6.1   Nailed Tension Splice*

A tension splice is shown in Figure 6.7. Using the data given design a suitable splice detail considering:

    i)   38 mm x 100 mm softwood splice plates,
    ii)   12 mm Finnish birch plywood,   and
    iii)   pre-drilled 1.5 mm thick mild steel plates

Timber   Douglas fir
              Service Class 2
              Strength Class C16
              Load duration considered long-term
Nails   3.35 mm diameter round wire x 65 mm long
              No pre-drilling

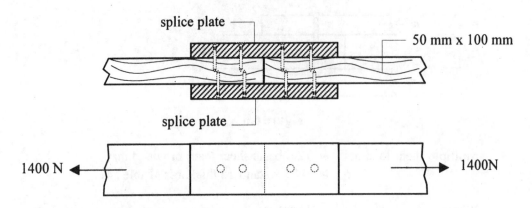

Figure 6.7

(i)   Timber-to-timber joint

Table 54   For nail diameter 3.35 mm, softwood not pre-drilled
                  Standard penetration   = 40 mm
                  Standard headside thickness   = 40 mm
                  Basic single shear lateral load = 369 kN

                  Actual headside thickness   = 38 mm   < standard

Clause 6.4.4.1 $\dfrac{\text{actual headside thickness}}{\text{standard headside thickness}}$ $= \dfrac{38}{40}$ = 0.95 > 0.66

                  Actual penetration thickness   = (65 – 38) = 27 mm   < standard

Clause 6.4.4.1 $\dfrac{\text{actual penetration thickness}}{\text{standard pointside thickness}}$ $= \dfrac{27}{40}$ = 0.68 > 0.66

Clause 6.4.4.2 Inner member   > 0.85 × standard thickness
Clause 6.4.4.3 penetration   = 27 mm   > minimum value of 15 mm

The Table 54 values should be multiplied by the smaller of the ratios in Clause 6.4.4.1 i.e. 0.68.

Basic single shear lateral load F = 369 × 0.68 = 251 N

Clause 6.4.9   Permissible load/nail F_{adm} = $F \times K_{48} \times K_{49} \times K_{50}$
where :
   F = basic load/nail
   K_{48} = load duration modification factor   long-term load K_{48} = 1.0
   K_{49} = moisture content modification factor   service class 2 K_{49} = 1.0
   K_{50} = number of nails in line modification factor   assume < 10 K_{50} = 1.0

$$F_{adm} = F \times K_{48} \times K_{49} \times K_{50} = 251 \times 1.0 \times 1.0 \times 1.0 = 251 \text{ N}$$

Number of nails required $= \dfrac{\text{Design load}}{F_{adm}} = \dfrac{1400}{251} = 5.6$ each side of splice

Adopt 6 nails each side   i.e. single line of three nails   or alternatively
Adopt 8 nails each side   i.e. two lines of two nails

Clause 6.4.3   Nail spacing
Table 53   (no pre-drilling)
Minimum End distance parallel to the grain $= 20d = (20 \times 3.35) = 67 \text{ mm}$
Minimum Edge distance perpendicular to the grain $= 5d = (5 \times 3.35) = 16.8 \text{ mm}$
Minimum distance between adjacent nails in any one line, parallel to the grain
$$= 20d = 67 \text{ mm}$$

Minimum distance between lines of nails perpendicular to the grain
$$= 10d = (10 \times 3.35) = 33.5 \text{ mm}$$

Nailing pattern assuming 6 nails each side

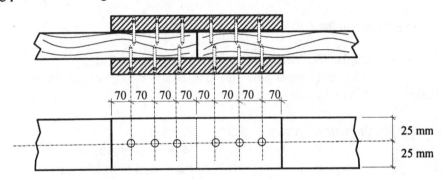

Total length of each splice plate $= 2 \times (4 \times 70) = 560 \text{ mm}$

Alternate pattern using 8 nails each side of the splice:

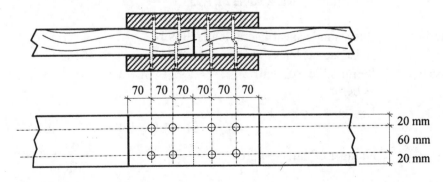

Total length of each splice plate $= 2 \times (3 \times 70) = 420 \text{ mm}$

(ii)   12 mm Finnish birch plywood-to-timber splice

Timber: Douglas fir, Strength Class C16, long-term loading
Nails: 3.35 mm diameter x 65 mm long in softwood, not pre-drilled

Table 56   Plywood is Group II (note 1 in Table 56)
Clause 6.4.6.2   minimum length of nail = 50 mm < actual length of 65 mm
                  Basic single shear lateral load = 353 N
Clause 6.4.9   Permissible load/nail $F_{adm} = F \times K_{48} \times K_{49} \times K_{50}$
                  as before:
                  $K_{48} = K_{49} = K_{50} = 1.0$

$$F_{adm} = 353 \times 1.0 \times 1.0 \times 1.0 = 353 \text{ N}$$

$$\text{Number of nails required} = \frac{\text{Design load}}{F_{adm}} = \frac{1400}{353} = 4$$

Adopt 4 nails in line or two lines of two nails similar to the previous splice. The Table 53 values for minimum nail spacings should be satisfied.

(iii)   Steel plate-to-timber splice

Timber: Douglas fir, Strength Class C16, long-term loading
Nails: 3.35 mm diameter x 65 mm long in softwood, not pre-drilled
Steel plate: 1.5 mm thick mild steel

Clause 6.4.5.1   minimum thickness of plate ≥ 1.2 mm
                                              ≥   0.3 × nail diameter
                                              = 0.3 × 3.35 = 1.005 mm
                  actual thickness of plate = 1.5 mm is adequate

Clause 6.5.4.2   Basic lateral load   = Table 54 value × K_{46}
                  Note: the hole diameter in the steel plate should equal the diameter of the nails, and K_{46} has a value of 1.25

Table 54   Basic single shear lateral load = 369 N
                  Basic lateral load   = 369 × 1.25 = 461 N
Clause 6.4.9   Permissible load/nail $F_{adm} = F \times K_{48} \times K_{49} \times K_{50}$
                  as before:
                  $K_{48} = K_{49} = K_{50} = 1.0$

$$F_{adm} = 461 \times 1.0 \times 1.0 \times 1.0 = 461 \text{ N}$$

$$\text{Number of nails required} = \frac{\text{Design load}}{F_{adm}} = \frac{1400}{461} = 3.04$$

Adopt 4 nails as in the case of Finnish-birch plywood splice plates.

6.3 Screws (Figure 6.8)

A very wide variety of shapes, finishes and types of screw are available. BS 5268 : Part 2 provides tables of basic lateral and withdrawal loads for screws ranging from 3.45 mm shank diameter (No. 6) to 7.72 mm shank diameter (No.18). As with nails, BS 5268 : Part 2 deals only with steel screws. The increased cost and slower rate of application limit the use of screws in purely structural work. The withdrawal resistance of screws is considerably greater than that of round wire nails whilst the lateral load-carrying capacity is nominally less since the yield strength of the threaded portion is smaller than the yield strength of the shank. The insertion of screws should be into pre-drilled holes with a diameter equal to the shank diameter and no deeper than the length of the shank. It is important to note that screws should not be driven by hammering since this significantly reduces the load-carrying capacity, particularly the withdrawal loads; they should be turned in the hole using a lubricant if necessary.

Screws are used for timber-to-timber connections, for fixing metal plates to timber and for plywood-to-timber joints. Basic single shear, lateral loads for screws into pre-drilled holes for timber-to-timber joints and for plywood-to-timber joints are given in Tables 60 and 62 respectively.

Where screws are driven into the end grain of timber, the Table 60 values should be multiplied by the end grain modification factor K_{43} which is equal to 0.7.
The Table 60 values apply provided:

♦ the headside member thickness is at least equal to the standard headside thickness given, and
♦ the penetration is at least twice the actual headside member thickness.

In situations where the headside member thickness is less than the tabulated standard value, provided

♦ the pointside screw penetration is at least twice the actual headside thickness, and
♦ the minimum headside member thickness is at least the shank diameter,

the basic loads are modified such that:

$$\text{Basic value} = \text{Table 60 value} \times \frac{\text{actual headside thickness}}{\text{standard headside thickness}}$$

In Table 62 the loads are dependent on a number of variables, i.e. plywood thickness and types, screw diameter and length and the timber strength class. The basic lateral loads for steel plate-to-timber joints is taken as the basic lateral load for timber-to-timber joints, (Table 60), multiplied by a modification factor K_{46} which equals 1.25.

The basic withdrawal loads for single screws is given in Table 61 for each 1 mm depth of penetration. As indicated in Figure 6.8(b), the pointside dimension is different when considering lateral loading and withdrawal resistance. The threaded length of most standard screws is approximately (0.67 × the overall length). As with nails, no withdrawal load should be assumed when a screw is driven into the end grain of timber.

The permissible load for a screwed joint is defined in Clause 6.6.6 as the product:

$$F_{adm} = F \times K_{52} \times K_{53} \times K_{54}$$

where:

F the basic load for a single screw,
K_{52} modification factor for duration of loading,
K_{53} modification factor for the moisture content,
K_{54} modification factor for the number of screws in each line
for each screw in the joint.

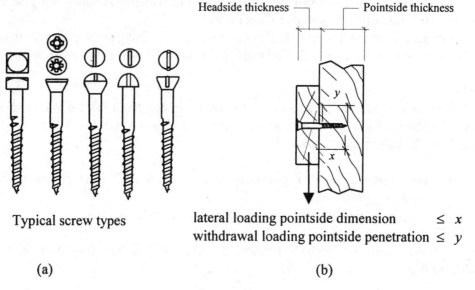

Headside thickness —   — Pointside thickness

Typical screw types   lateral loading pointside dimension   ≤ x
                             withdrawal loading pointside penetration ≤ y

(a)   (b)

Figure 6.8

6.3.1 Example 6.2 Screwed Tension Splice

A tension splice is shown in Figure 6.9. Using the data given determine the maximum medium-term load which can be transmitted by the screws indicated.

Data:

Timber: 50 mm thick x 100 mm wide softwood of strength class C18
Splice plates: 12 mm thick x 100 mm wide Swedish softwood plywood
Screws: No.8 (4.17 mm diameter), slotted, countersunk head woodscrews 38 mm
                 long in pre-drilled holes.
Service Class 2

Clause 6.5.3 and Table 59:   Screw spacing
minimum end distance parallel to grain   = 10d = 10 × 4.17= 4.17 mm
actual end distance parallel to grain   = 50 mm   adequate

minimum edge distance perpendicular to grain   = $5d$ = 5×4.17 = 20.9 mm
actual edge distance perpendicular to grain   = 25 mm   adequate
minimum distance between lines perpendicular to grain = $3d$ = 3×4.17 = 12.5 mm
actual distance between lines perpendicular to grain   = 50 mm   adequate
minimum distance between screws in line parallel to grain = $10d$ = 41.7 mm
actual distance between screws in line parallel to grain = 50 mm   adequate

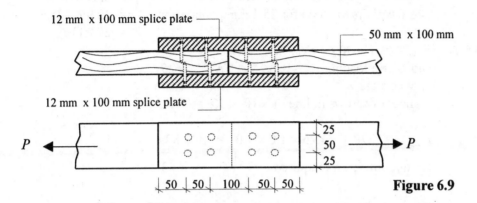

12 mm x 100 mm splice plate

50 mm x 100 mm

12 mm x 100 mm splice plate

P

25
50
25

P

50 50 100 50 50

Figure 6.9

The screw spacings, edge and end distances satisfy the Table 59 requirements.
Table 62 Basic single shear lateral loads
plywood thickness = 12 mm
plywood group   = I (see note 1 in Table 62)
screw size   = No.8
strength class   = C18
                   Basic single shear lateral load F = 385 N
Clause 6.5.7 $F_{adm} = F \times K_{52} \times K_{53} \times K_{54}$
                medium-term load K_{52} = 1.12
                service class 2 K_{53} = 1.0
                number of screws in line K_{54} = 1.0
          $F_{adm} = 385 \times 1.12 \times 1.0 \times 1.0$ = 431.2 N
Permissible load for eight screws = 8×431.2 = 3450 N

6.3.2 Example 6.3   *Wall Cladding Subject to Wind Suction*

A timber framed building has cladding screwed to timber studs as shown in
Figure 6.10. Using the data given, determine the number of screws required to resist the
wind suction pressure indicated.

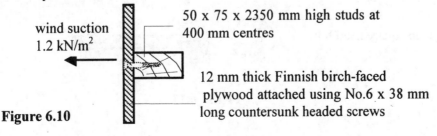

wind suction
1.2 kN/m^2

50 x 75 x 2350 mm high studs at
400 mm centres

12 mm thick Finnish birch-faced
plywood attached using No.6 x 38 mm
long countersunk headed screws

Figure 6.10

Load on one stud due to wind suction = $1.2 \times 0.4 \times 2.35$ = 1.13 kN

Clause 6.5.4.2 Basic withdrawal loads

Table 61   No. 6 screws x 38 mm long,   strength class C14 timber
     Basic withdrawal load/mm of penetration   = 10.96 kN
     minimum penetration of screw point   = 15 mm
     actual penetration of screw point   = $(38 - 12)$ = 26 mm
     length of threaded section of screw $\approx$ 0.67×38 = 25.4 mm
     Basic withdrawal load for 25.4 mm penetration   = 10.96×25.4
                 F = 278.3 N

Clause 6.5.7 F_{adm} = $F \times K_{52} \times K_{53} \times K_{54}$
     short-term loading K_{52} = 1.25
     service class 2 K_{53} = 1.0
     number of screws in line n < 10 K_{52} = 1.0

$$F_{adm} = 278.3 \times 1.25 \times 1.0 \times 1.0 = 347.8 \text{ N}$$

$$\text{Number of screws required} = \frac{1130}{347.8} = 3.25$$

$$\text{maximum spacing of screws} = \frac{2350}{3.25} = 723 \text{ say 700 mm}$$

Note: 3.35 mm diameter smooth round wire nails have a basic withdrawal load/mm of 1.62 N (see Table 55), and consequently many more nails would be required. Despite this the saving in time and effort may still justify using nails. This is particularly so if improved nails are used in which the basic withdrawal load can be enhanced by multiplying the smooth round nail value by K_{45}, which equals 1.5.

6.4 Bolts and Dowels

Bolts are normally made from ordinary mild steel with hexagonal or square heads and nuts, see Figure 6.11:

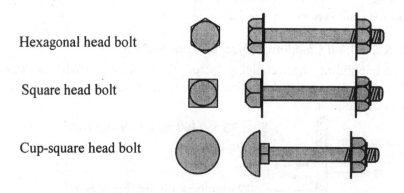

Hexagonal head bolt

Square head bolt

Cup-square head bolt

Figure 6.11

Generally bolts and dowels (pieces of round steel rod fitting tightly into drilled holes) are used in double or multiple shear joints as shown in Figures 6.12 to 6.14.

The recommendations for the design of bolted and dowelled joints are given in Section 6.6 of BS 5268 : Part 2. The code provides single shear loads for bolts and dowels ranging from 8 mm diameter to 24 mm in increments of 4 mm for long/medium/short and very short term loading. The threaded length of bolts is often inadequate (i.e. usually 2 × bolt diameter), and it may be necessary to order bolts with an extended threaded length. This is particularly so if they are to be used in conjunction with imbedded connectors (see section 6.8). Bolts should always be used with appropriate washers (diameter ≥ 3 × bolt diameter and thickness ≥ 0.25 × bolt diameter), fitted under the head of each bolt and under each nut unless an equivalent bearing area is provided by e.g. a steel plate. When the nut is tightened at least one complete turn of the thread of the bolt should protrude through.

Whilst a bolt hole should be drilled to a diameter as close as practicable to the nominal bolt diameter, and no more than 2 mm larger than the bolt diameter, dowels should be inserted in pre-bored holes having a diameter not greater than the dowel itself. Since clearance holes reduce the capacity of bolted joints, there is a tendency to adopt the use of dowels. In addition to an increased structural efficiency it is possible to insert dowels which do not fully penetrate the thickness of a member hence producing a more acceptable visual appearance.

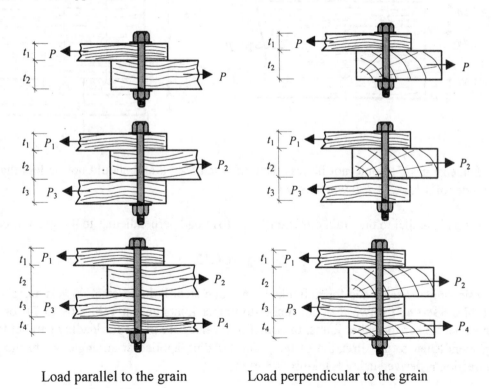

Load parallel to the grain	Load perpendicular to the grain
Figure 6.12	**Figure 6.13**

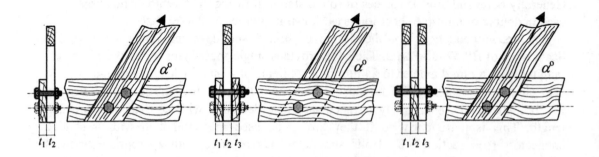

Load inclined at an angle α to the grain

Figure 6.14

The minimum spacings, end and edge distances of bolts are given in Table 75 and illustrated in Figure 6.15:

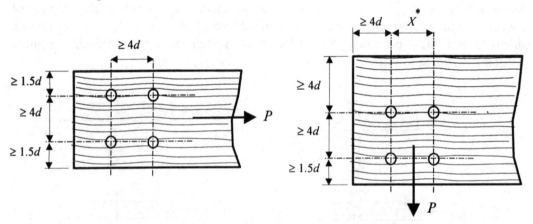

* Dimension 'X' should not be less than $5d$ when $t \geq 3d$ and should not be less than the greater of $3d$ or $(2 + t/d)$ when $t < 3d$.

(a) Load parallel to the grain direction   (b) Load perpendicular to the grain direction

Figure 6.15

Basic single shear loads for individual 4.6 grade steel bolts or steel dowels are given in Tables 63 to 68 for two member timber-to-timber joints and in Tables 69 to 74 for three member timber-to-timber joints. In each Table values are given for loading parallel to and perpendicular to the direction of the grain. Loading applied at an angle 'α' to the grain direction is derived using Hankinso's Formula:

$$F = F_{||} \, F_{\perp} \, (F_{||} \sin^2\alpha + F_{\perp}\cos^2\alpha)$$

where:

F is the basic load in a direction 'α' to the grain direction

$F_{||}$ is the basic load parallel to the direction of the grain

$F_{\perp}$ is the basic load perpendicular to the grain

The permissible load/bolt for a joint is specified in Clause 6.6.6 as:

$$F_{adm} = F \times K_{56} \times K_{57} \text{ (per shear plane)}$$

where:

F is the basic single shear load for a bolt,

K_{56} is the modification factor for moisture content,

K_{57} is the modification factor for the number of bolts in each line.

In the case of steel plate-to-timber bolted joints the steel plate should have a minimum thickness of 2.5 mm or 0.3 × bolt diameter, whichever is the greater as indicated in Clause 6.6.5.1. In addition, the basic single shear loads given in Tables 63 to 74 should be multiplied by the modification factor K_{46} (which has a value of 1.25), when the applied load is parallel to the grain. This factor **does not** apply when the load is perpendicular to the grain.

It is important to note that the effective cross-sectional area of a member at a bolted joint is determined by deducting the net projected area of the bolt holes from the gross area of the cross-section. When assessing the net projected area, all bolts that lie within a distance of two bolt diameters, measured parallel to the grain from the cross-section, should be considered as occurring at that cross-section.

6.4.1 Example 6.4   Bolted Joints with Load Parallel to the Grain Direction

Using the data provided, determine the permissible medium-term loads for the two member, three member and four member joints shown in Figure 6.16:

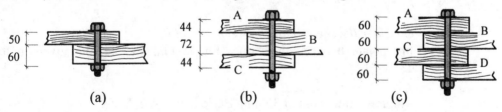

(a)   (b)   (c)

Figure 6.16

Data:

Timber strength class C24

Service class 2

M12 4.6 grade bolt

(a)   Two member joint:

Table 65:   Medium term loading,   Loading parallel to the grain, M12 bolts

Clause 6.6.4.1   Loading for the thinner member should be used to determine the basic load
Interpolation between thicknessses of timber indicated in the Tables is permitted.
Minimum thickness of 47 mm Basic load = 1.96 kN
Minimum thickness of 60 mm Basic load = 2.5 kN

Actual thickness used 50 mm   Basic load $= 1.96 + \dfrac{3}{10}(2.5 - 1.96)$

$= 2.12$ kN

Clause 6.6.6 $F_{adm} = F \times K_{56} \times K_{57}$
Service class is 2 K_{56} = 1.0
One bolt used K_{57} = 1.0
$F_{adm} = 2.12 \times 1.0 \times 1.0$ = 2.12 kN

Clause 6.6.3   Bolt spacing
Table 75   Loading parallel to the grain direction
loaded end distance $\geq \; 7d$ = (7×12) = 84 mm
loaded edge distance $\geq \; 1.5d$ = (1.5×12) = 18 mm

(b)   Three member joint:
Table 71:   Medium term loading,   Loading parallel to the grain, M12 bolts
The values given for three member joints apply where the outer members have the tabulated thickness and the inner member is twice as thick. In cases where the thicknesses are different interpolation between the given values is permitted.
In this case the inner thickness $< 2 \times$ outer thickness

i.e. $\dfrac{\text{inner thickness}}{2}$ $= \dfrac{72}{2}$ = 36 mm   < 44 mm

Consider the shear plane between A and B
Interpolate between the values for 35 mm and 44 mm given in the Table 71

Minimum thickness of 35 mm Basic load = 2.75 kN
Minimum thickness of 44 mm Basic load = 2.87 kN

Actual thickness used 36 mm   Basic load $= 2.75 + \dfrac{1}{9}(2.87 - 2.75)$

$= 2.76$ kN

Consider the shear plane between B and C
The same basic load applies as in the shear plane between A and B
Total basic load of bolt in double shear $F = 2 \times 2.76$ = 5.52 kN

Clause 6.6.6 $F_{adm} = F \times K_{56} \times K_{57}$
Service class is 2 K_{56} = 1.0
One bolt used K_{57} = 1.0
$F_{adm} = 5.52 \times 1.0 \times 1.0$ = 5.52 kN

Clause 6.6.3   Bolt spacing as in case (a)

(c)   Four member joint
Clause 6.6.4.2 indicates that multiple member joints should be regarded as a series of three member joints, i.e. use Tables 69 to 74 when considering each shear plane. It is important to remember that when a member has a shear plane on both sides its effective thickness should be taken as half the actual thickness; if a member has a shear plane on one side only, the effective thickness is equal to the actual thickness.

There are three shear planes in this connection, each of which must be considered seperately before adding together, to determine the basic load F.

Table 71:   Medium term loading,   Loading parallel to the grain, M12 bolts

In this case the inner thickness < 2 × outer thickness

$$\text{i.e.} \ \frac{\text{inner thickness}}{2} \ = \ \frac{60}{2} \ = \ 30 \text{ mm} \qquad < \ 60 \text{ mm}$$

Consider the shear plane between A and B
Interpolate between the values for 22 mm and 35 mm given in the Table 71

Minimum thickness of 22 mm   Basic load   = 2.21 kN
Minimum thickness of 35 mm   Basic load   = 2.75 kN
Actual thickness used 30 mm   Basic load $= 2.21 + \dfrac{8}{13}\left(2.75 - 2.21\right)$

$$F_{AB} = 2.54 \text{ kN}$$

Consider the shear plane between B and C
The same basic load applies as in the shear plane between A and B since both members have shear planes on each side and the effective thicknesses equal 30 mm
Basic load $F_{BC} = 2.54$ kN

Consider the shear plane between C and D
This shear plane is the same as the one between A and B
Basic load $F_{CD} = 2.54$ kN
Total basic load of bolt in multiple shear $F = 3 \times 2.54 = 7.62$ kN

Clause 6.6.6 $F_{\text{adm}} = F \times K_{56} \times K_{57}$
                    Service class is 2 K_{56} = 1.0
                    One bolt used K_{57} = 1.0
                    $F_{\text{adm}} = 7.62 \times 1.0 \times 1.0$ = 7.62 kN
Clause 6.6.3   Bolt spacing as in case (a)

6.4.2 *Example 6.5* *Bolted Joints with Load Perpendicular to the Grain Direction*

Using the data provided, determine the permissible medium-term loads for the two member, three member and four member joints shown in Figure 6.17:

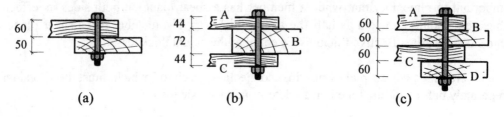

(a)   (b)   (c)

Figure 6.17

Data:
Timber strength class C22
Service class 2
M16 4.6 grade bolt

(a)   Two member joint:
Table 64:   Long term loading,   Loading perpendicular to the grain, M16 bolts
                    In this case the basic load must be evaluated for member A for loading parallel to the grain direction and for member B for loading perpendicular to the grain direction. The smaller of the two values is the required basic load.

                    Consider member A – load parallel to the grain direction
                    Minimum thickness of 60 mm Basic load   = 2.19 kN

                    Consider member B – load perpendicular to the grain direction
                    Actual thickness is 50 mm with a shear plane on one side only, use interpolation between the 47 mm and 60 mm values given in Table 64
                    Minimum thickness of 47 mm Basic load   = 1.43 kN
                    Minimum thickness of 60 mm Basic load   = 1.83 kN

                    Actual thickness 50 mm Basic load $= 1.43 + \dfrac{3}{13}(1.83 - 1.43)$

                                                              = 1.52 kN
                              Use the smaller value   F = 1.52 kN
Clause 6.6.6 $F_{\text{adm}} = F \times K_{56} \times K_{57}$
                    Service class is 2 K_{56} = 1.0

One bolt used $\quad K_{57} \quad = 1.0$
$F_{adm} = 1.52 \times 1.0 \times 1.0 \quad = 1.52 \text{ kN}$

Clause 6.6.3   Bolt spacing

Member A
Table 75   Loading parallel to the grain direction
loaded end distance $\quad\geq\quad 7d \quad = (7 \times 16) \quad = 112 \text{ mm}$
loaded edge distance $\quad\geq\quad 1.5d = (1.5 \times 16) \quad = 24 \text{ mm}$
Member B
Table 75   Loading perpendicular to the grain direction
loaded end distance $\quad\geq\quad 4d \quad = (4 \times 16) \quad = 64 \text{ mm}$
loaded edge distance $\quad\geq\quad 4d \quad = (4 \times 16) \quad = 64 \text{ mm}$

(b)   Three member joint:
Table 70:   Long term loading,   Loading perpendicular to the grain, M16 bolts

In this case the basic load must be evaluated for members A and C for loading parallel to the grain direction and for member B for loading perpendicular to the grain direction. The smaller of the two values is the required basic load for a particular shear plane. This must be carried out for both shear planes.

Shear plane between A and B
Consider member A – load parallel to the grain direction
Minimum thickness of 44 mm Basic load   = 3.88 kN

Consider member B – load perpendicular to the grain direction
Actual thickness is 72 mm with a shear plane on both sides, use an effective thickness of 36 mm
Interpolate between the 35 mm and 44 mm values given in Table 70

Minimum thickness of 35 mm Basic load   = 2.57 kN
Minimum thickness of 44 mm Basic load   = 3.23 kN

Actual thickness 50 mm Basic load $\qquad = 2.57 + \dfrac{1}{9}(3.23 - 2.57)$
$$= 2.64 \text{ kN}$$
Use the smaller value $\qquad F_{AB} = 2.64 \text{ kN}$

Shear plane between B and C
The joint is symmetrical and the same value of basic shear as for shear plane AB applies to plane BC   i.e. $F_{BC} = 2.64 \text{ kN}$

Total basic load of bolt in double shear $F = 2 \times 2.64 \quad = \quad 5.28 \text{ kN}$

Clause 6.6.6 $F_{adm} = F \times K_{56} \times K_{57}$
Service class is 2 K_{56} = 1.0
One bolt used K_{57} = 1.0
F_{adm} = 5.28 × 1.0 × 1.0 = 5.28 kN

Clause 6.6.3   Bolt spacing as in case (a)

(c)   Four member joint
There are three shear planes in this connection, each of which must be considered seperately before adding together, to determine the basic load F.

Table 70:   Long term loading, Loading perpendicular to the grain, M16 bolts

Shear plane between A and B
Consider member A – load parallel to the grain direction
Minimum thickness of 60 mm Basic load   = 4.06 kN

Consider member B – load perpendicular to the grain direction
Actual thickness is 60 mm with a shear plane on both sides, use an effective thickness of 30 mm
Interpolate between the 22 mm and 35 mm values given in Table 70

Minimum thickness of 22 mm Basic load   = 1.62 kN
Minimum thickness of 35 mm Basic load   = 2.57 kN

Actual thickness 30 mm Basic load $= 1.62 + \dfrac{8}{13}(2.57 - 1.62)$
                                         $= 2.20$ kN

Use the smaller value $F_{AB} = 2.20$ kN

Shear planes between B and C, and C and D give the same result
Total basic load of bolt in multiple shear $F = 3 \times 2.20 =$ 6.6 kN

Clause 6.6.6 $F_{adm} = F \times K_{56} \times K_{57}$
Service class is 2 K_{56} = 1.0
One bolt used K_{57} = 1.0
F_{adm} = 6.6 × 1.0 × 1.0   = 6.6 kN

Clause 6.6.3   Bolt spacing as in case (a)

6.4.3 Example 6.6   *Bolted Joints with Load Inclined to the Grain Direction*

Using the data provided, determine the permissible short-term loads for the two member, three member and four member joints shown in Figure 6.18:

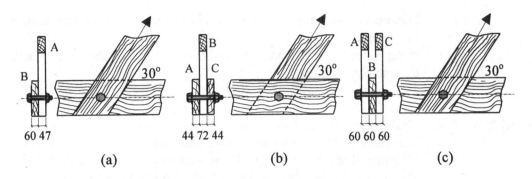

Figure 6.18

Data:
Timber strength class C14
Service class 2
1/M12 4.6 grade bolts

(a)   Two member joint:

Table 63:   Short term loading,   M12 bolts

Consider member A   the loading is parallel to the grain
Minimum thickness of 47 mm Basic load   = 1.83 kN

Consider member B   the loading is inclined at an angle of 30° to the grain direction and the basic load should be obtained using Hankinson's formula;

$$F = F_{||} \, F_{,\perp} / (F_{||} \, \sin^2\alpha + F_\perp \, \cos^2\alpha)$$

Minimum thickness of 60 mm Basic load parallel to grain   = 2.33 kN
Minimum thickness of 60 mm Basic load perpendicular grain = 2.02 kN
$$F = (2.33 \times 2.02)/(2.33 \times \sin^2 30° + 2.02 \times \cos^2 30°) = 2.24 \text{ kN}$$

Use the smaller value of the two i.e. $F = 1.83$ kN

Clause 6.6.6 $F_{adm} = F \times K_{56} \times K_{57}$
Service class is 2 K_{56} = 1.0
One bolt used K_{57} = 1.0
$F_{adm} = 1.83 \times 1.0 \times 1.0 = 1.83$ kN

The end and edge distances should satisfy the requirements of Table 75 as before.

(b)   Three member joint, load parallel to the inside single member

Table 71:   Short term loading,   M12 bolts
                   There are two shear planes. The maximum load is governed by the smaller of the sum of the two outer members each based on a minimum

thickness of 44 mm or the inner member based on a minimum thickness of 36 mm.

Note: since a shear plane occurs on *both* sides of the inner member 0.5 × thickness is used.

Table 69

Consider the shear plane between A and B
Consider member A load inclined at angle of 30^0 to the grain direction
Minimum thickness of 44 mm Basic load parallel   = 2.75 kN
Minimum thickness of 44 mm Basic load perpendicular = 2.52 kN
$F = (2.75 \times 2.52)/(2.75 \times \sin^2 30° + 2.52 \times \cos^2 30°) = 2.69$ kN

Consider member B load parallel to the grain direction
Interpolate between the values for 35 mm and 44 mm given in the Table 69 for short term M12 bolts
Minimum thickness of 35 mm   Basic load   = 2.65 kN
Minimum thickness of 44 mm   Basic load   = 2.75 kN

Actual thickness 36 mm   Basic load $= 2.65 + \dfrac{1}{9}(2.75 - 2.65)$

$= 2.66$ kN

Use the smaller value $F = 2.66$ kN
Consider the shear plane between B and C
The same basic load applies as in the shear plane between A and B
Total basic load of bolt in double shear $F = 2 \times 2.66 = 5.32$ kN

Clause 6.6.6 $F_{adm} = F \times K_{56} \times K_{57}$
Service class is 2 K_{56} = 1.0
One bolt used K_{57} = 1.0
$F_{adm} = 5.32 \times 1.0 \times 1.0 = 5.32$ kN

Clause 6.6.3   Bolt spacing as in case (a)

(c)   Three member joint, load parallel to the outside double member
Table 71:   Short term loading, Loading parallel to the inside single member, M12 bolts
As in (b) there are two shear planes. The maximum load is governed by the smaller of the sum of the two outer members each based on a minimum thickness of 60 mm or the inner member based on a minimum thickness of 30 mm.

Consider the shear plane between A and B

Consider member A load parallel to the grain direction
Minimum thickness of 60 mm Basic load parallel $\quad$ = 3.04 kN

Consider member B load inclined at angle of 30⁰ to the grain direction
Interpolate between the values for 22 mm and 35 mm given in the Table 69 for short term M12 bolts

Minimum thickness $\quad$ = 22 mm $\quad$ Basic load parallel $\quad$ = 2.05 kN
Minimum thickness $\quad$ = 35 mm $\quad$ Basic load parallel $\quad$ = 2.65 kN

Actual thickness $\quad$ = 30 mm $\quad$ Basic load $\quad$ $= 2.05 + \dfrac{8}{13}(2.65 - 2.05)$

$\quad = 2.42$ kN

Minimum thickness $\quad$ = 22 mm $\quad$ Basic load perpendicular = 1.79 kN
Minimum thickness $\quad$ = 35 mm $\quad$ Basic load perpendicular = 2.45 kN

Actual thickness $\quad$ = 30 mm $\quad$ Basic load $\quad$ $= 1.79 + \dfrac{8}{13}(2.45 - 1.79)$

$\quad = 2.20$ kN

$$F = (2.42 \times 2.2)/(2.42 \times \sin^2 30° + 2.2 \times \cos^2 30°) = 2.36 \text{ kN}$$

Use the smaller value $\quad F = 2.36$ kN

Consider the shear plane between B and C
The same basic load applies as in the shear plane between A and B
Total basic load of bolt in double shear $F = 2 \times 2.36 = 4.72$ kN

Clause 6.6.6 $\quad F_{adm} = F \times K_{56} \times K_{57}$
$\qquad\qquad$ Service class is 2 K_{56} $\quad$ = 1.0
$\qquad\qquad$ One bolt used $\quad K_{57}$ $\quad$ = 1.0
$\qquad\qquad F_{adm} = 4.72 \times 1.0 \times 1.0$ $\quad$ = 4.72 kN

Clause 6.6.3 $\quad$ Bolt spacing as in case (a)

In all cases above the permissible loads have been calculated for one bolt. In joints containing more than one bolt the total permissible load is determined by adding the permissible loads for each bolt in the joint.

6.4.4 Example 6.7   Bolted Knee-Brace

A structure is shown in Figure 6.19 in which two knee-braces are used to resist the lateral wind forces on a timber frame. Check the suitability of the bolt details to transmit the loading indicated.

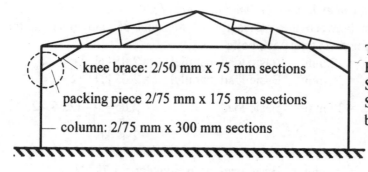

knee brace: 2/50 mm x 75 mm sections

packing piece 2/75 mm x 175 mm sections

column: 2/75 mm x 300 mm sections

Timber: Strength Class C27
Bolts: M20 grade 4.6
Service Class 2
Short Term loading in knee-brace = 30 kN

Figure 6.19

(a)   Column to packing connection
This connection is the same type as the three-member joint with the load parallel to the inside member in Example 6.5(b). Use Table 72 for shear values.

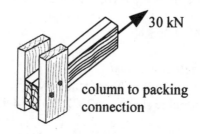

column to packing connection

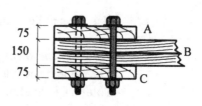

Consider shear plane between members A and B

Member A: Load applied at 40^0 to grain direction

Minimum thickness	= 72 mm	Basic load parallel	= 8.35 kN
Minimum thickness	= 97 mm	Basic load parallel	= 9.27 kN

$$\text{Actual thickness} \quad = 75 \text{ mm} \quad \text{Basic load} \quad = 8.35 + \frac{3}{25}(9.27 - 8.35)$$

$$= 8.46 \text{ kN}$$

Minimum thickness	= 72 mm	Basic load perpendicular	= 7.3 kN
Minimum thickness	= 97 mm	Basic load perpendicular	= 7.95 kN

$$\text{Actual thickness} \quad = 75 \text{ mm} \quad \text{Basic load} \quad = 7.3 + \frac{3}{25}(7.95 - 7.3)$$

$$= 7.38 \text{ kN}$$

$F = (8.46 \times 7.38)/(8.46 \times \sin^2 40° + 7.38 \times \cos^2 40°) = 7.98$ kN

Consider member B load parallel to the grain direction

$$\frac{\text{actual thickness}}{2} = \frac{150}{2} = 75 \text{ mm}$$

| Minimum thickness | = 72 mm | Basic load parallel to grain | = 8.35 kN |
| Actual thickness | = 75 mm | Basic load parallel to grain | > 8.35 kN |

Use the smaller value $F = 7.98$ kN

Consider the shear plane between members B and C
The same basic load applies as in the shear plane between A and B

Total basic load for single bolt in double shear $F = 2 \times 7.98 = 15.96$ kN
Total basic load for two bolts in double shear equals $2F = 2 \times 15.96 = 31.92$ kN

Clause 6.6.6 $F_{adm} = F \times K_{56} \times K_{57}$
Service class is 2 K_{56} $= 1.0$

Two bolt used K_{57} $= 1 - \dfrac{3(2-1)}{100} = 0.97$

$F_{adm} = 31.92 \times 1.0 \times 0.97 = 30.96$ kN $>$ applied load of 30 kN

(b)   Knee-brace to packing connection
This connection is the same type as the three-member joint with all members
subject to loading parallel to the grain, as in Example 6.3.

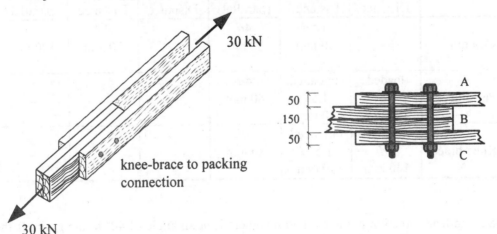

30 kN

knee-brace to packing
connection

50
150
50

A
B
C

30 kN

Consider the shear plane between A and B
Interpolate between the values for 47 mm and 60 mm given in Table 72.

Minimum thickness = 47 mm   Basic load parallel to the grain = 7.83 kN
Minimum thickness = 60 mm   Basic load parallel to the grain = 8.03 kN

Actual thickness used 50 mm

$$\text{Basic load} = 7.83 + \frac{3}{13}(8.03 - 7.83)$$

$$= 7.88 \text{ kN}$$

Consider the shear plane between B and C
The same basic load applies as in the shear plane between A and B
Total basic load of bolt in double shear $F = 2 \times 7.88$ $= 15.76$ kN

Total basic load for two bolts in double shear equals $2F = 2 \times 15.76 = 31.52$ kN

Clause 6.6.6 $F_{adm} = F \times K_{56} \times K_{57}$
Service class is 2 K_{56} $= 1.0$

Two bolts used K_{57} $= 1 - \dfrac{3(2-1)}{100} = 0.97$

$F_{adm} = 31.52 \times 1.0 \times 0.97$ $= 30.57$ kN $>$ applied load of 30 kN

The edge/end distances and spacing should be checked to ensure that the requirements of Table 75 are satisfied.

	Loading parallel to the grain			Loading perpendicular to the grain		
	End Distance	Edge Distance	Spacing (parallel)	End Distance	Edge Distance	Spacing (parallel)
Column	–	1.5d 30 mm	4d 80 mm	–	4d 80 mm	5d 100 mm
Packing	loaded 7d 140 mm	unloaded 1.5d 30 mm	4d 80 mm	–	–	–
Knee-brace	loaded 7d 140 mm	unloaded 1.57d 30 mm	4d 80 mm	–	–	–

Note: The load direction in the column members is at an angle of 40° to the grain. If the values relating to both the parallel and perpendicular directions are satisfied as in this case, they will also be satisfactory for the inclined load case.

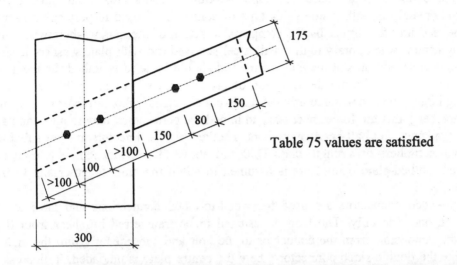

Table 75 values are satisfied

6.5 Connectored Joints

6.5.1 Toothed-plate Connectors

Toothed-plate connectors consist of a circular plate of steel with toothed edges as shown in Figure 6.20.

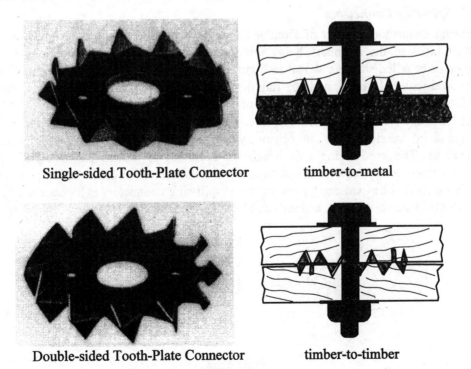

Single-sided Tooth-Plate Connector   timber-to-metal

Double-sided Tooth-Plate Connector   timber-to-timber

Figure 6.20

Double-sided connectors are used for timber-to-timber connections and have teeth projecting alternately on either side. This type of connector is used in permanent joints and is imbedded into the timber by the compressive action of the nuts/washers when the bolts are tightened. A temporary high tensile steel screwed rod with plate washers larger than the connectors and nuts at the ends of the rod should be used to imbed the teeth of toothed-plate connectors before the insertion of the permanent ordinary mild steel bolt. When using large connectors, some tropical hardwoods such as iroko, jarrah or teak, or in multiple member joints the forces necessary to imbed the connectors, may require the use of a ratchet spanner and ball-bearing washers. Toothed-plate connectors are not suitable for very dense timbers of strength class D50 and above. The permanent bolt used in double-sided toothed-plate connectors is assumed to stitch the units together and to be unloaded.

Single-sided connectors are used for wood-to-metal connections and have teeth projecting on one side only. The load is assumed to be transferred by shear from the timber to the connector, from the connector to the bolt and subsequently into the metal plate. Unlike the double-sided connector where the centre plate is unloaded, in this case the connector centre plate is loaded and consequently is stiffened as shown in Figure 6.20. The single-sided connector is utilised in temporary or demountable structures where each member has a separate connector imbedded. The connectors are then placed back-to-back when the structure is assembled. The transfer of load is similar to that above, i.e. timber – connector – bolt – connector – timber.

6.5.2 Split-ring Connectors

Split-ring connectors consist of circular bands of steel placed in pre-cut grooves in the contact faces of the members being joined. The connectors are available with either straight or bevelled sides as shown in Figure 6.21. Two connector sizes, 64 mm diameter to be used with M12 bolts, and 102 mm diameter to be used with M20 bolts, are given in BS 5268 : Part 2. Various manufacturers provide a wider range. Both versions transfer the same load; the bevelled type however is easier to position and produces less slip than the straight-sided version. This is obviously advantageous when considering structural deflections. The groove-ring into which the split-ring is placed has a slightly larger diameter than the connector and consequently the connector is slightly sprung open when it is in position. The load carrying capacity of split-ring connectors is higher than double-sided tooth-plate connectors, and they can be used more easily in very dense timbers.

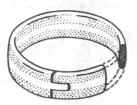 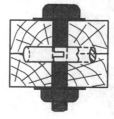

Split-ring connector

Figure 6.21

6.5.3 Shear-plate Connectors

Shear-plate connectors, as shown in Figure 6.22, are most frequently used for timber to structural steel joints or as in two single-sided tooth-plate connectors for demountable structures. Similar to split-ring connectors, with slightly lower load capacity, two sizes are given in BS 5268 : Part 2, 67 mm diameter and 102 mm diameter, both used with M20 bolts. The strength of the smaller connector is dependent on the strength of the central metal plate. The larger connector has a reinforced centre plate resulting in its strength being governed by the shear strength of the bolt. A recess is cut into the timber into which the shear-plate connector is placed. Unlike the split-ring connector, the diameter of the recess is the same as that of the connector.

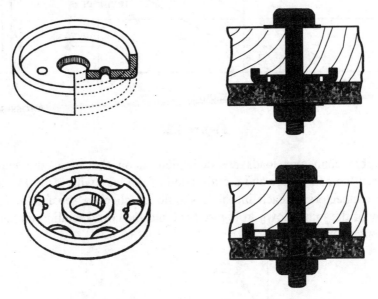

Figure 6.22   Shear-plate connectors

Care must be taken when preparing and assembling a connectored joint. Advice is given in the code with respect to each type of connector and should be followed. Since shrinkage is inherent in timber as it dries out and reaches an equilibrium moisture content, it is important to revisit timber joints which use bolts some time after erection and retighten any bolts which may have loosened.

6.6   Example 6.8   Connectored Joints

A node of a bolted, connectored lattice girder is shown in Figure 6.23. Using the loads given, check the suitability of the joint considering:

i)	tooth-plate connectors	(75 mm diameter M12 bolts),	
ii)	split-ring connectors	(64 mm diameter M12 bolts)	and
iii)	shear-plate connectors	(67 mm diameter M20 bolts)	

Data: Assume all loading to be medium-term
            Main tie: 2/50 x 225 mm   *Diagonal:*   1 /50 x 150 mm
            Upright: 1/50 x 150 mm   *Timber:*   Strength Class C27

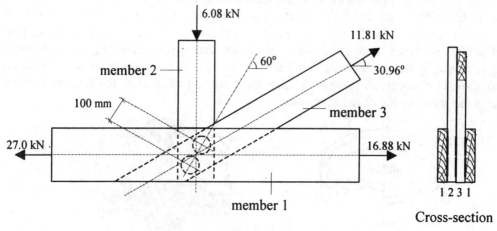

Figure 6.23

The allowable connector loads are dependent upon the edge, and end distances, spacing between the connectors and the direction of the load with respect to the grain. In this joint the connectors at each interface should be checked separately. Consider the exploded view of the joint shown in Figure 6.24 and the corresponding forces transferred through the connectors.

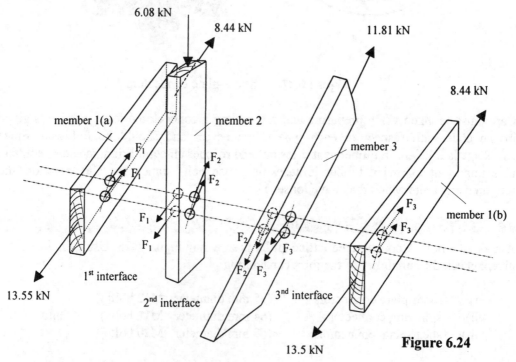

Figure 6.24

Consider the 1ˢᵗ· Interface: *(consider the left-hand side first)*

Member 1(a)

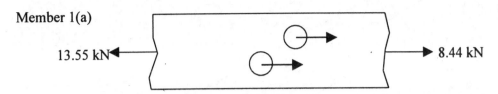

Resultant member force = (13.5 − 8.44)   = 5.06 kN ⟵   horizontal
Force on connectors   = 5.06 kN ⟶   horizontal
Grain direction is horizontal
Angle of connector force to grain direction   = 0°

Member 2

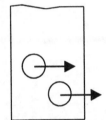

Connector force = 5.06 kN ⟶   horizontal
Grain direction is vertical
Angle of connector force to grain direction   = 90°

Consider the 2ⁿᵈ· Interface: *(consider the left-hand side first)*

Member 2

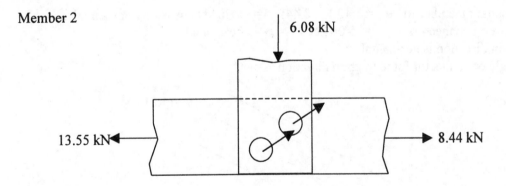

Resultant member force = $\sqrt{6.08^2 + (13.5 - 8.44)^2}$ = 7.91 kN

Angle of resultant force to vertical $\beta = \tan^{-1}\left(\dfrac{6.01}{5.06}\right)$ = 49.9°

Force on connectors   = 7.91 kN
Grain direction is vertical
Angle of connector force to grain direction   = 49.9°

Member 3

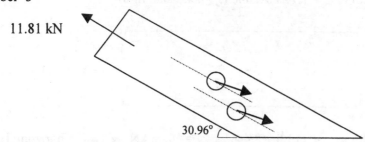

11.81 kN

30.96°

Connector force   = 7.91 kN   (49.9° to the vertical)
Grain direction is 30.96° to the horizontal (59.04° to the vertical)
Angle of connector force to grain direction   = (59.04° − 49.9°) = 9.14°

Consider the 3rd Interface: *(consider the right-hand side)*

Member 1(b)

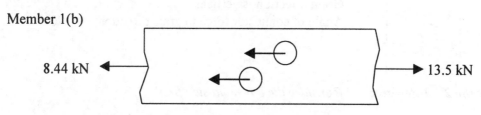

8.44 kN   13.5 kN

Resultant member force = (13.5 − 8.44)   = 5.06 kN ⟵   horizontal
Force on connectors   = 5.06 kN ⟶   horizontal
Grain direction is horizontal
Angle of connector force to grain direction   = 0°

Member 3   ⟱ 11.81 kN

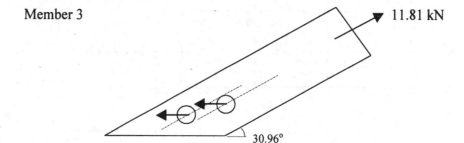

30.96°

Connector force = 5.06 kN   horizontal ⟵
Grain direction is vertical
Angle of connector force to grain direction   = 30.96°

The forces on each of the connectors in each of the members are summarised separately
for each interface in Table 6.2.

Summary of Applied Connector Forces - (2 connectors)						
	1st. Interface		2nd. Interface		3rd. Interface	
Member	Force (kN)	Angle to grain direction	Force (kN)	Angle to grain direction	Force (kN)	Angle to grain direction
1(a)	5.06	0°				
2	5.06	90°	7.91	49.9°		
3			17.55	9.14°	5.06	30.96°
1(b)					5.06	0°

Table 6.2

The capacity of connectors is dependent on the end and edge distance and the spacing of the units. In this joint, the details are given in Figures 6.25 – 27.

Member 1

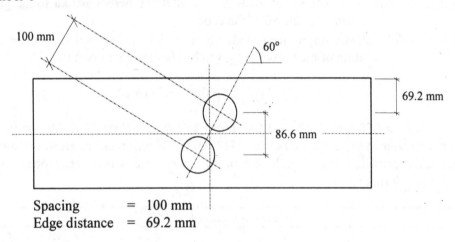

Spacing = 100 mm
Edge distance = 69.2 mm

Figure 6.25

Member 2

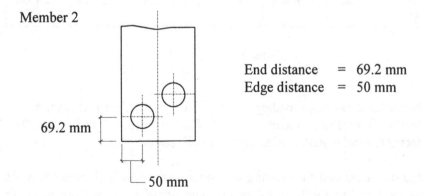

End distance = 69.2 mm
Edge distance = 50 mm

Figure 6.26

Member 3

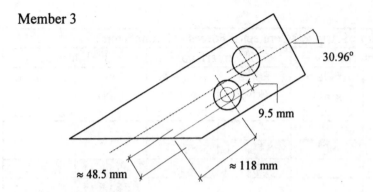

30.96°

9.5 mm

≈ 118 mm

≈ 48.5 mm

End distance   ≈ 118 mm
Edge distance   ≈ 48.5 mm   **Figure 6.27**

6.6.1   Toothed-plate Connectors   (Clause 6.7)

Clause 6.7.6   Permissible load/connector F_{adm} $=$ $F \times K_{58} \times K_{59} \times K_{60} \times K_{61}$

Clause 6.7.4.3 Basic values for loads (F), parallel and perpendicular to the grain, are given in Table 80 of the code.

Clause 6.6.4.1 Basic single shear loads where the load is inclined at an angle α° to the grain of the timber are given by Hankinson's Formula:

$$F = F_{||}F_\perp/(F_{||}\sin^2\alpha + F_\perp\cos^2\alpha)$$

All members are 50 mm thick, and the timber is strength class C27. All connectors are 76 mm diameter round connectors with M12 bolts. The information given in Table 6.3 is information extracted from Table 80 of the code and where appropriate applying Hankinson's formula.

Basic Connector Loads (F)					
	$F_{||}$	$F_\perp$	$F_{\alpha=9.14°}$	$F_{\alpha=30.96°}$	$F_{\alpha=49.9°}$
Connector on one side only	5.52 kN	4.59 kN	5.5 kN	5.25 kN	4.94 kN
Connectors on both sides and on the same bolt	5.18 kN	3.81 kN	3.84 kN	4.73 kN	4.28 kN

Table 6.3

Clause 6.6.7
Modification factor for duration of loading K_{58} $=$ 1.12 (medium term)
Modification factor for moisture content K_{59} $=$ 1.0   (service class 2)
Modification factor for end distance, edge distance and spacing K_{60}

If the end and edge distances and the spacing are equal to the standard values given in Tables 77, 78 and 79 respectively, then K_{60} = 1.0. The *Standard* values are given for specific values of 'α - *angle of load to grain*' in Tables 77, 78 and 79 and 'θ – *angle of connector axis to grain*' in Table 79. If actual values are less than the Standard values then K_{60} should have the lower of the values of K_C and K_S given in Tables 81, 82 and 79 respectively.

Summary of Actual End and Edge Distances and Spacing				
Member	End Distance	Edge Distance	Spacing	Angle of connector to grain direction (θ)
Member 1	-	69.2 mm	100 mm	60°
Member 2	69.2 mm	50.0 mm	100 mm	30°
Member 3	118.0 mm	48.5 mm	100 mm	29°

Table 6.4

Table 77   End Distances
Round toothed-plate connectors loaded end $0° \le \alpha \le 90°$
Minimum   = 51 mm
Standard   = 102 mm

Table 78   Edge Distances
Round toothed-plate connectors unloaded and loaded end $0° \le \alpha \le 90°$
Minimum   = 44 mm
Standard   = 44 mm

Table 79   Spacing modification factor K_S

1st Interface:

Member 1(a) $\alpha = 0°$, $\theta = 60°$

Extract from Table 79		Minimum value	Standard value
α	θ	$K_S = 0.75$	$K_S = 1.0$
0°	45°	89	102
	90°	89	89

Using interpolation the value for $\theta = 60°$ can be obtained.

α	θ	$K_S = 0.75$	$K_S = 1.0$
0°	60°	89	98

Actual spacing = 100 mm > standard value $\therefore K_s = 1.0$

Member 2   α = 90°,   θ = 30°

Extract from Table 79		Minimum value	Standard value
α	θ	$K_S = 0.75$	$K_S = 1.0$
60° to 90°	0°	89	89
	45°	89	102

Using interpolation the value for $\theta = 30°$ can be obtained.

α	θ	$K_S = 0.75$	$K_S = 1.0$
60° to 90°	30°	89	98

Actual spacing = 100 mm > standard value $\therefore K_S = 1.0$

2nd Interface:

Member 2   α = 49.9°,   θ = 30°

Extract from Table 79		Minimum value	Standard value
α	θ	$K_S = 0.75$	$K_S = 1.0$
	0°	89	95
45°	45°	89	102
	90°	89	108
	0°	89	89
60° to 90°	45°	89	102
	90°	89	114

Using interpolation the value for $\alpha = 49.9°$ can be obtained.

α	θ	$K_S = 0.75$	$K_S = 1.0$
49.9°	0°	89	93
	45°	89	102

Using interpolation the value for $\theta = 30°$ can be obtained.

α	θ	$K_S = 0.75$	$K_S = 1.0$
49.9°	30°	89	99

Actual spacing = 100 mm > standard value $\therefore K_S = 1.0$

Member 3 $\alpha = 9.14°$, $\theta = 29°$

Extract from Table 79		Minimum value	Standard value
α	θ	$K_S = 0.75$	$K_S = 1.0$
	0°	89	114
0°	45°	89	102
	90°	89	89
	0°	89	108
15°	45°	89	102
	90°	89	95

Using interpolation the value for $\alpha = 9.14°$ can be obtained.

α	θ	$K_S = 0.75$	$K_S = 1.0$
9.14°	0°	89	110
	45°	89	102

Using interpolation the value for $\theta = 29°$ can be obtained.

α	θ	$K_S = 0.75$	$K_S = 1.0$
49.9°	29°	89	105

Actual spacing = 100 mm < standard value

$$\therefore K_S = 0.75 + 0.25\left(\frac{100 - 89}{105 - 89}\right) = 0.92$$

3rd. Interface:

Member 3 $\alpha = 30.96°$, $\theta = 29°$

Extract from Table 79		Minimum value	Standard value
α	θ	$K_S = 0.75$	$K_S = 1.0$
	0°	89	102
30°	45°	89	102
	90°	89	102
	0°	89	95
45°	45°	89	102
	90°	89	108

Using interpolation the value for $\alpha = 30.96°$ can be obtained.

α	θ	$K_S = 0.75$	$K_S = 1.0$
30.96°	0°	89	102
	45°	89	102

Using interpolation the value for $\theta = 29°$ can be obtained.

α	θ	$K_S = 0.75$	$K_S = 1.0$
30.96°	29°	89	102

Actual spacing = 100 mm < standard value

$$\therefore K_S = 0.75 + 0.25\left(\frac{100 - 89}{102 - 89}\right) = 0.96$$

Member 1(b) $\alpha = 0°,$ $\theta = 60°$

Extract from Table 79		Minimum value	Standard value
α	θ	$K_S = 0.75$	$K_S = 1.0$
0°	0°	89	114
	45°	89	102
	90°	89	89

Using interpolation the value for $\theta = 60°$ can be obtained.

α	θ	$K_S = 0.75$	$K_S = 1.0$
0°	60°	89	106

Actual spacing = 100 mm < standard value

$$\therefore K_S = 0.75 + 0.25\left(\frac{100 - 89}{106 - 89}\right) = 0.91$$

Table 82   Loaded end distance modification factor K_C

1st Interface:

Member 1(a)   *end distance > 105 mm* $\alpha = 0°$ $\therefore K_C = 1.0$

Member 2   *end distance = 69.2 mm* $\alpha = 90°$

Extract from Table 82	76 mm diameter connector		
α End Distance	0°	45°	90°
65	0.75	0.81	0.87
70	0.78	0.83	0.89

Using interpolation the value for end distance = 69.2 mm $K_C = 0.89$

$2^{nd.}$ Interface:

Member 2   end distance = 69.2 mm $\alpha = 49.9^o$

Extract from Table 82	76 mm diameter connector		
α / End Distance	0°	45°	90°
65	0.75	0.81	0.87
70	0.78	0.83	0.89

Using interpolation the value for end distance = 69.2 mm

Extract from Table 82	76 mm diameter connector		
α / End Distance	0°	45°	90°
69.2	0.78	0.83	0.89

$\alpha = 49.9^o$ mm $\therefore K_C = 0.83 + 0.06 \left(\dfrac{49.9 - 45}{90 - 45} \right) = 0.84$

Member 3   end distance = 118 mm >105 $\therefore K_C = 1.0$

$3^{rd.}$ Interface:

Member 3   end distance > 118 mm >105 $\therefore K_C = 1.0$
Member 1(b)   end distance > 105 $\therefore K_C = 1.0$

Clause 6.7.6: $K_{61} = 1 - \dfrac{3(n-1)}{100}$ for $n < 10$

$\qquad\qquad\qquad\quad = 0.7$ for $n \geq 10$

where n is the number of connector units of the same size which are symmetrically arranged in one or more lines parallel to the line of action of the load in a primary axially loaded member in a structural framework.

In all other cases where more than one toothed-plate connector unit is used in a joint $K_{61} = 1.0$.

Since none of the lines of action of loads is parallel to the line of the connectors assume $K_{61} = 1.0$.

The permissible load for each connection is summarised in Table 6.5:

Interface	α	Member	F	K_{58}	K_{59}	K_{60}	K_{61}	F_{adm}	$F_{applied}$
1st	0°	1(a)	5.52	1.12	1.0	1.0	1.0	6.0	2.53
	90°	2	3.81	1.12	1.0	0.89	1.0	3.8	2.53
2nd	49.9°	2	4.28	1.12	1.0	0.84	1.0	4.0	3.96
	9.14°	3	3.84	1.12	1.0	0.92	1.0	3.9	3.96
3rd	30.96°	3	4.73	1.12	1.0	0.96	1.0	5.1	2.53
	0°	1(b)	5.52	1.12	1.0	0.98	1.0	6.0	2.53

Table 6.5

Note: Members 1(a) and 1(b) have a connector on one side only

Members 2 and 3 have connectors on both sides and on the same bolt

K_{60} is the lower value of K_S and K_C as calculated for each case

The applied load is the load per connector from Table 6.2

6.6.2   *Split-ring and Shear-plate Connectors*   *(Clauses 6.8 and 6.9)*

Clause 6.8.5   Permissible load/connector F_{adm} $=$ $F \times K_{62} \times K_{63} \times K_{64} \times K_{65}$

Clause 6.8.4.3   Basic values for loads (F), parallel and perpendicular to the grain, are given in Table 88 of the code.

Clause 6.6.4.1   As with tooth-plate connectors Hankinson's Formula applies to Basic single shear loads where the load is inclined at an angle $\alpha°$ to the grain of the timber, i.e.

$$F = F_{||}F_{\perp}/(F_{||}\sin^2\alpha + F_{\perp}\cos^2\alpha)$$

All members are 50 mm thick, and the timber is strength class C27. All connectors are 64 mm diameter round connectors with M12 bolts. The information given in Table 6.6 is information extracted from Table 88 of the code and, where appropriate, applying Hankinson's formula.

Basic Connector Loads (F)					
	$F_{||}$	$F_{\perp}$	$F_{\alpha=9.14°}$	$F_{\alpha=30.96°}$	$F_{\alpha=49.9°}$
Connector on one side only	9.21 kN	6.45 kN	7.66 kN	8.27 kN	7.36 kN
Connectors on both sides and on the same bolt	9.21 kN	6.45 kN	7.66 kN	8.27 kN	7.36 kN

Table 6.6

Clause 6.8.5

Modification factor for duration of loading K_{62} $=$ 1.25   (medium-term)

Modification factor for moisture content K_{63} $=$ 1.0   (service class 2)

Modification factor for end distance, edge distance and spacing K_{64}

If the end and edge distances and the spacing are equal to the standard values given in Tables 85, 86 and 87 respectively, then $K_{64} = 1.0$. The *Standard* values are given for specific values of 'α - *angle of load to grain*' in Tables 85, 86 and 87 and 'θ – *angle of connector axis to grain*' in Table 87. If actual values are less than the Standard values then K_{64} should have the lower of the values of K_S, K_C and K_D given in Tables 87, 89 and 90 respectively.

Table 85 End Distances
Split-ring and shear-plate connectors loaded end $0° \leq \alpha \leq 90°$
Minimum = 70 mm
Standard = 70 mm

In this case the actual end distance (see Table 6.4) for member 2 is slightly less than the minimum and should be increased e.g. to 75 mm.

Table 86 Edge Distances
Split-ring and shear-plate connectors Unloaded $0° \leq \alpha \leq 90°$
Minimum = 44 mm
Standard = 44 mm

Table 87 Spacing modification factor K_S

1st. Interface:

Member 1(a) $\alpha = 0°$, $\theta = 60°$

Extract from Table 87							
α	θ	Minimum		Spacing			Standard
		$K_s = 0.75$	$K_s = 0.80$	$K_s = 0.85$	$K_s = 0.90$	$K_s = 0.95$	$K_s = 1.0$
0°	60°	89	92	92	95	95	98

Actual spacing = 100 mm > standard value $\therefore K_S = 1.0$

Member 2 $\alpha = 90°$, $\theta = 30°$

Extract from Table 87							
α	θ	Minimum		Spacing			Standard
		$K_s = 0.75$	$K_s = 0.80$	$K_s = 0.85$	$K_s = 0.90$	$K_s = 0.95$	$K_s = 1.0$
90°	30°	89	89	89	92	92	93

Actual spacing = 100 mm > standard value $\therefore K_S = 1.0$

2nd *Interface:*

Member 2 $\alpha = 49.9^\circ$, $\theta = 30^\circ$

Extract from Table 87							
α	θ	Minimum	Spacing				Standard
		$K_s = 0.75$	$K_s = 0.80$	$K_s = 0.85$	$K_s = 0.90$	$K_s = 0.95$	$K_s = 1.0$
45°	30°	89	92	95	102	105	107
60° to 90°	30°	89	89	89	92	92	93

Using interpolation the value for $\alpha = 49.9^\circ$ can be obtained.

α	θ	Minimum	Spacing				Standard
		$K_s = 0.75$	$K_s = 0.80$	$K_s = 0.85$	$K_s = 0.90$	$K_s = 0.95$	$K_s = 1.0$
49.9°	30°	89	91	93	99	100	102

Actual spacing = 100 mm < standard value $\therefore K_s = 0.95$

Member 3 $\alpha = 9.14^\circ$, $\theta = 29^\circ$

Extract from Table 87							
α	θ	Minimum	Spacing				Standard
		$K_s = 0.75$	$K_s = 0.80$	$K_s = 0.85$	$K_s = 0.90$	$K_s = 0.95$	$K_s = 1.0$
0°	15°	89	102	117	130	146	157
	30°	89	98	108	114	124	132
15°	15°	89	102	111	124	133	145
	30°	89	98	105	114	124	129

Using interpolation the value for $\alpha = 9.14^\circ$ can be obtained.

α	θ	Minimum	Spacing				Standard
		$K_s = 0.75$	$K_s = 0.80$	$K_s = 0.85$	$K_s = 0.90$	$K_s = 0.95$	$K_s = 1.0$
9.14°	15°	89	102	113	126	138	150
	30°	89	102	106	114	124	130

Using interpolation the value for $\theta = 29^\circ$ can be obtained.

α	θ	Minimum	Spacing				Standard
		$K_s = 0.75$	$K_s = 0.80$	$K_s = 0.85$	$K_s = 0.90$	$K_s = 0.95$	$K_s = 1.0$
9.14°	29°	89	102	106	115	125	131

Actual spacing = 100 mm < standard value $\therefore K_s = 0.79$

3rd. *Interface:*

Member 3 $\quad \alpha = 30.96^\circ, \quad \theta = 29^\circ$

Extract from Table 87

α	θ	Minimum	Spacing					Standard
		$K_s = 0.75$	$K_s = 0.80$	$K_s = 0.85$	$K_s = 0.90$	$K_s = 0.95$	$K_s = 1.0$	
30°	15°	89	95	105	111	121	127	
	30°	89	95	102	108	114	119	
45°	15°	89	92	95	102	105	108	
	30°	89	92	95	102	105	107	

Using interpolation the value for $\alpha = 30.96^\circ$ can be obtained.

α	θ	Minimum	Spacing					Standard
		$K_s = 0.75$	$K_s = 0.80$	$K_s = 0.85$	$K_s = 0.90$	$K_s = 0.95$	$K_s = 1.0$	
30.96°	15°	89	95	104	110	120	125	
	30°	89	95	101	107	113	118	

Using interpolation the value for $\theta = 29^\circ$ can be obtained.

α	θ	Minimum	Spacing					Standard
		$K_s = 0.75$	$K_s = 0.80$	$K_s = 0.85$	$K_s = 0.90$	$K_s = 0.95$	$K_s = 1.0$	
30.96°	29°	89	95	101	107	113	118	

Actual spacing $= 100$ mm $<$ standard value $\quad \therefore K_s = 0.84$

Member 1(b) $\quad \alpha = 0^\circ, \quad \theta = 60^\circ$

Extract from Table 87

α	θ	Minimum	Spacing					Standard
		$K_s = 0.75$	$K_s = 0.80$	$K_s = 0.85$	$K_s = 0.90$	$K_s = 0.95$	$K_s = 1.0$	
0°	60°	89	92	92	95	95	98	

Actual spacing $= 100$ mm $>$ standard value $\quad \therefore K_S = 1.0$

Table 89 Loaded end distance modification factor K_C

1st. *Interface:*

Member 1(a) $\qquad$ *end distance* > 180 *mm* $\qquad \alpha = 0^\circ \qquad K_C = 1.0$

Member 2 $\qquad$ *end distance* $= 75$ *mm* $\qquad \alpha = 90^\circ$
$\qquad\qquad\qquad$ For $0^\circ \leq \alpha^\circ \leq 90^\circ$ $\qquad\qquad\qquad K_C = 0.65$

2$^{nd.}$ Interface:

      Member 2   *end distance = 75 mm* $\alpha = 49.9^o$

                                For $0° \le \alpha° \le 90°$ $K_C = 0.65$

      Member 3   *end distance = 118 mm* $\alpha = 9.14^o$

                                For $0° \le \alpha° \le 90°$ $K_C = 0.88$

3$^{rd.}$ Interface:

      Member 3   *end distance = 118 mm* $\alpha = 30.96^o$

                                For $0° \le \alpha° \le 90°$ $K_C = 0.88$

      Member 1(b)   *end distance > 180 mm* $\alpha = 0^o$ $K_C = 1.0$

Table 90   Loaded edge distance modification factor K_D

1$^{st.}$ Interface:

      Member 1(a)   *edge distance = 69.2 mm* $\alpha = 0^o$ $K_D = 1.0$

      Member 2   *edge distance = 50 mm* $\alpha = 90^o$

                                For $45° \le \alpha° \le 90°$ $K_C = 0.87$

2$^{nd.}$ Interface:

      Member 2   *edge distance = 50 mm* $\alpha = 49.9^o$

                                  For $45° \le \alpha° \le 90°$ $K_C = 0.87$

      Member 3   *edge distance = 48.5 mm* $\alpha = 9.14^o$

Edge Distance (mm)	Angle of load to grain α			
	0°	15°	30°	45° to 90°
45	1.00	0.94	0.89	0.83
50	1.00	0.98	0.93	0.87

Using interpolation the values for edge distance = 48.5 mm can be obtained.

Edge Distance (mm)	Angle of load to grain α			
	0°	15°	30°	45° to 90°
48.5	1.00	0.96	0.91	0.85

Using interpolation the value for $\alpha = 9.14°$ can be obtained, $K_D = 0.98$

3rd Interface:

Member 3   end distance = 48.5 mm $\alpha = 30.96^{o}$
Using interpolation the value for $\alpha = 30.96°$ can be obtained, $K_D \approx 0.92$

Member 1(b)   end distance = 69.2 mm $\alpha = 0^{o}$ $K_D = 1.0$

Clause 6.8.5: $K_{65} = 1 - \dfrac{3(n-1)}{100}$ for $n < 10$

                              $= 0.7$ for $n \geq 10$

where n is the number of connector units of the same size which are symmetrically arranged in one or more lines parallel to the line of action of the load in a primary axially loaded member in a structural framework.

In all other cases where more than one toothed-plate connector unit is used in a joint $K_{65} = 1.0$.

Since none of the lines of action of loads is parallel to the line of the connectors assume $K_{65} = 1.0$,

The permissible load for each connection is summarised in Table 6.6:

Interface	α	Member	F	K_{62}	K_{63}	K_{64}	K_{65}	F_{adm}	$F_{applied}$
1st	0°	1(a)	9.21	1.25	1.0	1.0	1.0	11.51	2.53
	90°	2	6.45	1.25	1.0	0.65	1.0	5.24	2.53
2nd	49.9°	2	7.36	1.25	1.0	0.65	1.0	5.98	3.96
	9.14°	3	7.66	1.25	1.0	0.8	1.0	7.66	3.96
3rd	30.96°	3	8.27	1.25	1.0	0.88	1.0	9.1	2.53
	0°	1(b)	9.21	1.25	1.0	1.0	1.0	11.51	2.53

Table 6.6

Note: Members 1(a) and 1(b) have a connector on one side only
          Members 2 and 3 have connectors on both sides and on the same bolt
          K_{64} is the lower value of K_S, K_C and K_D as calculated for each case
          The applied load is the load per connector from Table 6.2

6.7   Glued Joints   (Clause 6.10)

The manufacture of glued joints, e.g. finger joints in glued-laminated beams, web-to-flange connections in ply-web beams and lap-joints including splices, should comply with the requirements of BS 6446 : 1984 'Specification for manufacture of glued structural components of timber and wood based panel products'.

The provisions of Clause 6.10 in BS 5268 : Part 2 are restricted to the timber species listed in the code, i.e. softwoods in table A.1 of Annex A, plywoods listed in section 4, Clause 5.4 for tempered hardboard and wood particle board as described in section 9.

The types of structural joints to which the provisions of Clause 6.10 are limited are those between:

- *solid or laminated timber members of which the dimension at right angles to the plane of the glueline is not greater than 50 mm;*

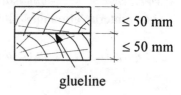

- *solid or laminated timber members of any dimension and plywood or wood particleboard no thicker than 29 mm;*

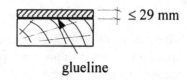

- *solid or laminated timber members of any dimension and tempered hardboard no thicker than 8 mm;*

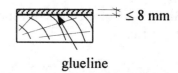

- *plywood members of any thickness, tempered hardboard members of any thickness, wood particleboard members of any thickness.*

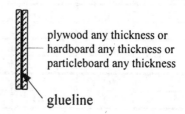

The possibility of differential shrinkage, distortion and stress concentrations at glued joints should also be considered. When mechanical fasteners are present in a glued joint, they are **not** considered to contribute to the strength of the joint.

Glued joints are designed on the basis of permissible shear stresses. When the components of a joint are loaded parallel to the grain, the lesser of the permissible shear stresses parallel to the grain for the timbers being joined is used in the calculations. In situations where one face is loaded at an angle to the grain, the permissible shear stress for the glue line should be calculated from:

$$\tau_\alpha = \tau_{adm,||} \, (1 - 0.67\sin\alpha)$$

where:

α is the angle between the direction of the load and the grain of the piece,

$\tau_{adm,||}$ is the permissible shear parallel to the grain stress for the timber.

When the bonding pressure is generated by nails or staples, the permissible shear stress for the glueline should be multiplied by the nail/glue modification factor K_{70} which has the value of 0.9. In the case of box beams, I-beams or stressed skin panels at the junction between the webs and flanges, Clause 5.7 of the code indicates that grade stresses should be multiplied by K_{37}, the stress concentration factor equal to 0.5. The implication is that this should also be applied to the permissible shear stress used for the glueline.

Most gluing is carried out in controlled factory conditions involving manufacturers who conduct full scale testing of their products to ensure that an adequate factor of safety is achieved. Some manufacturers believe that testing has indicated that the inclusion of the 0.5 concentration factor is too severe and unnecessary.

Since glue is always stronger than the timber being connected (assuming the recommended type of glue and manufacturing procedure have been adopted), the strength of the glueline is based on timber stresses. The load-duration and load-sharing factors apply when determining the glueline strength. It is important to recognise that tensile components of stress perpendicular to the plane of the glueline are unacceptable.

6.7.1   *Example 6.9   Glued Lap Joint*

Determine the minimum contact area required to transmit the forces given in Example 6.1 assuming appropriate adhesive is used to glue the component parts together.

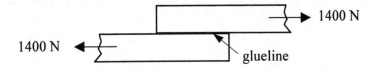

Data:
Timber: Strength Class C16,   Service Class 2,   Load-duration; long-term
Bonding is carried out by the use of nails.

The glueline is required to transmit 1400 N

Table 7   Strength Class C16 $\tau_{g,||}$ = 0.67 N/mm^2

$$\tau_{adm,||} = \tau_{g,||} \times K_3 \times K_8 \times K_{70}$$

$$\tau_{adm,||} = 0.67 \times 1.0 \times 1.1 \times 0.9 = 0.66 \text{ N/mm}^2$$

$$\text{Minimum Area required} = \frac{1400}{0.66} = 2120 \text{ mm}^2$$

6.8   Review Problems

6.1   Identify at least six methods of fastening timber elements.
        (see Section 6.1)

6.2   Explain the differences between the most commonly used type of nail,
        i.e. plain wire nails, improved nails, pneumatically driven nails.
        (see Section 6.2)

6.3   Define the terms: headside thickness, pointside thickness, standard
        penetration and actual penetration.
        (see Section 6.2.1)

6.4   Explain the difference between the three most commonly used timber
        connections.
        (see Section 6.8)

---

7. Roof Trusses

Objective: *The objective of this chapter is to illustrate the commonly used structural forms for pitched roofs and introduce BS 5268 : Part 3 : 1998 for the design of trussed rafters.*

7.1 Introduction

Timber pitched roof structures are used for two main reasons: firstly to ensure adequate weather-proofing and secondly, if required, to provide roof-space utilisation such as additional storage. Relatively low pitch angles such as 10° are acceptable for roofs surfaced with multi-layered bituminous felts or similar sheet materials. In situations where a roof is tiled, slated or covered with overlapping profile sheeting, the pitch must be sufficient to permit rapid drainage of water to prevent the ingress of water by wind driven rain. The minimum slope necessary is dependent on the type of covering, particularly the degree of overlap between individual units. Typically, large slates require approximately $22\frac{1}{2}^{o}$ slopes whilst small slates and single lap tiles may require nearer 35° slopes. Plain tiles require at least a 40° slope to inhibit water penetration.

The construction of a timber pitched roof can take one of many structural forms such as:

- ♦ monopitch roof,
- ♦ coupled roof,
- ♦ close coupled roof,
- ♦ collar roof,
- ♦ purlin roof   or
- ♦ trussed rafter roof.

as indicated in Figures 7.1 to 7.3:

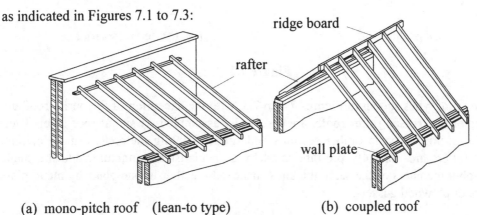

(a) mono-pitch roof   (lean-to type)   (b) coupled roof

Figure 7.1

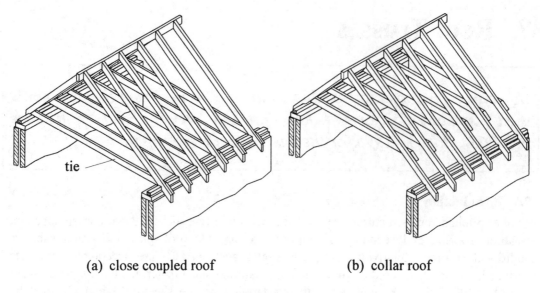

(a) close coupled roof   (b) collar roof

Figure 7.2

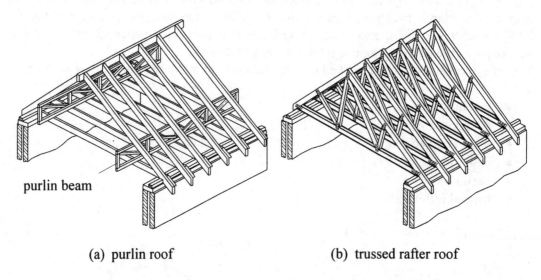

(a) purlin roof   (b) trussed rafter roof

Figure 7.3

All of the roof types shown in Figures 7.1 to 7.3, with the exception of the purlin roof and elements of the trussed rafter roofs, are essentially assembled on site at roof level. Their construction utilises basic timber sections and simple jointing methods, usually nailing. Trussed rafters are normally pre-fabricated by a specialist manufacturer and are made using timber members of the same thickness fastened together in one plane by metal plate fasteners or plywood gussets.

7.2 Monopitch Roof

Monopitch roofs comprise a series of single rafters supported on wall plates directly carried on two walls, or on a wall-plate directly carried on a wall at the lower end and another wall-plate fastened to, or corbelled from, a wall at the upper level as shown in Figure 7.1 (a). The latter method is often referred to as a lean-to construction.

Since there is a tendency for an inclined rafter to induce horizontal thrust at the support, provision must be made to transfer this force to the wall and prevent sliding. *Clearly the wall plate and the supporting wall must be capable of resisting the outward thrust from the rafter.*

The transfer of thrust is achieved by creating a notch (birdsmouth) in the rafter at the location where it meets the wall plate, as shown in Figure 7.4.

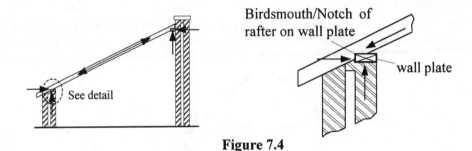

Figure 7.4

The wall plate is located at the top of the wall in a mortar bed to provide a level bearing for the rafters and distribute the end reaction evenly over the wall. The rafters are normally skew-nailed to the plate. A similar detail is used at the upper level. The covering material can be sheeted or tiled. When using sheeted materials care must be taken to ensure the appropriate rafter spacing is provided accurately to accommodate the standard sheet sizes. In tiled roofs softwood battens are provided, the size of which depends upon the spacing of the rafters which normally range from 400 mm to 600 mm centres. When using larger spacings care must be taken to ensure that the battens have adequate stiffness to enable tiling or slating nails to be driven in.

The economic spans of monopitch roofs of this type are limited to approximately 3 m to 4 m.

7.3 Coupled Roof

A coupled roof is assembled by nailing rafters to a ridge board at the upper level and to wall plates at the lower level as shown in Figure 7.1(b).

The horizontal thrust which is produced at the wall plate normally limits the economic clear span to approximately 3 m. Spans above this level require a significant increase in the depth of the rafter to control deflection, and in addition buttressing of the support walls may be necessary to resist the lateral thrust. The ridge board locates the rafters in opposite alignment on each side preventing lateral movement. This form of construction is sometimes used with very steeply pitched roofs in church buildings utilizing solid or glued laminated members and relatively low support walls. This structural arrangement, as indicated in Figure 7.5, significantly reduces the effects of horizontal thrust.

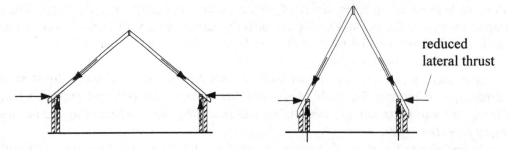

reduced
lateral thrust

Figure 7.5

7.4 Close Coupled Roof

Close coupled roofs are a development of coupled roofs, in which the horizontal thrust at the lower rafter ends is contained internally within a triangulated framework as shown in Figure 7.6.

Figure 7.6

The additional tie member, which is securely nailed at its junctions with the rafters, may also be used as a ceiling joist. In this instance a heavier section than is required simply for tying is usually required. Economic spans for this type of construction are approximately 5.0 m to 6.0 m. In spans of this value, the section size adopted for the ceiling joist can be minimised by the introduction of additional supports such as binders and hangers as shown in Figure 7.7.

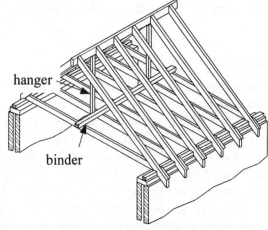

hanger

binder

Figure 7.7

7.5 Collar Roof

Close couple roofs in which the tie is placed at a level above the supporting walls, typically one third to one half of the rise as shown in Figure 7.8, are referred to as collar roofs. This form of construction is less efficient in resisting the spread of the main rafters. A disadvantage in this type of roof is that the section of rafter between the wall plate and the collar is subject to considerable bending. In addition, a bolted/connectored joint between the collar and the rafter is normally required to adequately resist the rafter thrust. Collar roofs are economic for relatively short spans not exceeding 5.0 m.

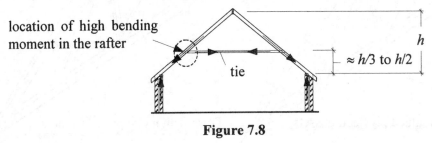

Figure 7.8

7.6 Purlin Roof

In couple roofs as the span increases the required increase in rafter depth produces a less efficient and economic structural solution. This can be overcome by providing an additional support system to the rafters in the form of purlin beams as shown in Figures 7.3(a) and 7.9.

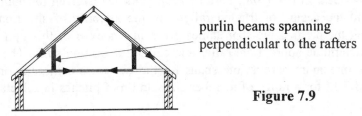

Figure 7.9

The purlins are beams spanning in a direction perpendicular to the rafters and providing intermediate support and hence reducing the effective span of the rafters. There are numerous possible structural configurations for the purlins; the most commonly used ones are illustrated in Figures 7.10(a) to 7.10(c). This form of construction is suited to spans exceeding 6.0 m.

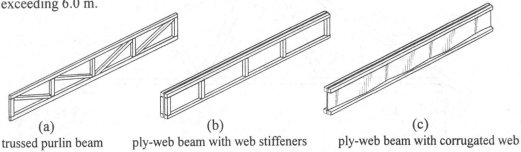

(a)	(b)	(c)
trussed purlin beam	ply-web beam with web stiffeners	ply-web beam with corrugated web

Figure 7.10

7.7   Trussed Rafters

Light trussed rafters normally span between external load-bearing walls without the requirement for intermediate supports. They are fabricated using glued plywood gussets or metal plate fasteners as shown in Figure 7.11.

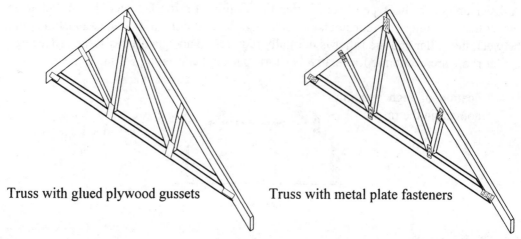

Truss with glued plywood gussets   Truss with metal plate fasteners

Figure 7.11

Ridge boards, hangers or binders are not required but *it is essential that adequate longitudinal and diagonal bracing of the whole roof and connection to the supporting structure are provided.* In BS 5268 : Part 3 : 1998 guidance is given for both the bracing requirements and the design of trussed rafters. In the majority of situations involving domestic housing the permissible span tables given in Annex B of this Part of the code can be used to determine appropriate rafter and ceiling tie section sizes. The permissible span tables give maximum permissible spans for the two truss configurations shown in Figures 7.12 and 7.13 for a range of member sizes and roof pitches in selected classes of timber.

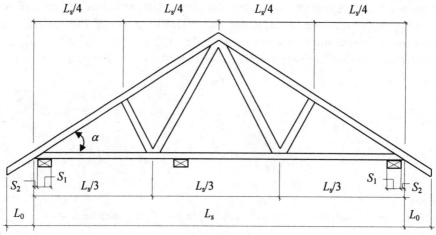

Figure 7.12

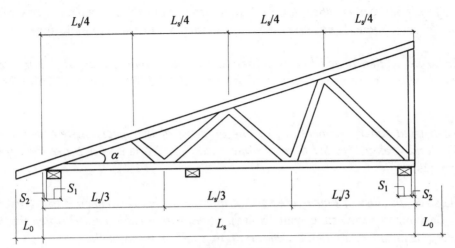

Figure 7.13

The information in the tables is limited to spans not exceeding 12.0 m and has been obtained from extensive programs of testing trussed rafters. A number of conditions must be satisfied before the tables can be used without requiring any additional calculation. They are:

a) *"The dead load on the rafter members does not exceed 0.41 kN/m measured along the slope. For lightweight roofs subject to wind uplift, checks should be made for possible stress reversal in members, the effects of such reversals on joint design, and the need to provide additional lateral restraint to members normally in tension. The adequacy of the holding down restraints should also be checked in accordance with **7.2.4**."* (clause 7.2.4 in the code refers to restraint of a roof against wind uplift)

b) *"The dead load on the ceiling tie does not exceed 0.15 N/m."*

c) *"The method of support and capacity of any water tank carried by the trussed rafters is in accordance with the details given in Figure 7"* (of the code).

d) *"The trussed rafters do not support any other plant or equipment".*

e) *"The imposed load does not exceed those recommended in **6.4.2**"* (clause 6.4.2 refers to imposed and wind loading), with the exception of snow loading, which should not exceed 0.75 kN/m^2.

f) *"Each trussed rafter supports load from a section of roof not more than 0.6 m wide and the spacing between centres of trussed rafters is not more than 0.6 m, except where it is necessary to accommodate chimneys and other openings as described in 7.6"* (clause 7.6 refers to limitation for hatch, chimney and other openings).

g) "The joints between members have adequate strength in service and can resist normal handling forces without damage (see 6.5.6)" (clause 6.5.6 refers to joint design).

h) "The cross-section dimensions, tolerances, moisture content and fabrication are in accordance with the recommendations of this part of BS 5268." (i.e. BS 5268 : Part 3 : 1998).

i) "The trussed rafter members are of one or more of the species listed in Table 1," (Part 3), *"and strength graded in accordance with 5.1.2"* (clause 5.1.2 specifies grading requirements).

j) "The strength class of timber used is not inferior to that recommended in Tables B.1 or B.2" (Maximum permissible span Tables), *"and within each trussed rafter the rafter and ceiling tie members are of the same strength grade or strength class."*

k) "The roof pitch is no greater than 35^0 and the supports are located in accordance with Figure 3" (Figure 3 indicates the wall plate location in relation to truss members if a simplified analysis is being carried out as shown in Figures 7.12 and 7.13 of this text), *"so that not less than half the width of each bearing is vertically below the eaves joint fastener and the distance S_2 is no greater than $S_1/3$ or 50 mm, whichever is the greater."*

l) "Any overhang of the rafter at the eaves (dimension L_o in Figure 11) does not exceed 0.6 mm unless justified by calculation" (Figure 11 indicates the two truss configurations, as indicated in Figures 7.12 and 7.13 of this text, to which the tables in Annex B apply).

m) "Proper consideration is given to the stability of both the complete roof and the individual trussed rafters in accordance with clause 7" (clause 7 refers to design responsibilities and overall stability).

BS 5268 : Part 3 : 1998   Annex B   Clause B.2 Internal members

"The internal members used for Fink trussed rafters which have been designed using the Tables in Annex B should be of the same size and strength class as the smaller of either the rafter members or the ceiling tie. Smaller sizes and other strength classes may be used where they can be justified by test or calculation. In no case however should the internal members be less than 60 mm in depth (see 5.1.3).

For monopitch trussed rafters, the internal members and the vertical end member should be justified by text or calculation but in no case should the depth be less than 60 mm (see Clause 5.1.3), and the length should not exceed the appropriate value given in Table 4."

Note: Clause 5.1.3 in Part 3 of the code relates to timber sizes in accordance with BS EN 336 and Table 4 in Part 3 provides maximum lengths of internal members for given depths and thicknesses of timber.

8. Eurocode 5

Objective: *to provide an introduction to Eurocode 5, the limit state design code for the design of structural timber elements.*

8.1 Introduction

This chapter provides an introduction to the contents of the Eurocode 5 and includes several examples of the design of simple structural elements. A more comprehensive treatment can be found in Timber Engineering - *STEP1 and STEP 2: Structural Timber Education Programme* (14,15). The Commission of the European Communities under the Comett programme supported this documentation.

The European Standards Organisation, CEN, is the umbrella organisation under which a set of common structural design standards (e.g. EC1, EC2, EC3, etc.) have been developed. The Structural Eurocodes are the result of attempts to eliminate barriers to trade throughout the European Union. Separate codes exist for each structural material, including EC5 : Part 1.1 for timber. The basis of design and loading considerations are included in EC 1.

Each country publishes its own European Standards (EN), e.g. in the UK the British Standards Institution (BSI) issues documents (which are based on the Eurocodes developed under CEN), with the designation BS EN.

Currently the Structural Eurocodes are issued as Pre-standards (ENV) which can be used as an alternative to existing national rules. In the UK the BSI has used the designation DD ENV; the pre-standards are equivalent to the traditional 'Draft for development' Documents.

In the UK the Eurocode for timber design is known as 'DD ENV 1995-1-1 Eurocode 5 : Design of timber structures : Part 1.1 General rules and rules for buildings (together with the United Kingdom National Application Document)'.

Eurocode 5 adopts the 'Limit State Design' philosophy as currently used in UK national standards.

8.1.1 National Application Document (NAD)

Each country which issues a European Standard also issues a NAD for use with the EN. The purpose of the NAD is to provide information to designers relating to product standards for materials, partial safety factors and any additional rules and/or supplementary information specific to design within that country.

A summary of the abbreviations used above is given in Table 8.1.

8.2 Terminology, Symbols and Conventions

The terminology, symbols and conventions used in EC5 : Part 1.1 differ from those used by BS 5268 : Part 2 : 1996. The code indicates **'Principles'** which are general statements and definitions which must be satisfied and **'Rules'** which are design procedures which comply with the principles. The rules can be substituted by alternative procedures provided that these can be shown to be in accordance with the principles.

There are two types of Annexe in EC5 : Part 1.1: normative and informative. Normative Annexes have the same status as the main body of the text whilst Informative Annexes provide additional information. The Annexes generally contain more detailed material or material which is used less frequently.

8.2.1   *Decimal Point*

Standard ISO practice has been adopted in representing a decimal point by a comma, i.e. $5,3 \equiv 5.3$

Abbreviation	Meaning
CEN	European Standards Organisation
EC	Eurocode produced by CEN
EN	European Standard based on Eurocode and issued by member countries
ENV	Pre-standard of Eurocode issued by member countries
DD ENV	UK version of Pre-standard (BSI)
NAD	National Application Document issued by member countries (BSI)
STEP 1	Timber Engineering: Basis of design, material properties, structural components and joints.
STEP 2	Timber Engineering: Design – Details and structural systems.

Table 8.1

8.2.2   *Symbols and Subscripts*

As in BS 5268 there are numerous symbols[*] and subscripts used in the code. The most frequently used are:

Symbols:
F: *action,*   a force (load) applied to a structure or an imposed deformation (indirect action), such as temperature effects or settlement,
  G: permanent action such as dead loads due to self-weight,
  Q: variable actions such as imposed, wind or snow loads,
  A: accidental actions such as explosions, fire or vehicle impact.
  E: *effect of actions* on structural elements, e.g. shear forces, bending moments, deformations etc.

---

[*] In most cases the Eurocode does not use italics for variables

R: *design resistance* of structural elements, e.g. bending strength of cross-section.

S: *design value of actions* factored values of externally applied loads or load effects such as axial load, shear force, bending moment etc.

X: *material property* physical properties such as tension, compression, shear and bending strength, modulus of elasticity etc. of timber being used.

A:	area	**k**:	coefficient or Factor (used with a subscript)
I:	second moment of area	**l, *l*** :	length or span
L:	length	**m**:	mass
M:	bending moment	**r**:	radius
N:	axial force	**s**:	spacing
V:	shear force	**t**:	thickness
W:	section modulus	α:	angle; ratio
a:	distance	β:	angle; ratio
b:	width	γ:	partial factor
d:	diameter	λ:	slenderness ratio (l_{eff}/i)
e:	eccentricity	ϕ:	rotational displacement
f:	strength of material	ρ:	mass density
h:	height or depth of beam	σ:	normal stress
i:	radius of gyration	τ:	shear stress

Subscripts:

c:	compression	**mod**:	modification
cr:	critical	**nom**:	nominal
d:	design value	**q or Q**:	variable action
ef:	effective	**sup**:	superior; upper
ext:	external	**ser**:	serviceability
f:	flange	**t**:	tension
fin:	final	**tor**:	torsion
inf:	inferior; lower	**u**:	ultimate
inst:	instantaneous	**v**:	shear
k:	characteristic	**w**:	web
l:	low; lower	α:	angle between force/stress and grain direction
l$_s$:	load sharing		
m:	material or bending	**0,90**:	relevant directions in relation to grain direction
max:	maximum		
min:	minimum		

Multiple subscripts are used to denote variables; e.g.

$\sigma_{m,y,d}$ is the design (d), bending (m) stress (σ) about the principal y-y axis (y)

$f_{m,y,d}$ is the corresponding design bending strength

8.3 Limit State Design

The limit states are states beyond which a structure can no longer satisfy the design performance requirements (see Chapter 1, section 1.6.3). The two classes of limit state adopted by EC5 : Part 1.1 are:

- ◆ *ultimate limit states:* These include failures such as full or partial collapse due to e.g. rupture of materials, excessive deformations, loss of equilibrium or development of mechanisms. Limit states of this type present a direct risk to the safety of individuals.
- ◆ *serviceability limit states:* Whilst not resulting in a direct risk to the safety of people, serviceability limit states still render the structure unsuitable for its intended purpose. They include failures such as excessive deformation resulting in unacceptable appearance or non-structural damage, loss of durability or excessive vibration causing discomfort to the occupants.

The limit states are quantified in terms of design values for actions, material properties and geometric characteristics in any particular design. Essentially the following conditions must be satisfied:

Ultimate limit state:

$$\textbf{Rupture} \qquad \mathbf{S_d} \le \mathbf{R_d}$$

where:

S_d is the design value of the effects of the actions imposed on the structure/structural elements,

R_d is the design resistance of the structure/structural elements to the imposed actions.

$$\textbf{Stability} \qquad \mathbf{S_{d,dst}} \le \mathbf{R_{d,stb}}$$

where:

$S_{d,dst}$ is the design value of the destabilizing effects of the actions imposed on the structure (including self-weight where appropriate).

$S_{d,stb}$ is the design value of the stabilizing effects of the actions imposed on the structure (including self-weight where appropriate).

Serviceability limit state:

$$\textbf{Serviceability} \qquad \mathbf{S_d} \le \mathbf{C_d}$$

where:

S_d is the design value of the effects of the actions imposed on the structure/structural elements,

C_d is a prescribed value, e.g. a limit of deflection.

8.3.1   Design Values

The term *design* is used for factored loading and member resistance

Design loading (F_d) =   partial safety factor (γ_F) × characteristic value (F_k)

e.g. $G_d = \gamma_G G_k$

where:

γ_G is the partial safety factor for permanent actions,

G_k is the characteristic value of the permanent actions.

Note: $G_{d,sup}$ $(= \gamma_{G,sup}G_{k,sup}$ or $\gamma_{G,sup}G_k)$ represents the 'upper' design value of a permanent action,

$G_{d,inf}$ $(= \gamma_{G,inf}G_{k,inf}$ or $\gamma_{G,inf}G_k)$ represents the 'lower' design value of a permanent action.

$$\text{Design resistance} \quad (R_d) \quad = \quad \frac{\text{material characteristic strength} \left(X_k\right) \times k_{mod}}{\text{material partial safety factor} \left(\gamma_m\right)}$$

where k_{mod} is a factor to allow for service class and duration of load

e.g.   ***design bending strength*** $=$ $f_{m,d}$ $=$ $\dfrac{f_{m,k} \times k_{mod}}{\gamma_m}$

Extract from NAD Table 1:

Table 1. Partial safety factors (γ factors)					
Reference in EC5 : Part 1.1	Definition	Symbol	Condition	Value	
				Boxed EC5	UK
2.3.3.2	Partial factors for materials	γ_m	Timber and wood based materials	1,3	1,3
		γ_m	Steel used in joints	1,1	1,1
		γ_m	Accidental	1,0	1,0
		γ_m	Serviceability	1,0	1,0

Table 8.2

Note: In addition to the k_{mod} factor it is necessary to consider other factors which may affect the bending strength e.g. size factor or load sharing.

The design values of the actions vary depending upon the limit state being considered. All of the possible load cases should be considered in different combinations as given in Clause 2.3.2.2 P(2) and Table 2.3.2.2 of the code; e.g. for persistent and transient design situations:

$$F_d \;=\; \Sigma\gamma_{G,j}\, G_{k,j} + \gamma_{Q,1}Q_{k,1} + \underset{i>1}{\Sigma\gamma_{Q,i}}\, \psi_{0,i}\, Q_{k,i}$$

Equation (1)
(Equation (2.3.2.2a) in EC5)

where:

$\gamma_{G,j}$ partial safety factor for permanent actions,   (Table 2.3.3.1)

$G_{k,j}$ characteristic values of permanent actions,

$\gamma_{Q,1}$ partial safety factor for 'one' of the variable actions,

$Q_{k,1}$ characteristic value of 'one' of the variable actions,

$\gamma_{Q,i}$ partial safety factor for the other variable actions,   (Table 2.3.3.1)

$\psi_{0,i}$ combination factor which is applied to the characteristic value Q_k of an action not being considered as $Q_{k,1}$,   (Eurocode 1 and NAD - Table 2)

$Q_{k,i}$ characteristic value of *'other'* variable actions.

Consider a design situation in which there are two characteristic dead loads, G_1 and G_2, in addition to three characteristic imposed loads, Q_1, Q_2 and Q_3. Assume the partial safety factors and combination factor are $\gamma_{Gj} = 1,5,$ $\gamma_{Q,1} = 1,5$ $\gamma_{Q,i} = 1,5$ $\psi_{0,i} = 0,7$

Combination 1:

$$F_d = (1,5G_1 + 1,5G_2) + 1,5\,Q_1 + (0,5 \times 0,7 \times Q_2) + (0,5 \times 0,7 \times Q_3)$$

$$F_d = 1,5(G_1 + G_2) + 1,5Q_1 + 0,35(Q_2 + Q_3)$$

Combination 2:

$$F_d = 1,5(G_1 + G_2) + 1,5Q_2 + 0,35(Q_1 + Q_3)$$

Combination 3:

$$F_d = 1,5(G_1 + G_2) + 1,5Q_3 + 0,35(Q_1 + Q_2)$$

When developing these combinations permanent effects are represented by their upper design values, i.e.

$$G_{d,sup} = \gamma_{G,sup}\, G_{k,sup} \quad \text{or} \quad \gamma_{G,sup}\, G_k$$

Those which decrease the effect of the variable actions (i.e. favourable effect) are replaced by their lower design values, i.e.

$$G_{d,inf} = \gamma_{G,inf}\, G_{k,inf} \quad \text{or} \quad \gamma_{G,inf}\, G_k$$

In most situations either the upper or lower design values are applied throughout the structure; specifically in the case of continuous beams, the same design value of self-weight is applied on all spans.

A similar approach is used when dealing with accidental actions.

8.3.2 *Partial Safety Factors*

The Eurocode provides indicative values for various safety factors: these are shown in the text as 'boxed values' e.g. $\boxed{1,35}$. Each country defines 'boxed values' within the NAD document to reflect the levels of safety required by the appropriate authority of the national government; in the UK the BSI

The boxed values of partial safety factors for actions in building structures for persistent and transient design situations are given in Table 2.3.3.1 of EC5 : Part 1.1 and in Table 8.2 of this text.

In Clause 2.3.3.1(5) two simplified expressions using the Table 2.3.3.1 values are given to replace Equation 1. They are:

considering the most unfavourable variable action

$$F_d = \Sigma\gamma_{Gj}\, G_{kj} + \boxed{1,5}\, Q_{k,1}$$

considering all unfavourable variable actions

$$F_d = \Sigma\gamma_{G,j}\, G_{k,j} + \boxed{1,35}\, \Sigma Q_{k,1}$$
$$i \geq 1$$

whichever is the greater.

EXTRACT FROM EC5:

Partial safety factors for actions in building structures for persistent and transient design situations.			
	Permanent actions (γ_G)	Variable actions one with its characteristic value	(γ_Q) others with their combination value
Normal partial coefficients			
favourable effect ($\gamma_{F,inf}$)	1,0*	-**	-**
unfavourable effect	1,35*	1,5	1,5
Reduced partial coefficients			
favourable effect	1,0*	-**	-**
unfavourable effect	1,2	1,35	1,35
Notes: * Where, because of the sensitivity of a structure to variations in the magnitude of permanent actions throughout the structure, favourable and unfavourable parts of these actions need to be considered separately, the favourable part should be associated with $\gamma_{G,inf} = \boxed{0,9}$ and the unfavourable part with $\gamma_{G,sup} = \boxed{1,1}$ ** In normal cases on building structures $\gamma_{Q,inf} = 0$ Reduced partial coefficients may be applied for one-storey buildings with moderate spans that are only occasionally occupied (storage buildings, sheds, green houses, and buildings and small silos for agricultural purposes), ordinary lighting masts, light partition walls, and sheeting.			

Table 8.3

8.4 Materials

The most recent revision of BS 5268: Part 2 (the 1996 version) incorporates some of the CEN standards on materials. This revision has provided a UK structural permissible stress design code which can run in parallel with *DD ENV 1995-1-1 Eurocode 5 : Design of timber structures, Part 1.1 General rules and rules for buildings (together with the United Kingdom National Application Document)*, (11), during the period of its introduction as a DD ENV until its publication as an EN. The main features, which have been included in the revision, are the **strength classes**, the **three service classes** and the approach to nailed, screwed and bolted **joints** all from DD ENV 1995-1-1.

The NAD provides three tables, i.e. Tables 7, 8, and 9, which give strength classes to which various visual grades and species of timber are assigned. As before, strength classes range from C14 to C30 for softwoods and D40 to D70 for hardwoods. The characteristic values for the various strength classes are given in EN 338 *"Structural timber – Strength classes"* and are reproduced in Tables 8.4 and 8.5 in this text.

	C14	C16	C18	C22	C24	C27	C30	C35	C40
in N/mm^2									
$f_{m,k}$	14	16	18	22	24	27	30	35	40
$f_{t,0,k}$	8	10	11	13	14	16	18	21	24
$f_{t,90,k}$	0,3	0,3	0,3	0,3	0,3	0,4	0,4	0,4	0,4
$f_{c,0,k}$	16	17	18	20	21	22	23	25	26
$f_{c,90,k}$	4,3	4,6	4,8	5,1	5,3	5,6	5,7	6,0	6,3
$f_{v,k}$	1,7	1,8	2,0	2,4	2,5	2,8	3,0	3,4	3,8
in kN/mm^2									
$E_{0,mean}$	7	8	9	10	11	12	12	13	14
$E_{0,05}$	4,7	5,4	6,0	6,7	7,4	8,0	8,0	8,7	9,4
$E_{90,mean}$	0,23	0,27	0,30	0,33	0,37	0,40	0,40	0,43	0,47
G_{mean}	0,44	0,50	0,56	0,63	0,69	0,75	0,75	0,81	0,88
in kg/m^3									
ρ_k	290	310	320	340	350	370	380	400	420

Table 8.4   Strength classes and characteristic values according to EN 338 coniferous species

	D30	D35	D40	D50	D60	D70
in N/mm^2						
$f_{m,k}$	30	35	40	50	60	70
$f_{t,0,k}$	18	21	24	30	36	42
$f_{t,90,k}$	0,6	0,6	0,6	0,6	0,7	0,9
$f_{c,0,k}$	23	25	26	29	32	34
$f_{c,90,k}$	8,0	8,4	8,8	9,7	10,5	13,5
$f_{v,k}$	3,0	3,4	3,8	4,6	5,3	6,0
in kN/mm^2						
$E_{0,mean}$	10	10	11	14	17	20
$E_{0,05}$	8,0	8,7	9,4	11,8	14,3	16,8
$E_{90,mean}$	0,64	0,69	0,75	0,93	1,13	1,33
G_{mean}	0,60	0,65	0,70	0,88	1,06	1,25
in kg/m^3						
ρ_k	530	560	590	650	700	900

Table 8.5   Strength classes and characteristic values according to EN 338 deciduous species

8.5 Conventions

The difference in conventions most likely to cause confusion with UK engineers is the change in the symbols used to designate the major and minor axes of a cross-section. Traditionally in the UK the **y-y axis** has represented the minor axis; in EC5 this represents the **MAJOR axis,** the minor axis is represented by the z-z axis. The **x-x axis** defines the **LONGITUDINAL axis**. All three axes are shown in Figure 8.1.

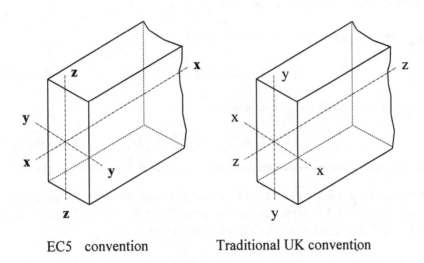

EC5   convention   Traditional UK convention

Figure 8.1

8.6 Use of EC5

A selection of examples are used in this chapter to illustrate the use of EC5 for the design of structural elements. Where necessary extracts from appropriate Tables in EC5 have been included. The clause reference numbers relate to those used in EC5.

8.7 Example 8.1 Solid Timber Flexural Member

A solid rectangular beam is simply supported with a clear unsupported span of 5,0 m. Using the design data given, check the suitability of a 100 mm x 300 mm section with respect to:

- ◆ bending   (Clause 5.1.6)
- ◆ lateral stability (Clause 5.2.2)
- ◆ shear   (Clause 5.1.7)
- ◆ bearing   (Clause 5.1.5)
- ◆ deflection   (Clause 4.3.1)
- ◆ vibration   (Clause 4.4)

Design Data:
Characteristic dead load G_k = 0,13 kN/m
Characteristic imposed load (medium-term) Q_k = 1,8 kN/m
Strength class of timber   = C16

Assume the beam is situated inside a heated building and protected from damp conditions. The beam is part of a load sharing system with tongue and groove boarding attached to the compression side.

Solution:
Design loads   (Clause 2.3.2.3 P(5))
The design load is calculated as the larger of:
(i)
considering the most unfavourable variable action

$$F_d = \Sigma\gamma_{G,j}\,G_{k,j} + \boxed{1,5}\,Q_{k,1} \qquad\qquad \text{Equation (2.3.3.1a)}$$

(ii)
considering all unfavourable variable actions

$$F_d = \Sigma\gamma_{G,j}\,G_{k,j} + \boxed{1,35}\,\Sigma Q_{k,1} \qquad\qquad \text{Equation (2.3.3.1b)}$$
$$i \geq 1$$

In this example there is only one variable action (Q_k) and therefore Equation (2.3.3.1b) is not required. The UK NAD currently has the same 'boxed' values of partial safety factors as EC5 given in Table 2.3.3.1 (see Table 8.2 in this text).

Table 2.3.3.1   Permanent actions (unfavourable effect) γ_g = 1,35

$$F_d = (1,35 \times 0,13) + (1,5 \times 1,8) = 2,88 \text{ kN/m}$$

Assume the span equals the clear distance between the bearings + 50 mm

$$L = 5,0 + 0,05 = 5,05 \text{ m}$$

Stresses due to applied actions:

Design bending stress $\qquad\qquad\qquad \sigma_{m,d} = \dfrac{M_d}{W}$

where $\quad W = \dfrac{bd^2}{6} = \dfrac{100 \times 300^2}{6} = 1,5 \times 10^6 \text{ mm}^3$

$\qquad\quad M_d = \dfrac{F_d L^2}{8} = \dfrac{2,88 \times 5,05^2}{8} = 9,18 \text{ kNm}$

$\qquad\quad \sigma_{m,d} = \dfrac{9,18 \times 10^6}{1,5 \times 10^6} = 6,12 \text{ N/mm}^2$

Design shear force $\qquad\quad V_d = \dfrac{F_d \times L}{2} = \dfrac{2,88 \times 5,05}{2} = 7,27 \text{ kN}$

Design shear stress $\qquad\quad \tau_{v,d} = \dfrac{3V_d}{2A}$

where $\quad A = (b \times d) = 100 \times 300 = 3 \times 10^4 \text{ mm}^2$

$$\tau_{v,d} \;=\; \frac{3 \times 7,27 \times 10^3}{2 \times 3 \times 10^4} = 0,36 \text{ N/mm}^2$$

Bending: (Clause 5.1.6)

The code states that the following conditions shall be satisfied:

$$k_m \frac{\sigma_{m,y,d}}{f_{m,y,d}} + \frac{\sigma_{m,z,d}}{f_{m,z,d}} \;\leq\; 1$$

$$\frac{\sigma_{m,y,d}}{f_{m,y,d}} + k_m \frac{\sigma_{m,z,d}}{f_{m,z,d}} \;\leq\; 1$$

where:

$\sigma_{m,y,d}$ and $\sigma_{m,z,d}$ are the design bending stresses about the principal axes and $f_{m,y,d}$ and $f_{m,z,d}$ are the corresponding design strengths (in this problem $\sigma_{m,z,d} = 0$).

k_m should be taken as 0,7 for rectangular sections and 1,0 for other cross-sections.

Clause 2.2.3.2

The design value of a material property X_d is given by $\quad X_d = \dfrac{k_{mod} X_k}{\gamma_m}$

Design bending strength $\qquad f_{m,d} \;=\; \dfrac{k_{mod} f_{m,k}}{\gamma_m}$

The values of γ_m and k_{mod} are given in Table 2.3.3.2 and Table 3.1.7 of the code respectively. Extract from these tables are given here.

Extract from EC5 : Part 1.1:

Table 2.3.3.2 Partial coefficients for material properties (γ_m)	
Ultimate limit states	
- fundamental combinations: timber and wood-based materials	1,3
steel used in joints	1,1
- accidental combinations:	1,0
Serviceability limit states	1,0

Extract from EC5 Table 3.1.7

Table 3.1.7   Values of k_{mod}

Material/ load-duration class	Service class 1	2	3
Solid and glued laminated timber plywood			
Permanent	0,60	0,60	0,50
Long-term	0,70	0,70	0,55
Medium-term	0,80	0,80	0,65
Short-term	0,90	0,90	0,70
Instantaneous	1,10	1,10	0,90

The service classification of sections for use in Table 3.1.7 is given in Clause 3.1.5 of the code with examples being given in Table 6 of the NAD. Table 6 of the NAD is illustrated below.

Extract from NAD

Table 6 Examples of appropriate service class	
Service class	Environmental conditions
1	Timber in buildings with heating and protected from damp conditions. Examples are internal walls, internal floors (other than ground floors) and warm roofs.
2	Timber in covered buildings. Examples are ground floor structures where no free moisture is present, cold roofs, the inner leaf of cavity walls and external cladding.
3	Timber fully exposed to the weather. Examples are the exposed parts of open buildings and timber used in marine structures.

The beam is classified as service class 1 with medium-term load-duration. From Table 3.1.7 the modification factor $k_{mod} = 0,8$.

EN 338   (Table 8.4 of this text) $f_{m,k}$ = 16 N/mm^2
Clause 2.3.3.2   (NAD – Table 1) γ_m = 1,3

(Table 8.2 of this text) $f_{m,d} = \dfrac{0,8 \times 16}{1,3} = 9,8$ N/mm^2

As with BS : 5268: Part 2 a number of additional modification factors must be considered.

Clause 3.2.2P(5)   (depth of section factor)
'*For depths in bending or widths in tension of solid timber less than 150 mm, the characteristic values for $f_{m,k}$ and $f_{t,0,k}$ ....may be increased by the factor k_h where:*

$$k_h = \min \left\{ \begin{array}{c} (150/h)^{0,2} \\ 1,3 \end{array} \right\}$$

with h *in mm for depth in bending or width in tension.'*

In this case h (= 300 mm) > 150 mm $\therefore$ $k_h = 1,0$

Clause 5.4.6(2)   (load sharing factor)
The load sharing factor k_{ls} is assumed to be 1,1 provided the load-distribution system, as described in Table 5.4.6 of the code), satisfies the following conditions:

   ♦ it is designed to support the applied permanent and variable loads,
   ♦ each element of the system is continuous over at least two spans, and any joints are staggered.

Extract from EC5

Table 5.4.6	Description of assemblies and load distribution systems
Assembly	Load-distribution system
Flat roof or floor joists (maximum span 6 m)	Boards or sheathing
Roof trusses (maximum span 12 m)	Tiling battens, purlins or sheathing
Rafters (maximum span 6 m)	Tiling battens or sheathing
Wall studs (maximum height 4 m)	Head and sole plates, sheathing at least one side

span = 5,05 m < 6 m   (as indicated in Table 5.4.6)
Assume the tongue and groove boarding satisfies the conditions in Clause 5.4.6.(2):
load sharing can be assumed to take place and $k_{ls} = 1,1$

Design bending strength $f_{m,d}$ = $9,8 \times k_h \times k_{ls}$ = $9,8 \times 1,0 \times 1,1$ = $10,78 \text{ N/mm}^2$

$$\frac{\sigma_{m,d}}{f_{m,d}} = \frac{6,12}{10,78} = 0,57 < 1,0$$

Section is adequate with respect to bending

Lateral stability: (Clause 5.2.2)
In the calculation above it was assumed that the tongue and groove boarding was attached to the compression side of the beam and provided full restraint against lateral torsional buckling of the beam (see Chapter 3, Section 3.3.5 of this text). In cases in which full restraint is not provided, the lateral torsional buckling strength should be checked.

The lateral torsional buckling strength of the beam is found by introducing another modification factor k_{crit}. The following condition should then be satisfied:

$$\sigma_{m,d} \leq k_{crit}f_{m,d}$$

where:
$\sigma_{m,d}$ and $f_{m,d}$ are as before,
k_{crit} can be found using the equations 5.2.2 (c-e) given in Clause 5.2.2 P(4).

Equation 5.2.2.c

$\lambda_{rel,m} \leq 0,75$ $k_{crit} = 1$

Equation 5.2.2.d

$0,75 < \lambda_{rel,m} \leq 1,4$ $k_{crit} = 1,56 - 0,75\lambda_{rel,m}$

Equation 5.2.2.e

$1,4 < \lambda_{rel,m}$ $k_{crit} = 1/\lambda^2_{rel,m}$

where:
$\lambda_{rel,m} = \sqrt{f_{m,k}/\sigma_{m,crit}}$ and

$\sigma_{m,crit} = \dfrac{0,75E_{0,05}b^2}{hL_{ef}}$ (this expression can be found in the NAD Clause 6.5)

In the NAD, Clause 6.5 guidance is given to determine L_{ef}, i.e.

'where full restraint is provided against rotation in plan at both ends, $L_{ef} = 0,7L$,
where partial restraint against rotation in plan is provided at both ends or full restraint at one end $L_{ef} = 0,85L$,
where partial restraint against twisting is provided at one or both ends, $L_{ef} = 1,2L$.'

For a homogeneous material there is only one value of E. In timber the modulus depends on the angle between the direction of stress and the grain. In general, the E value parallel to the grain should be used. The expression for $\sigma_{m,crit}$ enables the critical value of uniform moment (M), occurring along the length of a beam (see Table 8.6) above which lateral instability will occur, to be determined. This load case can be considered as a basic load case and all others related to it and referred to as *'equivalent uniform moment'* load cases. Similar expressions for the critical stress (or moment) can be derived for the other load cases and *'equivalent uniform moment'* factors determined to relate these to the basic load case. Table 8.6 gives a range of '*equivalent uniform moment factors*' for some of the most common load cases used.

Beam and loads	Actual bending moment	Equivalent uniform moment	Equivalent uniform moment factor
Basic Case (M ... M)	M ☐ M	M	1,00
q/m, L	M = qL²/8	0,88M	0,88
F, L	M = FL/4	0,74M	0,74
M	M	0,57M	0,57
M ... M	M ... M	0,43M	0,43

Table 8.6

$$\lambda_{rel,m} = \sqrt{\frac{f_{m,k}}{\sigma_{m,crit}}} \qquad \text{where} \qquad \sigma_{crit} = \frac{0,75E_{0,05}b^2}{hL_{ef}}$$

Assume the beam has torsional restraints at its supports, but is not restrained along the length of the compression edge.

EN 338 (Table 8.4 of this text)

$$E_{0,05} = 5,4 \text{ kN/mm}^2$$

$$\sigma_{crit} = \frac{0,75E_{0,05}b^2}{hL_{ef}} = \frac{0,75 \times 5400 \times 100^2}{300 \times 5050} = 26,73 \text{ N/mm}^2$$

The characteristic bending strength $f_{m,k}$ should be modified to allow for the particular load case being considered. In this problem the load is assumed to be uniformly distributed and therefore the value of the equivalent uniform moment factor from Table 8.5 is 0,88.

$$f_{m,k} = 16 \times 0,88 = 14,08 \text{ N/mm}^2 \qquad \lambda_{rel,m} = \sqrt{\frac{14,08}{26,73}} = 0,73 \quad (< 0,75)$$

Clause 5.2.2 P(4) $k_{crit} = 1,0$ $f_{m,d} = 10,78 \times 1,0 = 10,78 \text{ N/mm}^2$

Equation 5.2.2(c) ($\sigma_{m,d} = 6{,}12 \text{ N/mm}^2$) $\sigma_{m,d} < k_{crit} f_{m,d}$

> Section is adequate with respect to lateral stability

Shear: (Clause 5.17)
The design shear stress must not exceed the design shear strength; this is represented in Equation (5.1.7.1) of the code as:

$$\tau_d \leq f_{v,d}$$

The design shear strength is determined from:

$$f_{v,d} = \frac{k_{mod}f_{v,g,k}}{\gamma_m}$$

From Table 3.1.7 as before $k_{mod} = 0{,}8$

EN 338   (Table 8.4 of this text) $f_{v,g,k} = 1{,}8 \text{ N/mm}^2$

Table 2.3.3.2   (NAD, Table 1) $\gamma_m = 1{,}3$
                 (Table 8.2 of this text)

$$f_{v,d} = \frac{0{,}8 \times 1{,}8}{1{,}3} = 1{,}1 \text{ N/mm}^2$$

Clause 5.4.6   Load-sharing $k_{ls} = 1{,}1$
                                       $f_{v,d} = 1{,}1 \times 1{,}1 = 1{,}21 \text{ N/mm}^2$

From previous calculations $\tau_{v,d} = 0{,}36 \text{ N/mm}^2$
                                       $\tau_{v,d} \leq f_{v,d}$

> Section is adequate with respect to shear

As with BS : 5268: Part 2, if beams are notched at the ends the design shear stress is calculated on the basis of an effective depth of section h_e as indicated in Clause 5.1.7.2 and the following condition must be satisfied:

$$\tau_{v,d} \leq k_v f_{v,d}$$

where:
$\tau_d = 1{,}5V/bh_e$ (as before but using a reduced shear area)
k_v is a modification factor applied to the design strength, i.e.

For beams notched at the unloaded side:

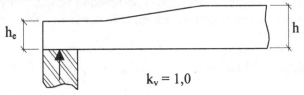

$k_v = 1{,}0$

For beams notched at the loaded side:

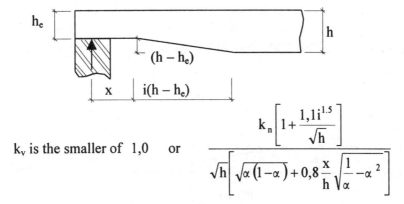

k_v is the smaller of 1,0   or $$\dfrac{k_n\left[1+\dfrac{1,1i^{1.5}}{\sqrt{h}}\right]}{\sqrt{h}\left[\sqrt{\alpha\left(1-\alpha\right)}+0,8\dfrac{x}{h}\sqrt{\dfrac{1}{\alpha}-\alpha^2}\right]}$$

where:
for solid timber k_n = 5
for glued laminated timber k_n = 6,5
h is the beam depth in mm
x is the distance from the line of action to the corner
α is h_e/h
i is the notch inclination

In addition to the above modification for a notch there is another factor included in EC5 to allow for a reduction in applied shear stress which occurs when point loads are near the supports. This effect is not accounted for in elastic beam theory nor is it allowed for in BS 5268 : Part 2. Its inclusion in EC5 : Part 1.1 is a result of observations during experimental work.

In Clause 5.1.7 P(2) EC5 : Part 1.1 states :
'At beam ends, the contribution to the total shear force of a point load F within a distance of 2h of the support may be reduced according to the influence line shown in figure 5.1.7.1.'

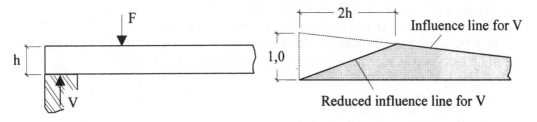

Figure 5.1.7.1 (from EC5)

Consider the effect of this reduction on a simply supported beam carrying a uniformly distributed load and a point load as shown in Figure 8.2.

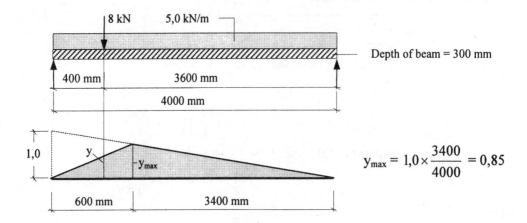

Figure 8.2

Without the reduction $\quad V = \left(\dfrac{5,0 \times 4,0}{2}\right) + \dfrac{8,0 \times 3,6}{4,0} \quad = \quad 10,0 + 7,2 \quad = \quad 17,2$ kN

With the reduction $\qquad V \;=\; 10,0 + (8,0 \times y)$

From the influence line $\quad y \;=\; y_{max} \times \dfrac{400}{600} \;=\; 0,85 \times 0,67 \;=\; 0,57$

$\qquad\qquad$ Reduced $\quad V \;=\; 10,0 + (8,0 \times 0,57) = \quad 14,06$ kN

The section can then be checked for the reduced value of shear force at the support.

Bearing: (Clause 5.1.5)

At the supports the bearing stress should be checked to ensure that the following condition is satisfied:

$$\sigma_{c,90,d} \;\le\; k_{c,90} \, f_{c,90,d} \qquad\qquad \text{(Equation 5.1.5a in EC5)}$$

where:

$\sigma_{c,90,d}$ the design compressive stress perpendicular to the grain

$f_{c,90,d}$ the design compressive strength perpendicular to the grain

$k_{c,90}$ is a factor which enhances the design strength if the loaded length on a beam is short as shown in Figure 5.1.5a and given in Table 5.1.5 of the code.

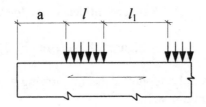

Figure 5.1.5a EC5

Extract from EC5

Table 5.1.5   Values of $k_{c,90}$

	$l_1 \leq 150$ mm	$l_1 > 150$ mm	
		$a \geq 100$ mm	$a < 100$ mm
$l \geq 150$ mm	1	1	
150 mm $> l \geq 15$ mm	1	$1 + \dfrac{150 - 1}{170}$	$1 + \dfrac{a(150 - 1)}{17000}$
15 mm $> l$	1	1,8	$1 + a/125$

Note: there is no increase in $f_{c,90,d}$ (i.e. $k_{c,90} = 1,0$) when $l \geq 150$ mm

$$\text{Design bearing stress} \quad = \quad \frac{V_d}{\text{Bearing Area}} \quad = \quad \frac{7,27 \times 10^3}{100 \times 50} \quad = \quad 1,45 \text{ N/mm}^2$$

EN 338   (Table 8.4)   Characteristic bearing strength = 4,6 N/mm^2
Clause 5.4.6   Load sharing exists k_{ls} = 1,1
Table 5.1.5 $a = 0$, and $l = 50$ mm $l_1 = 0$ $k_{c,90}$ = 1,0

$$\text{Design bearing strength} \qquad f_{c,90,d} \;=\; 1,0 \times 4,6 \times 1,1 \;=\; 5,06 \text{ N/mm}^2$$
$$\sigma_{c,90,d} \;<\; f_{c,90,d}$$

Section is adequate with respect to bearing

EC5 : Part 1.1 also specifies the following condition in situations where the compression stresses are applied at an angle of α to the grain, i.e.

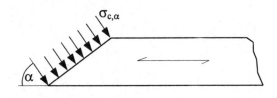

Equation 5.1.5b in EC5

$$\sigma_{c,\alpha,d} \;\leq\; \frac{f_{c,0,d}}{\dfrac{f_{c,0,d}}{f_{c,90,d}} \sin^2\alpha + \cos^2\alpha}$$

Deflection   (Clause 4.3)
In EC5 : Part 1.1 the deflections of beams are considered as '*instantaneous*' or '*final*' values. The final values take into account the increases in deformation with time due to the combined effect of creep and moisture. Deflection is considered to be the combined effect of three separate components:

♦ u_0 pre-camber   (if applied)
♦ u_1 deflection due to permanent loads,   and
♦ u_2 deflection due to variable loads.

as shown in Figure 4.3.1 of the code.

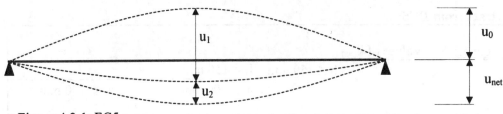

Figure 4.3.1 EC5

The resulting '*net*' deflection is given by:

$$u_{net} = u_1 + u_2 - u_0 \qquad \text{Equation 4.3.1 EC5}$$

The calculated values of u_1 and u_2 are based on the characteristic loading as defined in equation (4.1a) of EC5 : Part 1.1:

$$\Sigma G_{kj} + Q_{k,1} + \Sigma \psi_{1,i}\, Q_{k,i}$$
$$i > 1$$

where:

G_{kj} characteristic values of permanent actions
$Q_{k,1}$ characteristic values of 'one' of the variable actions
$\psi_{1,i}$ combination coefficient   (EC 1 and EC5, NAD, Table 2)
$Q_{k,i}$ as previously defined

The magnitude of the instantaneous bending deflection (u_m) can be calculated using standard elastic techniques (e.g. see Section 2.9 in Chapter 2), and assuming the mean value of the appropriate stiffness modulus. In the case of a simply supported rectangular timber beam with a uniformly distributed load, the shear deflection can be estimated using:

$$u_v = 0{,}96 \left(\frac{E}{G}\right)\left(\frac{h}{L}\right)^2 u_m$$

where:
E, G, h and L have their usual definitions.

Extract from EC5 : Part 1.1, NAD

Table 2. Combination factors (ψ factors)				
Variable action	**Building type**	ψ_0	ψ_1	ψ_2
Imposed floor loads	Dwellings	0,5	0,4	0,2
	Other occupancy classes[1]	0,7	0,6	0,3
	Parking	0,7	0,7	0,6
Imposed ceiling loads	Dwellings	0,5	0,4	0,2
	Other occupancy classes[1]	0,7	0,2	0,0
Imposed roof loads Wind loads	All occupancy classes[1]	0,7	0,2	0,0
[1] As listed and defined in table 1 of BS 6399 : Part 1 : 1984.				

The 'final' value of deflection can be estimated by modifying the equation for u_{inst} as indicated in equation (4.1b) of EC5 : Part 1.1:

$$u_{fin} = u_{inst}(1 + k_{def})$$

where:

k_{def} is the factor allowing for the combined effect of moisture and creep and is given in Table 4.1 of EC5 : Part 1.1.

Extract from Table 4.1, EC5 : Part 1.1

Table 4.1 Values of k_{def} for timber, wood-based materials and joints			
Material/	Service class		
load-duration class	1	2	3
Solid timber*, glued laminated timber			
Permanent	0,60	0,80	2,00
Long-term	0,50	0,50	1,50
Medium-term	0,25	0,25	0,75
Short-term	0,00	0,00	0,30
* For solid timber which is installed at or near fibre saturation points, and which is likely to dry out under load, the value of k_{def} should be increased by 1,0.			

The k_{def} factor is applied to the deflection calculations for each load separately depending upon the load duration and service class in each case. The final value of deflection is the sum of the values for each relevant load case.

The recommended limits given in Clause 4.3.1(2) of the code for the instantaneous deflection due to variable actions are:

$$u_{2,inst} \leq l/300 \text{ for beams and } \leq l/150 \text{ for cantilevers}$$

and those for the final deflection given in Clause 4.3.1(3) are:

$$u_{2,fin} \leq l/200 \text{ for beams and } \leq l/100 \text{ for cantilevers}$$
$$u_{net,fin} \leq l/200 \text{ for beams and } \leq l/100 \text{ for cantilevers}$$

The appropriate criterion to be considered is dependent on the particular circumstances in each case, e.g. $u_{2,inst}$ may be suitable when limiting deflection to avoid damage to non-structural elements and $u_{net,fin}$ when considering aesthetics.

The UK NAD gives additional information in Clause 6.4 relating to serviceability limit states. In the case of a solid timber member acting alone the appropriate 5-percentile modulus of elasticity ($E_{0,05}$) and/or 5-percentile shear modulus ($G_{0,05}$) should be used when calculating the instantaneous deformation. In the case of two or more pieces of solid timber joined together and acting as a single member, the mean value of elastic modulus may be used. In addition, it can be assumed that for solid timber, $G_{0,05} = 0,063E_{0,05}$. A modified combination factor $k_{def,ef}$ may be used in equation (4.1b) of EC5 : Part 1.1 when evaluating the final deformation (u_{fin}) of an element or structure which is subject to a combination of uniformly distributed actions with different load durations. The value of the effective k_{def} is given by:

$$k_{def,ef} = \frac{1}{Q_{tot}}\left(0.8\sum G_{kj} + Q_{k,1}k_{def,1} + \sum \psi_{1,i}Q_{k,i}k_{def,i}\right)$$

where:

$k_{def,ef}$ is the effective deformation factor for the element or structure being considered under combined action Q_{tot},

Q_{tot} is the combined action calculated from equation (4.1a) of EC5 : Part 1.1,

$k_{def,1}$ is the deformation factor from Table 4.1 of EC5 : Part 1.1 appropriate to the duration of action $Q_{k,1}$,

$k_{def,i}$ is the deformation factor from Table 4.1 of EC5 : Part 1.1 appropriate to the duration of action $Q_{k,i}$,

$G_{k,1}$, $Q_{k,1}$ and $Q_{k,i}$ are as before.

In the problem being considered here assume that the deflection with respect to aesthetic consideration is important, i.e. $u_{net,fin}$ should be less than the recommended limiting value.

$$G_{k,i} = 0.13 \text{ kN/m} \quad \text{(long-term)}$$
$$Q_{k,i} = 1.8 \text{ kN/m} \quad \text{(medium-term)}$$
Service Class 1

EC5 : Part 1.1   Equation 4.1(a),   NAD – Clause 6.4

$$Q_{tot} = \Sigma G_{kj} + Q_{k,1} + \boxed{\begin{array}{c}\Sigma\psi_{1,i} Q_{k,i} \\ i > 1\end{array}}$$

this term is not required in this case

$$Q_{tot} = 0.13 + 1.8 = 1.93 \text{ kN/m}$$

Effective deformation factor:

$$k_{def,ef} = \frac{1}{Q_{tot}}\left(0.8\sum G_{kj} + Q_{k,1}k_{def,1} \boxed{+ \sum \psi_{1,i}Q_{k,i}k_{def,i}}\right)$$

this term is not required in this case

EC5 : Part 1.1   Table 4.1 $k_{def,1} = 0.25$

NAD Clause 6.4 $k_{def,ef} = \dfrac{1}{1.93}\{(0.8 \times 0.13) + (1.8 \times 0.25)\} = 0.29$

EC5 : Part 1.1   Clause 4.1 P(4)

$$u_{fin} = u_{inst}(1 + k_{def,ef})$$

where :

u_{inst} is determined using the combined actions and $k_{def,ef}$ allows for different load durations.

Since load-sharing exists $E = E_{0,mean} = 8 \text{ kN/mm}^2$

Chapter 2   Table 2.1 $u_{inst} = \dfrac{5WL^3}{384EI}$

$W = 1,93 \times 5,05 = 9,75$ kN $I = \dfrac{100 \times 300^3}{12} = 225 \times 10^6$ mm^4

$u_{inst} = \dfrac{5 \times 9,75 \times 5050^3}{384 \times 8 \times 225 \times 10^6} = 9,1$ mm

$u_{fin} = 9,1(1 + 0,29) = 11,74$

EC5 : Part 1.1 Clause 4.3.1(3)   Recommended limiting value $\leq l/200$

$= 5050/200 = 25$ mm

$u_{fin} < 25$ mm

Section is adequate with respect to deflection

Note: In this case the shear deflection, which is less than the bending deformation, will not increase the estimated deflection above the limiting value.

Vibration: (Clause 4.4)

In EC5 : Part 1.1, Clause 4.4 guidance is given for the consideration of vibration in floors. Various criteria should be satisfied with respect to the maximum vertical deflection caused by a vertical concentrated static force, the unit impulse velocity response and the fundamental natural frequency. The UK NAD Clauses 6.4 (e) and (f) indicate that the control of vibration given in EC5 : Part 1.1 is not appropriate to most traditional UK floors. The recommendation given is to ensure that the total instantaneous deflection of the floor joists under load does not exceed 14 mm or $l/333$, whichever is the lesser. In this problem $l/333 = 15,2$ mm; since u_{inst} (= 9,1 mm) is less than 14 mm, the section is also adequate with respect to vibration.

8.8 Example 8.2   Solid Timber Tension Member

A tie member in a structural frame is required to transmit a long-term load of 1,0 kN and a medium-term load of 2,0 kN. Check the suitability of a 75 mm x 50 mm section of Strength Class C14 assuming Service Class 2.

Solution:

In EC5 : Part 1.1, Clause 5.1.2P(1) the following condition relating to tension parallel to the grain in solid timber must be satisfied:

$$\sigma_{t,0,d} \leq f_{t,0,d} \qquad \text{Equation 5.1.2 EC5}$$

where:
$\sigma_{t,0,d}$ the design stress in tension parallel to the grain,
$f_{t,0,d}$ the design strength in tension parallel to the grain.
The design strength is obtained by applying the appropriate modification factors to the characteristic value.

EC5 : Part 1.1   Clause 2.2.3.2 P(10) $f_{t,0,d} = \dfrac{k_{mod} f_{t,0k}}{\gamma_m} \times k_h$

Table 2.3.3.2 $\gamma_m = 1,3$
EN 338 (Table 8.4) characteristic strength $f_{t,0,d} = 8 \text{ N/mm}^2$
EC5 : Part 1.1   Table 3.1.7 $k_{mod} = 0,8$

Note: If a load combination consists of actions belonging to different load-duration classes, a value of k_{mod} should be chosen which corresponds to the action with the shortest duration.

EC5 : Part 1.1   Clause 3.2.2 P(3) and P(5)
For widths in tension parallel to the grain which are less than 150 mm the characteristic value $f_{t,0,k}$ can be increased by the factor k_h where:

$$k_h = \min \left\{ \begin{array}{c} (150/h)^{0,2} \\ 1,3 \end{array} \right\} \quad \text{with h in mm}$$

In this case $h = 75$ mm $k_h = \min \left\{ \begin{array}{c} (150/75)^{0,2} = 1,15 \\ 1,3 \end{array} \right\} \quad \therefore k_h = 1,15$

Design tensile strength $f_{t,0,d} = \dfrac{0,8 \times 8,0 \times 1,15}{1,3} = 5,66 \text{ N/mm}^2$

Design tensile stress $\sigma_{t,0,d} = \dfrac{N_{t,d}}{A}$

EC5 : Part 1.1   Clause 2.3.3.1P(5)   Equation 2.3.3.1a

$$N_{t,d} = \Sigma \gamma_{G,j} G_{k,j} + 1,5\, Q_{k,1}$$

EC5 : Part 1.1   Table 2.3.3.1   (Table 8.1) $\gamma_{G,j} = 1,35$

$$N_{t,d} = (1,35 \times 1,0) + (1,5 \times 2,0) = 4,35 \text{ kN}$$
$$\sigma_{t,0,d} = \dfrac{4,35 \times 10^3}{75 \times 50} = 1,16 \text{ N/mm}^2$$
$$\sigma_{t,0,d} < f_{t,0,d}$$

Section is adequate in tension

In the case of glued laminated timber the width factor (k_h), in tension parallel to the grain, is related to a width of 600 mm and is given by:

$$k_h = \min \left\{ \begin{array}{c} (600/h)^{0,2} \\ 1,15 \end{array} \right\} \quad \text{with h in mm}$$

In the case of timber subject to tension perpendicular to the grain there are different criteria for both solid and glued laminated timber.

For solid timber: $\quad\quad\quad\quad \sigma_{t,90,d} \leq f_{t,90,d}$ $\quad\quad\quad$ Equation 5.1.3a $\quad$ EC5

The UK NAD, in Clause 6.3(f), states *'No size adjustments to tension perpendicular to grain and shear stresses are applicable for solid timber.'*

In the case of glued laminated timber when considering tension perpendicular to the grain the ultimate limit state is influenced by the uniformly stressed volume V in m³ and a reference volume (V_0) of 0,01m³; as given in Clause 3.3.2 P(3). The condition to be satisfied is given in the code as:

$$\sigma_{t,90,d} \leq f_{t,90,d}(V_0/V)^{0,2} \quad\quad\quad \text{Equation 5.1.3b} \quad \text{EC5}$$

8.9 Example 8.3 Member Subject to Combined Tension and Bending

A 125 mm x 50 mm timber member is required to support long-term design loads of 12 kN in axial tension and 0,8 kNm in bending about the y-y axis. Check the suitability of the section assuming the timber to be of Strength Class C18 used under Service Class 2 conditions and not part of a load sharing system.

Solution:
Members subject to combined bending and axial tension must satisfy the interaction equations (5.1.9a) and (5.1.9b) given in EC5 : Part 1.1. They are:

$$\frac{\sigma_{t,0,d}}{f_{t,0,d}} + \frac{\sigma_{m,y,d}}{f_{m,y,d}} + k_m\frac{\sigma_{m,z,d}}{f_{m,z,d}} \leq 1 \quad\quad\quad \text{Equation 5.1.9a} \quad \text{EC5}$$

$$\frac{\sigma_{t,0,d}}{f_{t,0,d}} + k_m\frac{\sigma_{m,y,d}}{f_{m,y,d}} + \frac{\sigma_{m,z,d}}{f_{m,z,d}} \leq 1 \quad\quad\quad \text{Equation 5.1.9b} \quad \text{EC5}$$

Since bending does not occur about the z-z axis in this problem only Equation (5.1.9a) need be considered, with the third term equal to zero:

$$\frac{\sigma_{t,0,d}}{f_{t,0,d}} + \frac{\sigma_{m,y,d}}{f_{m,y,d}} \leq 1$$

Design tensile stress $\quad\quad\quad\quad \sigma_{t,0,d} = \dfrac{12,0\times10^3}{125\times50} = 1,92 \text{ N/mm}^2$

Design bending stress $\quad\quad\quad\quad \sigma_{m,y,d} = \dfrac{0,8\times10^6 \times 6}{50\times125^2} = 6,14 \text{ N/mm}^2$

EN 338 (Table 8.4) $\quad\quad\quad\quad \sigma_{t,0,k} = 11,0 \text{ N/mm}^2$

EC5 : Part 1.1 Clause 2.2.3.2 P(1) $\quad f_{t,0,d} = \dfrac{k_{mod}f_{t,0,k}}{\gamma_m} \times k_h$

$\quad\quad\quad\quad$ Table 2.3.3.2 $\quad\quad\quad\quad \gamma_m = 1,3$

$\quad\quad\quad\quad$ Table 3.1.7 $\quad\quad\quad\quad\quad k_{mod} = 0,7$

$\quad\quad\quad\quad$ Clause 3.2.2 P(5) $\quad\quad$ Since the width < 150 mm the k_h factor applies:

$$k_h = \min \left\{ \begin{array}{l} (150/h)^{0,2} \\ 1,3 \end{array} \right\} \quad \text{with h in mm}$$

In this case   h = 50 mm $k_h = \min \left\{ \begin{array}{l} (150/50)^{0,2} = 1,24 \\ 1,3 \end{array} \right\}$ $\therefore k_h = 1,24$

Design tensile strength $f_{t,0,d} = \dfrac{0,7 \times 11,0 \times 1,24}{1,3} = 7,34 \text{ N/mm}^2$

Design bending strength $f_{m,y,d} = \dfrac{k_{mod} f_{m,y,k}}{\gamma_m} \times k_h$

EN 338   (Table 8.4) $f_{m,y,k} = 18 \text{ N/mm}^2$

EC5   Clause 3.2.2 P(5) $k_h = \min \left\{ \begin{array}{l} (150/125)^{0,2} = 1,03 \\ 1,3 \end{array} \right\}$

Design bending strength $f_{m,y,d} = \dfrac{0,7 \times 18,0}{1,3} \times 1,03 = 9,98 \text{ N/mm}^2$

$$\frac{\sigma_{t,0,d}}{f_{t,0,d}} + \frac{\sigma_{m,y,d}}{f_{m,y,d}} = \frac{1,92}{7,34} + \frac{6,14}{9,98} = 0,88 < 1$$

Section is adequate with respect to combined tension and bending

8.10 Compression Members

EC5 : Part 1.1, Clause 5.1.4 states that for compression parallel to the grain two conditions must be satisfied:

(i) $\sigma_{c,0,d} \leq f_{c,0,d}$ Equation 5.1.4   EC5
(ii)   *'A check shall also be made of the stability condition (see 5.2.1)'*

EC5 : Part 1.1   Clause 5.2.1 P(1)   *'The bending stresses due to initial curvature, eccentricities and induced deflection shall be taken into account, in addition to those due to any lateral load'*

In EC5 : Part 1.1 second order effects such as additional bending stresses induced by lateral deflection and initial curvature are allowed for by the use of buckling curves (in the form of equations), which accounts for the decrease in strength of a real column compared to one which is infinitely stiff in bending. The stress conditions to be satisfied fall into two categories:

(i)   For both $\lambda_{rel,y} \leq 0,5$ and $\lambda_{rel,z} \leq 0,5$ then

$$\left(\frac{\sigma_{c,0,d}}{f_{c,0,d}} \right)^2 + \frac{\sigma_{m,y,d}}{f_{m,y,d}} + k_m \frac{\sigma_{m,z,d}}{f_{m,z,d}} \leq 1 \qquad \text{Equation (5.1.10a)}$$

and

$$\left(\frac{\sigma_{c,0,d}}{f_{c,0,d}}\right)^2 + k_m \frac{\sigma_{m,y,d}}{f_{m,y,d}} + \frac{\sigma_{m,z,d}}{f_{m,z,d}} \leq 1 \qquad \text{Equation (5.1.10a)}$$

where:

$\sigma_{c,0,d}$	design compressive stress parallel to the grain
$f_{c,0,d}$	design compressive strength parallel to the grain
$\sigma_{m,y,d}$	design bending stress corresponding to bending about the y-y axis
$f_{m,y,d}$	design bending strength corresponding to bending about the y-y axis
$\sigma_{m,z,d}$	design bending stress corresponding to bending about the z-z axis
$f_{m,z,d}$	design bending strength corresponding to bending about the z-z axis
k_m	factor = 0,7 for rectangular sections
	= 1,0 for other sections (given in Clause 5.1.6)

(ii)   For both $\lambda_{rel,y} > 0,5$ and $\lambda_{rel,z} > 0,5$ then

$$\frac{\sigma_{c,0,d}}{k_{c,z} f_{c,0,d}} + \frac{\sigma_{m,z,d}}{f_{m,z,d}} + k_m \frac{\sigma_{m,y,d}}{f_{m,y,d}} \leq 1 \qquad \text{Equation (5.2.1e)}$$

and

$$\frac{\sigma_{c,0,d}}{k_{c,y} f_{c,0,d}} + k_m \frac{\sigma_{m,z,d}}{f_{m,z,d}} + \frac{\sigma_{m,y,d}}{f_{m,y,d}} \leq 1 \qquad \text{Equation (5.2.1f)}$$

with

$$k_{c,y} = \frac{1}{k_y + \sqrt{k_y^2 - \lambda_{rel,y}^2}} \quad \text{and} \quad k_{c,z} = \frac{1}{k_z + \sqrt{k_z^2 - \lambda_{rel,z}^2}} \qquad \text{Equation (5.2.1g)}$$

$$k_y = 0,5\left\{1 + \beta_c\left(\lambda_{rel,y} - 0,5\right) + \lambda_{rel,y}^2\right\}$$
$$\hspace{9cm} \text{Equation (5.2.1h)}$$
$$k_z = 0,5\left\{1 + \beta_c\left(\lambda_{rel,z} - 0,5\right) + \lambda_{rel,z}^2\right\}$$

where:

σ_m is the bending stress due to any lateral loads

β_c is a factor for members within the straightness limits defined in Chapter 7 of the code:

Clause 7.2 P(1):   '*The deviation from straightness measured midway between the supports shall for columns and beams where lateral instability can occur and members in frames be limited to 1/500 of the length for glued laminated members and to 1/300 of the length for structural timber*'

Note: The limitations on bow in most strength grading rules are inadequate for the selection of material for these members and particular attention should therefore be paid to their straightness.

For solid timber $\beta_c = 0,2$
For glued laminated timber $\beta_c = 0,1$

where:

$$\lambda_{rel,y} = \sqrt{\frac{f_{c,0,k}}{\sigma_{c,crit,y}}} \quad \text{and} \quad \lambda_{rel,z} = \sqrt{\frac{f_{c,0,k}}{\sigma_{c,crit,z}}}$$

8.11 Example 8.4 Solid Timber Compression Member

A 3000 mm long member in a structural frame is required to transmit a design axial load ($N_{c,d}$) of 2,0 kN. Check the suitability of a 75 mm x 50 mm section of Strength Class C14 assuming Service Class 2.

Solution:

EC5 : Part 1.1   Clause 5.1.4 P(1) $\sigma_{c,0,d} \le f_{c,0,d}$

EC5 : Part 1.1   Clause 2.2.3.2 P(1) $f_{c,0,d} = \dfrac{k_{mod} f_{t,o,k}}{\gamma_m}$

EC5 : Part 1.1   Table 2.3.3.2 $\gamma_m = 1,3$
EN 338   (Table 8.4) $f_{c,o,d} = 16 \text{ N/mm}^2$
EC5 : Part 1.1   Table 3.1.7 $k_{mod} = 0,8$

Design compressive strength parallel to the grain $f_{c,0,d} = \dfrac{0,8 \times 16}{1,3} = 9,85 \text{ N/mm}^2$

Design compressive stress parallel to the grain $\sigma_{c,0,d} = \dfrac{2,0 \times 10^3}{(75 \times 50)} = 0,53 \text{ N/mm}^2$

$$\sigma_{c,0,d} < f_{c,0,d}$$

Section is adequate with respect to strength

EC5 : Part 1.1   Clause 5.1.4 P(2)   Check the instability condition

EC5 : Part 1.1   Clause 5.2.1 P(2) $\lambda_{rel,y} = \sqrt{\dfrac{f_{c,0,k}}{\sigma_{c,crit,y}}}$ where $\sigma_{c,crit,y} = \dfrac{\pi^2 E_{0,05}}{\lambda_y^2}$

EN 338   (Table 8.4) $E_{0,05} = 4,7 \text{ kN/mm}^2$

Slenderness

$$\lambda_y = \frac{L_e}{i_y} = \frac{\sqrt{12} \times 3000}{100} = 103,5; \quad \sigma_{c,crit,y} = \frac{\pi^2 4,7 \times 10^3}{103,5^2} = 4,33 \text{ N/mm}^2$$

$$\lambda_z = \frac{L_e}{i_z} = \frac{\sqrt{12} \times 3000}{50} = 207,0; \quad \sigma_{c,crit,z} = \frac{\pi^2 4,7 \times 10^3}{207^2} = 1,08 \text{ N/mm}^2$$

$$\lambda_{rel,y} = \sqrt{\frac{f_{c,0,k}}{\sigma_{c,crit,y}}} = \sqrt{\frac{16}{4,33}} = 1,92 \quad \lambda_{rel,z} = \sqrt{\frac{f_{c,0,k}}{\sigma_{c,crit,z}}} = \sqrt{\frac{16}{1,08}} = 3,85$$

Since $\lambda_{rel,y}$ and $\lambda_{rel,z} > 0,5$ the expressions given in Clause 5.2 P(4) should be satisfied, i.e.

$$\frac{\sigma_{c,0,d}}{k_{c,z}f_{c,0,d}} + \boxed{\frac{\sigma_{m,z,d}}{f_{m,z,d}} + k_m \frac{\sigma_{m,y,d}}{f_{m,y,d}}} \leq 1 \qquad \text{Equation 5.2.1e} \quad \text{EC5}$$

$$\frac{\sigma_{c,0,d}}{k_{c,y}f_{c,0,d}} + \boxed{k_m \frac{\sigma_{m,z,d}}{f_{m,z,d}} + \frac{\sigma_{m,y,d}}{f_{m,y,d}}} \leq 1 \qquad \text{Equation 5.2.1f} \quad \text{EC5}$$

These terms are not required in this problem since there are no lateral loads

Consider the y-y axis:

$$k_{c,y} = \frac{1}{k_y + \sqrt{k_y^2 - \lambda_{rel,y}^2}} \qquad k_y = 0.5\left\{1 + \beta_c\left(\lambda_{rel,y} - 0.5\right) + \lambda_{rel,y}^2\right\}$$

$$\beta_c = 0.2 \qquad\qquad k_y = 0.5\left\{1 + 0.2(1.92 - 0.5) + 1.92^2\right\} = 2.49$$

$$k_{c,y} = \frac{1}{2.49 + \sqrt{2.49^2 - 1.92^2}} = 0.25$$

$$\frac{\sigma_{c,0,d}}{k_{c,y}f_{c,0,d}} = \frac{0.53}{0.25 \times 9.85} = 0.22 \ < \ 1$$

Consider the z-z axis:

$$k_{c,z} = \frac{1}{k_z + \sqrt{k_z^2 - \lambda_{rel,z}^2}} \qquad k_z = 0.5\left\{1 + \beta_c\left(\lambda_{rel,z} - 0.5\right) + \lambda_{rel,z}^2\right\}$$

$$\beta_c = 0.2 \qquad\qquad k_z = 0.5\left\{1 + 0.2(3.85 - 0.5) + 3.85^2\right\} = 8.25$$

$$k_{c,z} = \frac{1}{8.25 + \sqrt{8.25^2 - 3.85^2}} = 0.064$$

$$\frac{\sigma_{c,0,d}}{k_{c,z}f_{c,0,d}} = \frac{0.53}{0.064 \times 9.85} = 0.84 \ < \ 1$$

Section is adequate with respect to instability

8.12 Example 8.5 Member Subject to Combined Compression and Bending

A timber column is subject to loading which induces both axial compression and biaxial bending stresses. Using the data given, check the suitability of a 200 mm x 200 mm section.

Data:

Buckling length $(l_{ey} = l_{ez})$	3000 mm
Strength Class	C22
Service Class	2
Design axial load (long-term)	100 kN
Design bending moment $M_{y,d}$ (short-term)	8.0 kNm
Design bending moment $M_{z,d}$ (short-term)	4.0 kNm

Solution:
Members subject to combined bending and axial compression must satisfy the interaction
equations (5.1.10a) and (5.1.10b) given in EC5 : Part 1.1:

$$\left(\frac{\sigma_{c,0,d}}{f_{c,0,d}}\right)^2 + \frac{\sigma_{m,y,d}}{f_{m,y,d}} + k_m \frac{\sigma_{m,z,d}}{f_{m,z,d}} \quad \leq \ 1 \qquad \text{Equation (5.1.10a)}$$

and

$$\left(\frac{\sigma_{c,0,d}}{f_{c,0,d}}\right)^2 + k_m \frac{\sigma_{m,y,d}}{f_{m,y,d}} + \frac{\sigma_{m,z,d}}{f_{m,z,d}} \quad \leq \ 1 \qquad \text{Equation (5.1.10a)}$$

In addition to the strength requirements of these equations, the instability condition given
in Clause 5.2.1 must also be checked.

Design axial stress $\qquad \sigma_{c,0,d} \ = \ \dfrac{N_{c,d}}{A} \ = \ \dfrac{100\times10^3}{200\times 200} \ = \ 2{,}5 \ \text{N/mm}^2$

Design bending stress $\qquad \sigma_{m,y,d} \ = \ \dfrac{M_{y,d}}{W} \ = \ \dfrac{8{,}0\times10^6\times6}{200\times 200^2} \ = \ 6{,}0 \ \text{N/mm}^2$

Design bending stress $\qquad \sigma_{m,z,d} \ = \ \dfrac{M_{z,d}}{W} \ = \ \dfrac{4{,}0\times10^6\times6}{200\times 200^2} \ = \ 3{,}0 \ \text{N/mm}^2$

EN 338   (Table 8.4) $\qquad f_{c,0,k} \ = \ 20 \ \text{N/mm}^2 \quad f_{m,k} \ = \ 22 \ \text{N/mm}^2 \quad E_{0,05} \ = \ 6{,}7 \ \text{kN/mm}^2$

EC5 : Part 1.1   Clause 2.2.3.2 P(1) $\qquad f_{c,0,d} \ = \ \dfrac{k_{mod}f_{c,0,d}}{\gamma_m}$

$\qquad\qquad\qquad$ Table 2.3.3.2 $\qquad\qquad \gamma_m \ = \ 1{,}3$
$\qquad\qquad\qquad$ Table 3.1.7 $\qquad\qquad k_{mod} = \ 0{,}9$

$\qquad\qquad\qquad$ Design axial strength $\qquad f_{c,0,d} = \ \dfrac{0{,}9\times 20}{1{,}3} \ = \ 13{,}8 \ \text{N/mm}^2$

$\qquad\qquad\qquad$ Clause 2.2.3.2 (P1) $\qquad f_{m,y,d} \ = \ f_{m,z,d} \ = \ \dfrac{k_{mod}\times f_{m,k}}{\gamma_m}$

Note: Since h > 150 mm the k_h factor does not apply to bending strength.

Design bending strength $\qquad f_{m,y,d} \ = \ f_{m,z,d} \ = \ \dfrac{0{,}9\times 22}{1{,}3} \ = \ 15{,}23 \ \text{N/mm}^2$

EC5 : Part 1.1   Clause 5.1.6 $\quad$ For rectangular sections $\ k_m = \ 0{,}7$

Equation 5.1.10(a)

$$\left(\frac{\sigma_{c,0,d}}{f_{c,0,d}}\right)^2 + \frac{\sigma_{m,y,d}}{f_{m,y,d}} + k_m \frac{\sigma_{m,z,d}}{f_{m,z,d}} \ = \ \left(\frac{2{,}5}{13{,}8}\right)^2 + \frac{6{,}0}{15{,}23} + 0{,}7\frac{3{,}0}{15{,}23} \ = \ 0{,}56 \ < \ 1$$

Equation 5.1.10(b)

$$\left(\frac{\sigma_{c,0,d}}{f_{c,0,d}}\right)^2 + k_m \frac{\sigma_{m,y,d}}{f_{m,y,d}} + \frac{\sigma_{m,z,d}}{f_{m,z,d}} = \left(\frac{2,5}{13,8}\right)^2 + 0,7\frac{6,0}{15,23} + \frac{3,0}{15,23} = 0,51 \ < \ 1$$

Section is adequate with respect to strength

EC5 : Part 1.1   Clause 5.1.10 P(3)   Check the instability condition

EC5 : Part 1.1   Clause 5.2.1 P(2) $\lambda_{rel,y} = \sqrt{\dfrac{f_{c,0,k}}{\sigma_{c,crit,y}}}$ where $\sigma_{c,crit,y} = \dfrac{\pi^2 E_{0,05}}{\lambda_y^2}$

Slenderness

$$\lambda_y = \frac{L_e}{i_y} = \frac{\sqrt{12} \times 3500}{200} = 60,62; \quad \sigma_{c,crit,y} = \frac{\pi^2 6,7 \times 10^3}{60,62^2} = 17,99 \ N/mm^2$$

$$\lambda_z = \frac{L_e}{i_z} = \frac{\sqrt{12} \times 3500}{200} = 60,62; \quad \sigma_{c,crit,z} = \frac{\pi^2 6,7 \times 10^3}{60,62^2} = 17,99 \ N/mm^2$$

$$\lambda_{rel,y} = \sqrt{\frac{f_{c,0,k}}{\sigma_{c,crit,y}}} = \sqrt{\frac{20,0}{17,99}} = 1,05 \qquad \lambda_{rel,z} = \sqrt{\frac{f_{c,0,k}}{\sigma_{c,crit,z}}} = \sqrt{\frac{20,0}{17,99}} = 1,05$$

Since $\lambda_{rel,y}$ and $\lambda_{rel,z} > 0,5$ the expressions given in Clause 5.2 P(4) should be satisfied, i.e.

$$\frac{\sigma_{c,0,d}}{k_{c,z}f_{c,0,d}} + \frac{\sigma_{m,z,d}}{f_{m,z,d}} + k_m \frac{\sigma_{m,y,d}}{f_{m,y,d}} \le 1 \qquad \text{Equation 5.2.1e} \quad EC5$$

$$\frac{\sigma_{c,0,d}}{k_{c,y}f_{c,0,d}} + k_m \frac{\sigma_{m,z,d}}{f_{m,z,d}} + \frac{\sigma_{m,y,d}}{f_{m,y,d}} \le 1 \qquad \text{Equation 5.2.1f} \quad EC5$$

Consider the y-y axis

$$k_{c,y} = \frac{1}{k_y + \sqrt{k_y^2 - \lambda_{rel,y}^2}} \qquad k_y = 0,5\left\{1 + \beta_c\left(\lambda_{rel,y} - 0,5\right) + \lambda_{rel,y}^2\right\}$$

$$\beta_c = 0,2 \qquad\qquad k_y = 0,5\left\{1 + 0,2(1,05 - 0,5) + 1,05^2\right\} = 1,1$$

$$k_{c,y} = \frac{1}{1,1 + \sqrt{1,1^2 - 1,05^2}} = 0,7$$

Similarly for the z-z axis $\qquad\qquad k_{c,z} = 0,7$

EC5 : Part 1.1   Equation (5.2.1e)

$$\frac{\sigma_{c,0,d}}{k_{c,z}f_{c,0,d}} + \frac{\sigma_{m,z,d}}{f_{m,z,d}} + k_m\frac{\sigma_{m,y,d}}{f_{m,y,d}} = \frac{2,5}{0,7\times13,8} + \frac{3,0}{15,23} + 0,7\frac{6,0}{15,23} = 0,73 < 1$$

EC5 : Part 1.1   Equation (5.2.1e)

$$\frac{\sigma_{c,0,d}}{k_{c,y}f_{c,0,d}} + k_m\frac{\sigma_{m,z,d}}{f_{m,z,d}} + \frac{\sigma_{m,y,d}}{f_{m,y,d}} = \frac{2,5}{0,7\times13,8} + 0,7\frac{3,0}{15,23} + \frac{6,0}{15,23} = 0,79 < 1$$

Section is adequate with respect to instability

9. Overall Structural Stability

Objective: *to introduce the concepts of structural stability, robustness and accidental damage.*

9.1 Introduction

In the previous chapters the requirements of strength, stiffness and stability of individual structural components has been considered in detail. It is also **essential** in any structural design to consider the requirements of **overall** structural stability.

BS 5268 : Part 2 states the following in Clause 1.6.1.1:

'*To ensure that a design is robust and stable:*
   a) *the geometry of the structure should be considered;*
   b) *required interaction and connections between timber load bearing elements and between such elements and other parts of the structure should be assumed;*
   c) *suitable bracing and diaphragm effects should be provided in planes parallel to the direction of the lateral forces acting on the whole structure.*

In addition, the designer should state in the health and safety plan.......... any special precautions or temporary propping necessary at each and every stage in the construction process to ensure overall stability of all parts of the structure.'

The term **stability** has been defined in 'Stability of Buildings' published by the Institution of Structural Engineers (18) in the following manner:

'*Provided that displacements induced by normal loads are acceptable, then a building may be said to be stable if:*
   ● *a minor change in its form, condition, normal loading or equipment would not cause partial or complete collapse and*
   ● *it is not unduly sensitive to change resulting from accidental or other actions.*
Normal loads include the permanent and variable actions for which the building has been designed.
The phrase 'is not unduly sensitive to change' should be broadly interpreted to mean that the building should be so designed that it will not be damaged by accidental or other actions to an extent disproportionate to the magnitudes of the original causes of damage.'

This publication, and the inclusion of stability, robustness and accidental damage clauses in current design codes, is largely a consequence of the overall collapse or significant partial collapse of structures e.g. the collapse of pre-cast concrete buildings under erection at Aldershot in 1963 (19) and notably the Ronan Point Collapse due to a gas explosion in 1968 (20).

The inclusion of such clauses in codes and building regulations is not new. The following is an extract from the 'CODE OF LAWS OF HAMMURABI (2200 BC), KING OF BABYLONIA' (the earliest building code yet discovered):

A. *If a builder builds a house for a man and do not make its construction firm and the house which he has built collapse and cause the death of the owner of the house - that builder shall be put to death.*

B. *If it cause the death of the son of the owner of the house - they shall put to death a son of that builder.*

C. *If it cause the death of a slave of the owner of the house - he shall give to the owner of the house a slave of equal value.*

D. *If it destroy property, he shall restore whatever it destroyed, and because he did not make the house which he built firm and it collapsed, he shall rebuild the house which collapsed at his own expense.*

E. *If a builder build a house for a man and do not make its construction meet the requirements and a wall fall in, that builder shall strengthen the wall at his own expense.*

Whilst this code is undoubtedly 'harsh' it probably did concentrate the designer's mind on the importance of structural stability! An American structural engineer, Dr. Jacob Feld, spent many years investigating structural failure and suggested ten basic rules to consider when designing and/or constructing any structure (21):

1. *Gravity always works, so if you don't provide permanent support, something will fail.*

2. *A chain reaction will make a small fault into a large failure, unless you can afford a fail-safe design, where residual support is available when one component fails. In the competitive private construction industry, such design procedure is beyond consideration.*

3. *It only requires a small error or oversight - in design, in detail in material strength, in assembly, or in protective measures - to cause a large failure.*

4. *Eternal vigilance is necessary to avoid small errors. If there are no capable crew or group leaders on the job and in the design office, then supervision must take over the chore of local control. Inspection service and construction management cannot be relied on as a secure substitute.*

5. *Just as a ship cannot be run by two captains, a construction job cannot be run by a committee. It must be run by one individual, with full authority to plan, direct, hire and fire, and full responsibility for production and safety.*

6. *Craftsmanship is needed on the part of the designer, the vendor, and the construction teams.*

7. *An unbuildable design is not buildable, and some recent attempts at producing striking architecture are approaching the limit of safe buildability, even with our most sophisticated equipment and techniques.*

8. *There is no foolproof design, there is no foolproof construction method, without guidance and proper and careful control.*

9. *The best way to generate a failure on your job is to disregard the lessons to be learnt from someone else's failures.*

10. *A little loving care can cure many ills. A little careful control of a job can avoid many accidents and failures.*

An appraisal of the overall stability of a complete structure during both the design and construction stages should be carried out by, and be the responsibility of, one individual. In many instances a number of engineers will be involved in designing various elements or sections of a structure but never the whole entity. It is **essential,** therefore, that one identified engineer carries out this vital appraisal function, including consideration of any temporary measures which may be required during the construction stage.

9.2 Structural Form

Generally, instability problems arise due to an inadequate provision to resist lateral loading (e.g. wind loading) on a structure. There are a number of well established structural forms which when used correctly, will ensure adequate stiffness, strength and stability. It is important to recognise that stiffness, strength and stability are three different characteristics of a structure. In simple terms:

- the *stiffness* determines the deflections which will be induced by the applied load system,
- the *strength* determines the maximum loads which can be applied before acceptable material stresses are exceeded and,
- the *stability* is an inherent property of the structural form which ensures that the building will remain stable.

The most common forms of structural arrangements which are used to transfer loads safely and maintain stability are:

- braced frames,
- unbraced frames,
- shear cores/walls,
- cellular construction,
- diaphragm action.

In many structures a combination of one or more of the above arrangements is employed to ensure adequate load paths, stability and resistance to lateral loading. All buildings behave as complex three-dimensional structures with components frequently interacting compositely to resist the applied force system. Analysis and design processes are a simplification of this behaviour in which it is usual to analyse and design in two dimensions with wind loading considered separately in two mutually perpendicular directions.

9.3 Braced Frames

In braced frames lateral stability is provided in a structure by utilising systems of diagonal bracing in at least two vertical planes, preferably at right angles to each other. The bracing systems normally comprise a triangulated framework of members which are either in tension or compression. The horizontal floor or roof plane can be similarly braced at an appropriate level, as shown in Figure 9.1, or the floor/roof construction may be designed as a deep horizontal beam to transfer loads to the vertical, braced planes, as shown in Figure 9.2. There are a number of configurations of bracing which can be adopted to accommodate openings, services etc. and are suitable for providing the required load transfer and stability.

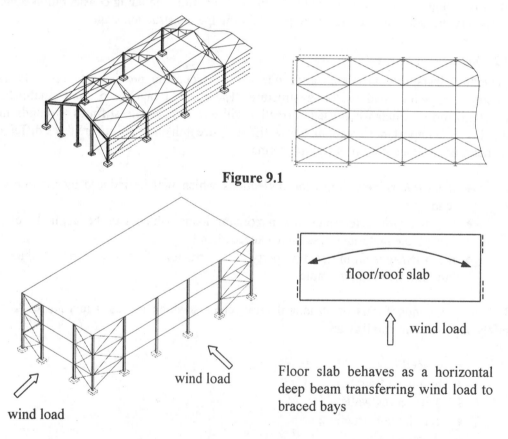

Figure 9.1

Figure 9.2 Braced frames

In such systems the entire wind load on the building is transferred to the braced vertical planes and hence to the foundations at these locations.

9.4 Unbraced Frames

Unbraced frames comprise structures in which the lateral stiffness and stability are achieved by providing an adequate number of rigid (moment resisting) connections at appropriate locations. Unlike braced frames in which 'simple connections' only are required, the connections must be capable of transferring moments and shear forces. This is illustrated in the structure in Figure 9.3 in which stability is achieved in two mutually perpendicular directions using rigid connections. In wind direction A each typical transverse frame transfers its own share of the wind load to its own foundations through the moment connections and bending moments/shear forces/axial forces in the members. In wind direction B the wind load on either gable is transferred through the members and floors to stiffened bays (i.e. in the longitudinal section), and hence to the foundation at these locations. It is not necessary for *every* connection to be moment resisting.

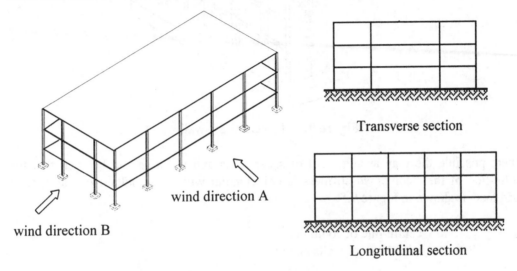

wind direction A

Transverse section

wind direction B

Longitudinal section

Figure 9.3 Unbraced frame

It is common for the portal frame action in a stiffened bay in wind direction B to be replaced by diagonal bracing whilst still maintaining the moment resisting frame action to transfer the wind loads in direction A.

9.5 Shear Cores/Walls

The stability of modern high-rise buildings can be achieved using either braced or unbraced systems as described in Sections 9.3 and 9.4, or alternatively by the use of shear-cores and/or shear-walls. Such structures are generally considered as three-dimensional systems comprising horizontal floor plates and a number of strong-points provided by cores/walls enclosing stairs or lift shafts. A typical layout for such a building is shown in Figure 9.4.

In most cases the vertical loads are generally transferred to the foundations by a conventional skeleton of beams and columns whilst the wind loads are divided between several shear-core/wall elements according to their relative stiffness.

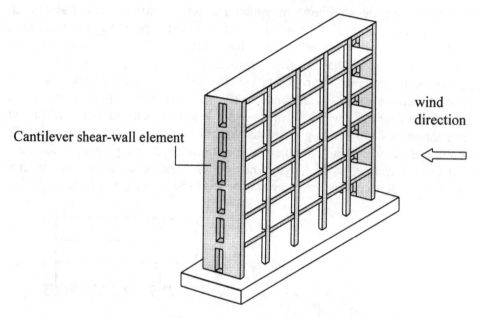

Figure 9.4　Typical shear-wall

Where possible the plan arrangement of shear-cores and walls should be such that the centre-line of their combined stiffness is coincidental with the resultant of the applied wind load as shown in Figure 9.5.

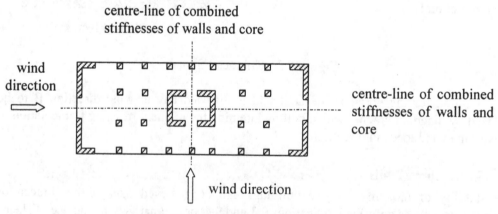

Figure 9.5　Efficient layout of shear-core/walls

If this is not possible and the building is much stiffer at one end than the other, as in Figure 9.6, then torsion may be induced in the structure and must be considered. It is better at the planning stage to avoid this situation arising by selecting a judicious floor-plan layout. The floor construction must be designed to transfer the vertical loads (which are perpendicular to their plane) to the columns/wall elements in addition to the horizontal wind forces (in their own plane) to the shear-core/walls. In the horizontal plane they are designed as deep beams spanning between the strong-points.

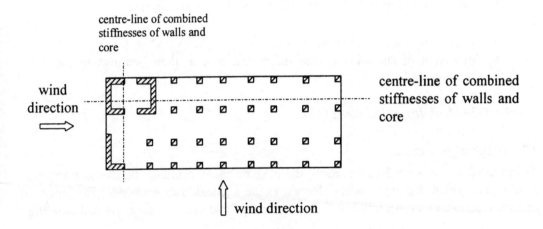

Figure 9.6   Inefficient layout of shear-core/walls

There are many possible variations, including the use of concrete, steel, masonry and composite construction, which can be used to provide the necessary lateral stiffness, strength and stability.

9.6   Cellular Construction

It is common in masonry structures for the plan layout of walls to be irregular with a variety of exterior and interior walls as shown in Figure 9.7.

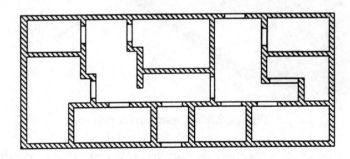

Figure 9.7   Cellular construction

The resulting structural form is known as 'cellular construction', in which there is an inherent high degree of interaction between the intersecting walls. The provision of stair-wells and lift-shafts can also be integrated to contribute to the overall bracing of the structure.

It is important in masonry cellular construction to ensure the inclusion of features such as:

- bonding or tying together of all intersecting walls
- provision of returns where practicable at ends of load-bearing walls
- provision of bracing walls to external walls
- provision of internal bracing walls
- provision of strapping of the floors and roof at their bearings to the load-bearing walls

as indicated in *Stability of Buildings* (18).

9.7 Diaphragm Action

As indicated in Section 9.3 floors, roofs and in some cases, cladding, behave as horizontal diaphragms which distribute lateral forces to the vertical wall elements. This form of structural action, as shown in Figure 9.8, is typical of that used in timber framed building.

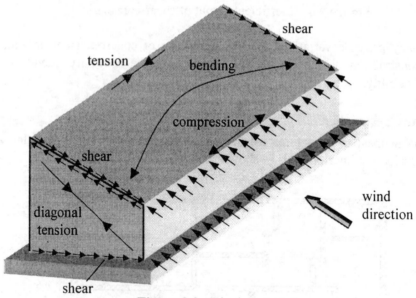

Figure 9.8 Diaphragm action

The roof/floor construction is normally built up from various types of sheathing materials nailed or screwed to timber joists. The wall elements normally consist of vertical studs with top and bottom plates and sheathing on either one or both sides. In addition to the wind loading shown in Figure 9.8, the structural elements must also transmit the dead and imposed loads.

It is essential when utilizing diaphragm action to ensure that the connections between the various elements are capable of transferring the appropriate forces and providing adequate load-paths.

9.8   Accidental Damage and Robustness

It is inevitable that accidental loading such as vehicle impact or gas explosions will result in structural damage. A structure should be sufficiently robust to ensure that damage to small areas or failure of individual elements does not lead to progressive collapse or significant partial collapse. There are a number of strategies which can be adopted to achieve this, e.g.

- ♦ enhancement of continuity which includes increasing the resistance of connections between members and hence load transfer capability,
- ♦ enhancement of overall structural strength including connections and members,
- ♦ provision of multiple load paths to enable the load carried by any individual member to be transferred through adjacent elements in the event of local failure,
- ♦ the inclusion of load-shedding devices such as venting systems to allow the escape of gas following an explosion or specifically designed weak elements/details to prevent transmission of load.

The robustness required in a building may be achieved by 'tying' the elements of a structure together using peripheral and internal ties at each floor and roof level as indicated in Figure 9.9.

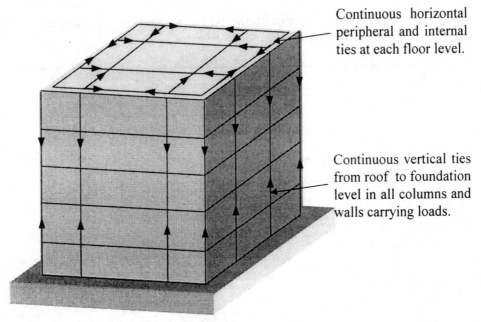

Continuous horizontal peripheral and internal ties at each floor level.

Continuous vertical ties from roof to foundation level in all columns and walls carrying loads.

Figure 9.9

An alternative to the 'fully tied' solution is one in which the consequences of the removal of each load bearing member are considered in turn. If the removal of a member results in an unacceptable level of damage then this member must be strengthened to become a protected member (i.e. one which will remain intact after an accidental event), or the structural form must be improved to limit the extent of the predicted collapse. This process is carried out until all non-protected horizontal and vertical members have been removed one at a time.

9.9   Review Problems

9.1   Distinguish between the strength, stiffness and stability of a building.
         (see Section 9.2)

9.2   Identify five methods of providing lateral stability to a building.
         (see Section 9.2)

9.3   Identify five features which are important for stability in buildings of
         cellular construction.
         (see Section 9.7)

9.4   Explain the importance of connections in diaphragm action.
         (see Section 9.7)

9.5   Explain the purpose of horizontal and vertical ties in a building.
         (see Section 9.8)

Appendix A - Continuous Beam Coefficients

Coefficients to determine the maximum support and span moments and reactions in multi-span beams are given in this appendix.

A.1 Uniformly Distributed Loads

It is assumed that all spans are equal and W is the **total UDL load/span**. Positive reactions are upwards and positive bending moments induce tension on the underside of the beams.

A.1.1 Two-span beams

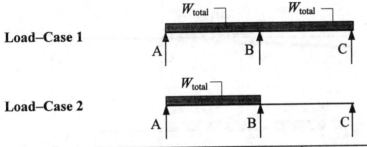

Load–Case 1

Load–Case 2

Load Case	Support R_A	Support R_B	Support R_C	Span AB M_{AB}	Support B M_B	Span BC M_{BC}
1	0.375	1.250	0.375	0.070	− 0.125	0.070
2	0.438	0.625	− 0.063	0.096	− 0.063	

Coefficients for Reactions and Bending Moments

Vertical Reaction = **coefficient** × W
Bending Moment = **coefficient** × W × **span** (L)

Example: Determine the reaction at A and bending moment at support B for the beam shown in Figure A.1.

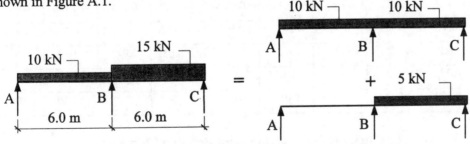

Figure A.1

R_A = $(0.375 \times 10) - (0.063 \times 5)$ = $+3.345$ kN
M_B = $-(0.125 \times 10 \times 6.0) - (0.063 \times 5 \times 6.0)$ = -9.39 kNm

A.1.2 Three-span beams

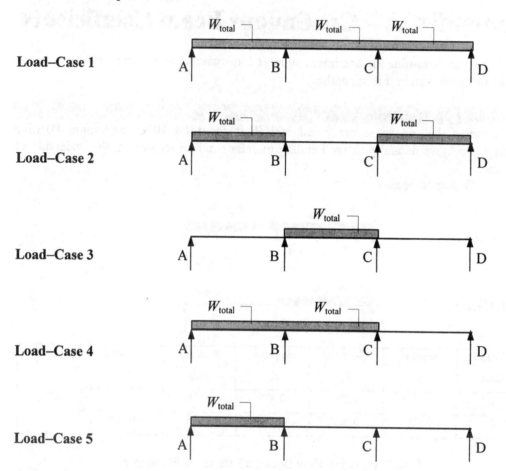

Load Case	Support R_A	Support R_B	Support R_C	Support R_D	Span AB M_{AB}	Support B M_B	Span BC M_{BC}	Support C M_C	Span CD M_{CD}
1	0.4	1.1	1.1	0.4	0.080	− 0.100	0.025	− 0.100	0.080
2	0.45	0.55	0.55	0.45	0.101	− 0.050	-	− 0.050	0.101
3	− 0.05	0.55	0.55	− 0.05	-	− 0.05	0.075	− 0.05	-
4	0.383	1.2	0.45	− 0.033	0.073	− 0.117	0.054	−0.033	-
5	0.433	0.65	−0.10	0.017	0.094	− 0.067	-	−0.10	0.017

Coefficients for Reactions and Bending Moments

A.1.3 *Four-span beams*

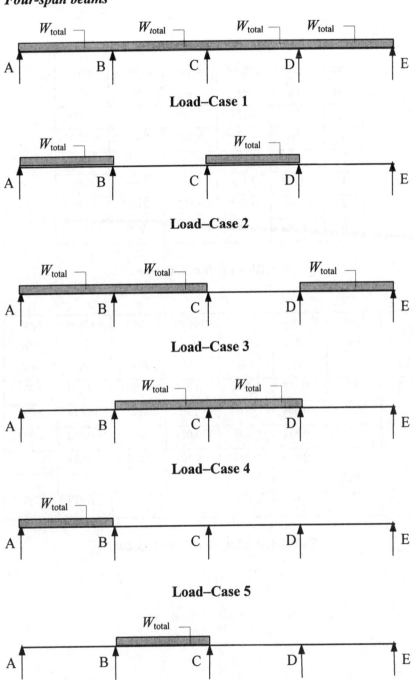

(Four-span beams cont.)

Load Case	Support R_A	Support R_B	Support R_C	Support R_D	Support R_D
1	0.393	1.143	0.929	1.143	0.393
2	0.446	0.572	0.464	0.572	− 0.054
3	0.38	1.223	0.357	0.598	0.442
4	− 0.036	0.464	1.143	0.464	− 0.036
5	0.433	0.652	0.107	0.027	− 0.005
6	− 0.049	0.545	0.571	− 0.080	0.013

Coefficients for Reactions

Load Case	Span AB M_{AB}	Support B M_B	Span BC M_{BC}	Support C M_C	Span CD M_{CD}	Support D M_D	Span DE M_{DE}
1	0.077	− 0.107	0.036	− 0.071	0.036	− 0.107	0.077
2	0.1	− 0.054	-	− 0.036	0.081	− 0.058	0.098
3	0.072	− 0.121	0.061	− 0.018	-	− 0.058	0.098
4	-	− 0.036	0.056	− 0.107	0.056	− 0.036	-
5	0.094	-	-	-	-	-	-
6	-	− 0.094	0.074	− 0.054	-	+ 0.014	-

Coefficients for Bending Moments

A.2 Point Loads

It is assumed that all spans are equal and W is the **total central point-load/span**. Positive reactions are upwards and positive bending moments induce tension on the underside of the beams.

A.2.1 Two-span beams

Load–Case 1

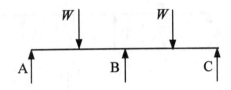

Load–Case 2

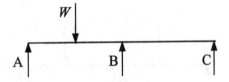

Load Case	Support R_A	Support R_B	Support R_C	Span AB M_{AB}	Support B M_B	Span BC M_{BC}
1	0.313	1.375	0.313	0.156	-0.188	0.156
2	0.406	0.688	-0.094	0.203	-0.094	-

Coefficients for Reactions and Bending Moments

Vertical Reaction = **coefficient** × W

Bending Moment = **coefficient** × W × **span** (L)

A.2.2 Three-span beams

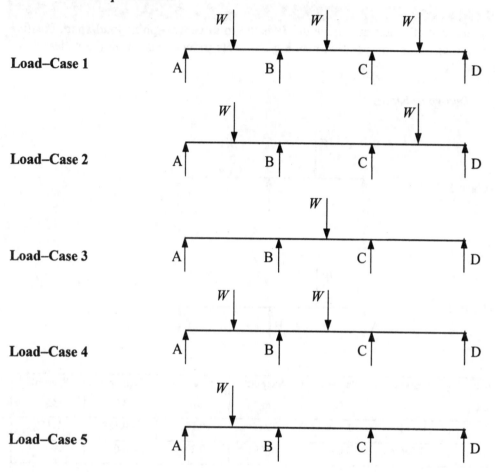

Load–Case 1

Load–Case 2

Load–Case 3

Load–Case 4

Load–Case 5

Load Case	Support R_A	Support R_B	Support R_C	Support R_D	Span AB M_{AB}	Support B M_B	Span BC M_{BC}	Support C M_C	Span CD M_{CD}
1	0.35	1.15	1.15	0.35	0.175	− 0.150	0.100	− 0.150	0.175
2	0.425	0.575	0.575	0.425	0.213	− 0.075	-	− 0.075	0.213
3	− 0.075	0.575	0.575	− 0.075	-	− 0.075	0.175	− 0.075	-
4	0.325	1.3	0.425	− 0.05	0.163	− 0.175	0.138	− 0.050	-
5	0.4	0.725	− 0.15	0.025	0.2	− 0.100	-	+ 0.025	0.025

Coefficients for Reactions and Bending Moments

A.2.3 Four-span beams

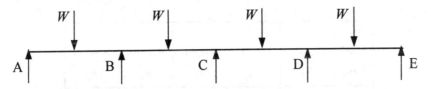

Load–Case 1

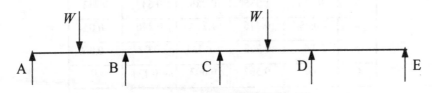

Load–Case 2

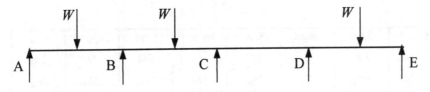

Load–Case 3

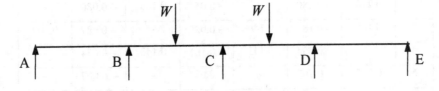

Load–Case 4

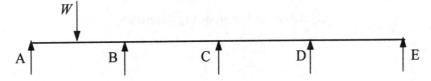

Load–Case 5

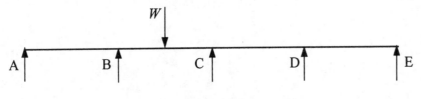

Load–Case 6

(Four-span beams cont.)

Load Case	Support R_A	Support R_B	Support R_C	Support R_D	Support R_D
1	0.339	1.214	0.893	1.214	0.339
2	0.420	0.607	0.446	0.607	− 0.08
3	0.319	1.335	0.286	0.647	0.413
4	− 0.054	0.446	1.214	0.446	− 0.054
5	0.4	0.728	− 0.161	0.04	− 0.007
6	− 0.074	0.567	0.607	− 0.121	0.02

Coefficients for Reactions

Load Case	Span AB M_{AB}	Support B M_B	Span BC M_{BC}	Support C M_C	Span CD M_{CD}	Support D M_D	Span DE M_{DE}
1	0.170	− 0.161	0.116	− 0.107	0.116	− 0.161	0.170
2	0.210	− 0.080	-	− 0.054	0.183	− 0.080	-
3	0.160	− 0.181	0.146	− 0.027	-	− 0.087	0.207
4	-	− 0.054	0.143	− 0.161	0.143	− 0.054	-
5	0.200	− 0.100	-	+ 0.027	-	− 0.007	-
6	-	− 0.074	0.173	− 0.080	-	+ 0.020	-

Coefficients for Bending Moments

Bibliography

1.   **BS 648: Schedule of weights of building materials**
     BSI, 1964

2.   **BS 4978: Specification for softwood grades for structural use**
     BSI, 1996

3.   **BS 5268: Structural use of timber:**
     Part 2: Code of practice for permissible stress design, materials and workmanship
     Part 3: Code of practice for trussed rafter roofs
     Part 4: Fire resistance of timber structures
     BSI, 1996, 1998, 1978

4.   **BS 6399: Loading for buildings:**
     Part 1: Code of practice for dead and imposed loads
     Part 2: Code of practice for wind loads
     Part 3: Code of practice for imposed roof loads
     BSI, 1996, 1997, 1988

5.   **BS 6446: Specification for manufacture of glued structural components of timber and wood based panel products**
     BSI, 1984

6.   **BS EN 385: Finger jointed structural timber – Performance requirements and minimum production requirements**
     BSI, 1995

7.   **BS EN 518: Structural timber – Grading – Requirements for visual strength grading standards**
     BSI, 1995

8.   **BS EN 519: Structural timber – Grading – Requirements for machine strength graded timber and grading machines**
     BSI, 1995

9.   **Fir Plywood Web Beam Design**
     Publication by COFI: Council of Forest Industries of British Columbia

10. **Eurocode 1: Basis of design and actions on structures   DD ENV 1991 – 1 – 1**
     Part 1: Basis of design (together with United Kingdom National Application Document)
     BSI, 1996

11.   ***Eurocode 5 : Design of timber structures   DD ENV 1995 – 1 – 1***
       Part 1.1: General rules and rules for buildings (together with United Kingdom
       National Application Document)
       BSI, 1994

12.   **Freudenthal, A.M.**
       The Safety of Structures
       Proceedings of the American Society of Civil Engineers, October 1945

13.   **Baird J.A. and Ozelton E.C.**
       Timber Designers' Manual, 2nd Edition, Blackwell Science (UK), 1984

14.   ***Step 1 : Structural Timber Education Programme***
       Volume 1 First Edition, Centrum Hout, The Netherlands, 1995

15.   ***Step 2 : Structural Timber Education Programme***
       Volume 2 First Edition, Centrum Hout, The Netherlands, 1995

16.   **Roark, R.J.**
       Formulas for Stress and Strain, 4th Edition, McGraw-Hill, New York, 1956
       BSI, 1994

17.   ***Extracts from British Standards for students of structural design***
       4th Edition
       BSI, 1998

18.   ***Stability of Buildings***
       Institution of Structural Engineers, 1998

19.   ***The collapse of a precast concrete building under construction***
       Technical statement by the Building Research Station, London
       HMSO, 1963

20.   ***Report of the inquiry into the collapse of flats at Ronan Point, Canning Town,
       London***
       HMSO, 1968

21.   **Kaminetzky, Dov**
       Design and Construction Failures: lessons from forensic investigations
       McGraw-Hill, 1991

Index